Informal
Primary Education
Today

Essays and Studies

CONTEMPORARY ANALYSIS IN EDUCATION SERIES
General Editor: Philip Taylor, University of Birmingham, UK.

Contemporary Analysis in Education Series

Informal Primary Education Today

Essays and Studies

Edited by

Alan Blyth

The Falmer Press

(A member of the Taylor & Francis Group)

London, New York and Philadelphia

UK   The Falmer Press, Falmer House, Barcombe, Lewes, East Sussex, BN8 5DL

USA   The Falmer Press, Taylor & Francis Inc., 242 Cherry Street, Philadelphia, PA 19106-1906

First published 1988

Library of Congress Cataloging in Publication Data is available on request
ISBN 1 85000 269 X
ISBN 1 85000 270 3 (pbk.)

Jacket design by Len Williams

Typeset in 11/13 Garamond by
Imago Publishing Ltd, Thame, Oxon

Printed in Great Britain by Taylor & Francis (Printers) Ltd, Basingstoke

Contents

Contents

General Editor's Preface

The idea of informal education in English primary education is alive and well. This collection of papers is testimony to this fact. Its practice, however, is not widespread at least in any full blown form, though its influence is present in the minds and teaching of most Primary School teachers.

The roots of informal education lie largely outside this country but its cultivation since the Second World War has been almost entirely English and the export of the practices which constitute informal education reached their peak in the late 1960s and early 1970s. Today many of these practices are not so widespread nor so well understood as then. It is thus timely that Alan Blyth, an educationist who understands primary education so well, should have taken on the task of reawakening our understanding of informal education and its practices by bringing together a group of able and informed contributors. He is to be congratulated.

Philip Taylor
Birmingham

Preface

When Professor Philip Taylor invited me to edit a book on informal primary education, to take its place in the *Contemporary Analysis in Education* series, I looked for contributors who could enrich the subject from their own different kinds of experience and who would write in a suitably analytic vein. The response from those whom I approached was most encouraging, and has made my editorial function a pleasure rather than a task. They each developed the book's theme as they thought best. I should like to thank them all for their willingness to write freshly and promptly, amid their many preoccupations, for an enterprise which I have coordinated in the alleged indolence of partial retirement.

Acknowledgement and thanks are made to Messrs. Routledge and Kegan Paul for their kind permission to reproduce the table on p. 76 from one of their many well-known publications in the field of educational studies. I should also like to thank Malcolm Clarkson, Managing Director of Falmer Press, for his courteous help and support in the production of this book, and my wife, Joan Blyth, for putting up with my editorial activities and for finding the opportunity to assist those activities with timely and necessary advice, alongside the writing of her own, more practical, books on primary history.

Alan Blyth
Department of Education,
University of Liverpool

Introduction

Alan Blyth

Today in 1987 public education is a matter for public debate. After more than a decade of ferment, education is now to be the subject of major legislation that will affect the entire structure and process of public schooling in England and Wales.

Within public education, primary education will receive its full share of scrutiny, as the legislative process begins to roll. This will be something almost unknown for half a century. Since the 1930s, and even more so since the widespread elimination of selection for secondary education, the political searchlight has been focussed elsewhere, while primary education, and especially nursery-infant education, has been left to develop an optimistic autonomy of its own, behind what it has now become fashionable to describe as a screen of secrecy. But now, again, primary education has become problematic.

The debate about primary education will centre around several issues, two of which are particularly relevant to the theme of this book. The first of these is about the nature of primary education itself. Should it be based essentially on the needs and present interests of children, or should primacy be accorded to the acquisition of skills needed in secondary education and afterwards? Should it be essentially formal and traditional, or essentially informal and progressive? These are questions that the public, encouraged by the media and by some politicians, would like answered. Although each question permits of a continuum of answers from one extreme to the other, the ballot box, and the impending legislation, may give the impression that they can be answered in a simple, straightforward way.

The second issue arises directly from the first, and is exemplified by that impression. At one extreme are found those who believe, with Matthew Arnold (in an uncharacteristic moment), that primary education is a simple, easy matter that can be understood by any competent parent or employer or businessman or shop steward in a few weeks, though the grasp required by a Secretary of State might take a little longer. It is these who believe that a simple choice is possible on the first issue. At the other end of the continuum are the professionals, differing among themselves, but all in some measure experienced in the practice and study of primary education, who are obliged by the very nature of their commitment to engage in constructive criticism, rather than to endorse simple answers to simple questions such as 'Is informal primary education good or bad?'. The public reception of Neville Bennett's first major study of teaching styles (Bennett *et al.*, 1976) showed clearly how readily the two issues can become entangled. For the attempts made to use his carefully-designed research and carefully-qualified findings as ammunition in the first debate inevitably involved his study itself in the second. In its more extreme form, this second controversy is really about the nature of professional competence. The accumulated experience of all who have been concerned with primary education is now sometimes alleged to be nothing more than pseudo-expertise, an Emperor's-clothes facade for personal aggrandizement or political subversion and for an annexation of parental rights which is now to be countered by repossession through the agency of a resolute government. Of course there have been a handful of instances that have given substance to such allegations, but not such as to warrant an indictment of an entire profession whose responsible evolution is itself the best guarantee against perversion or excess. As with child health, so with child education, the basis for effectiveness is a genuine partnership between parents who must in some ways know their own children as nobody else can, and professionals with an expertise based on wider knowledge and experience. That is the stance that must, inevitably, be taken by teachers and others involved in primary education against the populist claims of today.

So this book does not purport to give a simple answer to the kind of question raised on the first issue, such as 'Is informal primary education good or bad?'. Nor, for that matter, does it offer a do-it-yourself manual for primary teachers who want to go informal: there are plenty of those. What is does do is to assert, and try to exemplify, the claim of professional educators to influence the course of events and to justify that influence. It takes a central theme in the first controversy, that of *informal primary education*, and tries to illuminate it through a series of Enigma Variations, each adding something distinctive of its author's study and reflection about primary education. Thus it cannot yield a verdict of the sort that the public often wants. But at the same time it takes a firm stand in the second controversy. Although the authors of these 'variations' differ noticeably among themselves in emphasis and interests, they are uniformly and unequivocally committed to an assertion of the claims of professional stature.

Since the various chapters in the book are not all directly based on specific research, the sub-title *essays and studies* has been added. Each chapter (save one) has been specially commissioned for this volume and represents its author's most recent thinking. The essays and studies consider in turn the historical origins and recent fortunes of informal primary education in England; the nature of children's learning and its significance for primary teaching; the foundations of curriculum and organization at different age-levels within the 'primary phase'; and the ways in which primary teachers' perceptions and values influence the performance of their roles. The general theme of informality runs through them all.

Therefore the term 'informal' itself demands some scrutiny. All the contributors point out that necessity and, as Alexander shows, informality defies simple logical definition. It certainly should not be thought to imply flabbiness or aimlessness, as is sometimes believed. In practice, it is as likely to be opposed to 'traditional' as to 'formal'. It invokes much the same images of educational ideology and practice as are summoned up by 'progressive', 'child-centred' (the one shrewdly analyzed by Harold Entwistle, 1970), 'developmental' (selected by Kelly in his chapter as a distinctly more constructive term), or even 'open'. Yet all of these adjectives are themselves rather cavalier ways of grouping together ideas which, in detail, display considerable discrepancies and even contradictions. In order to impart some additional structure to the book itself, as well as to extend a little the analysis of informal primary education, five aspects of informality are selected for particular attention here and in chapter 1, and reconsidered, in the light of the intervening chapters and of recent developments generally, in the conclusion. These five aspects are presented, for the sake of clarity, in an ideal form; as the various contributors themselves indicate, and as many others might gleefully reiterate, reality does not always match the ideal.

The first of these aspects is informality in *pedagogy*. By this is meant an emphasis on educational play, and subsequently on experimentation, problem-solving, exploration, guided discovery, and data search, rather than on formal instruction. It implies the strenuous engagement of all children in these procedures.

A second aspect that sits easily alongside the first is informality in *curriculum*. Here, projects and topics and centres of interest take the place of separate subjects, though these procedures should not only foster a balanced development in skills, concepts, interests and attitudes across the curriculum, but should also lead progressively towards appreciation and understanding of different subjects as collective human achievements. In that process (and process is the essence of informal curriculum) relevant knowledge, though not necessarily uniform knowledge, in subjects is cumulatively acquired, all the more effectively because of its meaningful relationship to children's experience and interests in school and beyond.

The third kind of informality refers to *organisation* and is closely linked with both the others. Informal organization involves a departure from a strict timetable (except for activities that must use facilities at specific times) and the introduction of such practices as team teaching, open-plan architecture, vertical grouping across age-categories, and flexibility in grouping and in the use of space. On a wider plane, it can involve the design of administrative structures and contexts within which informal pedagogy and curriculum can be most readily encouraged.

Informality also calls for its own means of *evaluation*. This applies both to the assessment of pupil progress and to the evaluation of the effectiveness of informal primary education itself. For both purposes it is inadequate to rely exclusively on means devised to suit more traditional practices. Informal pedagogy and curriculum require their own evaluation, by their own different, but no less demanding, criteria.

Finally, informality often implies a characteristic kind of *personal style*. An informal style is one that depends on friendliness rather than on status in a hierarchy, and is also one that attempts to promote democratic values through informality in dress and manner, thereby minimizing the social distance between teachers and children. First names and even nicknames are more likely to figure than the conventional Mrs. Jones or Mr. Smith (or the older Sir or Miss). Sometimes, informality in personal style also implies irreverence towards social institutions and customs regarded as incompatible with the purposes of informal education.

These five aspects of informality — pedagogy, curriculum, organization, evaluation, and personal style — are independent but related threads in the texture of this book. They were not indicated in advance to the contributors, yet they are illuminated by what the various authors have to say. The conclusion attempts to show how. The five aspects are not all essential to every example of informal primary education — indeed, it is unusual to find all five of them at once — yet they do cohere in a recognizable fashion in a description of informality in English primary education today.

The focus of this book is on English schools and English society, though wider matters are necessarily referred to. Concurrent developments elsewhere in the United Kingdom, for example in Wales since the publication of Plowden's counterpart, the Gittins Report from the Central Advisory Council for Education (Wales) in 1967, really merit consideration in their own right; and indeed, to avoid the taint of parochilism, a world survey would be required. Yet the English story has resonances elsewhere, and may be of positive interest to those who may recognize in it issues similar to their own, viewed from another perspective.

There is a final adverb in the book's title: *today*. Primary education is undergoing rapid transitions — that is almost a truism — and so what is said today can have its full meaning only for today. By tomorrow, it will have grown tawdry and begun the transition that will metamorphose it first into an outdated reference on a reading list, and then, if it survives at all, into a source for the recent history of education. So perhaps it will still be of some interest, when the next millenium begins, to read again what some writers in England thought about informal primary education in the climacteric year 1987, when 1987 was still **Today**.

Five Aspects of Informality in Primary Education: An Historical Sketch

Alan Blyth

Almost everywhere, during almost the whole of human history and pre-history, and even in pre-human life, education has been informal. It has comprised elements of nurture and instruction, within the limits of cultural reproduction and transmission. By comparison, the 3000 or so years of formal educational institutions appear dwarfed, especially since those institutions catered until a mere century ago for a relatively small part of the population of a relatively small part of the human race, destined for few, if socially powerful, occupations. Even then, those institutions absorbed the attentions of that small minority for only a relatively short part of their lives, and for only a relatively short part of the day and year even while they were at their most effective. For the rest, informality in education was unbroken.

Yet it was mainly through those institutions that human thought acquired systematic independence from custom and tradition and at least some of its major achievements. Now the very nature of that separated, liberating, institutional education impelled it towards formality of organization and procedure. The education that was 'fit for free men' and made free men (rarely women) — 'liberal education' — was thus far from free in its own structure. As methods of instruction, courses of study, specialist premises and specialist teaching roles were developed, so there emerged all the characteristics of a distinctive occupation and, at best, a profession. What began as a social necessity for such purposes as the development of the skills and mystiques of priests and administrators, medical experts and technologists, eventually gave an opportunity for the emergence of creative speculation and systematic knowledge, and for the creation of new paradigms that ultimately superseded what had come to be regarded as certainty. From the centres in which such intellectual activity was concentrated, a content of education was thinly diffused through the rest of society. Yet that content tended always to become pedantic, perpetuated by inertia, justified by appeals to its own tradition, and eventually challenged both intellectually and socially.

This process of challenge began almost as soon as formal education itself, and can be traced in societies from Rome to Beijing and from the ancient world to the age of European expansion. But since the eighteenth century the acceleration of change in ideas has impelled a more coherent series of attacks upon the whole conception of education as something necessarily formal and restricted, a process that was given greater impetus with the rise of modern industrial cultures.

It is against this background that the origins of what we may term modern informal education can be traced. In one sense it developed as a conscious attempt to improve on what were seen as the drawbacks of formal education; in another, it looked backwards and also sideways to those age-old processes of informal education that were grounded in the folk culture. Thus, informal education gladdened the hearts of those who saw the key to the future in the allegedly unsullied past, before the ills of existing society were invented; the Rousseaus and Wordsworths of educational romanticism.

This romantic image has been particularly characteristic of primary education. For one thing, preadolescent children, especially girls, were always relatively untouched by formal education and thus appeared most ripe for informality. Then again, when formal education was criticized, it was often the rigidity and inhumanity of its earlier phases that were singled out for the strongest attack, because here the mismatch between child behaviour and the claims of knowledge-based teaching was seen at its starkest, at the point nearest to the prison-house door. When societies, or parts of them, became prosperous enough to indulge children rather than to exploit them, this kind of argument acquired greater force. As the seventeenth century gave way to the eighteenth, and the concept of educational reform acquired currency, it was in the primary years that the challenge to formal education was most likely to take shape.

A new species of intellectual began to emerge, that of the educationist. In the manner of the time, members of that species did not hesitate to design whole systems of education embodying their principles. Alice-wise, they usually began at the beginning, the primary phase, and many spent a lifetime finding how much there was to learn about the education of children, so that they wrote more fully about those early years than about adolescence and adulthood. This tradition has continued into the twentieth century when the task of an educationalist became so much more complicated. So much of the most vivid writing about education, and much of the richness of rhetoric and metaphor that belong to the vocabulary of informal education, are inextricably associated with primary education. It has become the age of informality *par excellence.*

The story of the great educationists and educational reformers is a part of every standard history of education or of educational thought. Indeed, ritual gestures towards the giants of those days are a part of the professional culture of teachers, even if they are rather vague about chronological detail, or even about why that detail matters. So it would be wearisome to try to recount the story yet again. Instead, the origins of the five aspects of informality outlined in the introduction will be indicated in turn, with some reference to their impact on English primary education down to the 1960s when the other contributors to the book take up the story in their various ways.

This sketch is based on a general study of the history of educational thought, not on specific research. It may be liable to correction in detail where recent research has corrected a perspective; if so, such correction would be necessary and welcome. As regards the structure of the chapter, it should be remembered that the five aspects selected are nothing more than convenient descriptors. They are neither entirely separate, nor entirely bound up together. Nor can they be reified in a Whig or a Marxist sense, as entities that persist as lines of development or arenas of dialectic. What does appear true is that some of them emerged sooner than others, in the historical record.[1]

Informality in Pedagogy

The first kind of informality to take effect in primary education was in the way in which children were taught. From classical and Biblical times, there have been voices concerned with education and sympathetic to children who have inveighed against the notion that children should be treated like adults, or animals, or machines. For many centuries, those voices did little more than make humane but random suggestions for the improvement of learning through more 'child-friendly' approaches. Even the advent of massive schemes for educational regeneration such as those proposed by J.A. Comenius in the seventeenth century, or for the application of new approaches to philosophy within the field of education as developed by thinkers of the calibre of John Locke later in the same century, or of Jean-Jacques Rousseau in the next, did little to systematize an informal approach to the teaching of young children; a few flashes of inspiration or crumbs of wisdom were really not enough. It was Rousseau's successors in the early nineteenth century, and especially J.H. Pestalozzi, who first attempted, however inefficiently, to stimulate informal learning within a specific institutional context. Pestalozzi saw himself as a cognitive psychologist and, however dismissively a modern psychologist might consider his practices, he did try to develop a step-by-step approach to the beginnings of primary education which mothers, and teachers, themselves often with little formal education, could enact. In one sense these guidelines were themselves very formal, yet they embodied an honest attempt to adjust teaching to learning, and they were based on leading rather than on driving, and on a loving yet progressive introduction to the natural and moral worlds, by means appropriate for young children, especially the children of the poor as the industrial era began.

Despite his notorious administrative naivety, Pestalozzi attracted the attention of the crowned heads of Europe and also of its educationists. One of these was Friedrich Froebel, whose admiration for Pestalozzi came to be tempered by criticism of his apparently pragmatic improvization and his lack of overarching philosophy. Froebel tried to devise a pedagogy in which the teacher should be a 'passive, following' catalyst, rather than an instructor, in the interaction between children and their environment. He was also among the first to exalt the significance of educative play in young children's development. He and his followers evolved a systematic pedagogy more informal in nature than Pestalozzi's, one which, following Rousseau, was thought to be in accordance with nature and was epitomized by Froebel's introduction of the horticultural metaphor, Kindergarten, whose longstanding association with the subsequent development of informal primary education is pointedly discussed by Alexander in chapter 8.

Others with a less mystical bent developed different kinds of informal pedagogy during the nineteenth century, taking into account the concurrent developments in (mainly positivist) psychology in Europe and the USA. The most significant development, in the USA at the very end of the century, was based on the instrumentalist philosophy of John Dewey. He added collective problem-solving, involving social activity, to the repertoire of informal pedagogy, and his followers developed and systematized his contribution in the guise of the project method. Meanwhile in Europe Maria Montessori was developing a 'scientific pedagogy' emphasizing sensory training and the use of didactic apparatus whose stepwise use Dewey rejected as unduly formal — he had similar views about the pedagogic apparatus devised by Pestalozzi and Froebel — but which was for children to use at their own pace, rather than at the behest of a teacher. This Montessori termed 'auto-education', and it was to be under the supervision of a 'directress' who was to be an observer and facilitator of the child's widening sensory and spiritual experience. The early twentieth century saw the burgeoning of many other experiments in informal pedagogy, but those associated with Dewey and Montessori have probably had the widest and most permanent impact.

Informal pedagogy figured spasmodically in English education from quite early in the industrial age, and even before. It was associated in particular with the emergence of the separate infant school as a distinctive educational institution. Robert Owen, and, a little later, Samuel Wilderspin, were prophets of this development, while the Home and Colonial Infant Schools Society provided it with an institutional base. One aim of the relatively few genuine early infant schools was to shield the youngest children from industrial activity; later, after the introduction of the Codes for the conduct of elementary schools, they received some mitigation of the rigours of the annual examination, since it was considered impracticable to expect children under the age of 6— later 7[2]— to perform in the same prescribed way as was expected of older children. This did not in itself imply that the pedagogy in infant schools, or subsequently in infant classes, was informal. Often it was as formal as teachers could manage with such young children. Yet the absence of tight direction of pedagogy at the infant level meant that here, at least, informal pedagogy could be fostered, and sometimes took root. More importantly, the separation of the training of infant teachers from that of other teachers led to the growth of a distinctive ethos in infant schools, the forerunner of the ideology discussed by King in chapter 5, especially as separate infant schools became more and more usual.

Meanwhile, from the middle of the nineteenth century onwards, informality in the Froebelian mode came to be introduced into the education of the younger children in middle-class private schools, through the education of their teachers. This kind of protected informality was subsequently reinforced by other, home-grown, approaches. Later still, it was challenged, first by the Montessorians, and then also by experimental schools whose pedagogy was based either on one of the current psychologies, as in Susan Isaacs' Malting House School, or on current reformist aspirations. In the twentieth century, these newer developments coalesced with developments within infant schools, spreading upwards into the new junior schools, to form a loose federation of informal pedagogies under a recognizable 'progressive' label. Writers and innovators such as Edmond Holmes, Norman McMunn, Caldwell Cook, and most notably A.S. Neill drew eclectically from the intellectual currents of their age, though they probably owed as much to their own intuitive artistry as to any outside source for their distinctive brands of informality. Much the same was true of the McMillan sisters, though Margaret McMillan, by emphasizing the importance of nursery education as well as infant education, illuminated an important additional area in which informal pedagogy was virtually essential. Blenkin's account in chapter 3 indicates how impressively that illumination has been pursued.

Informality in pedagogy has continued to develop during the twentieth century. It has been adapted to the contributions of Freud, Piaget and Bruner, and others almost as influential. It has been subjected to increasingly penetrating scrutiny, including searching questions about whether informality in pedagogy is equally viable in all educational and social contexts, or whether it appears effective only in those situations in which social attitudes and aspirations seem propitious. On one point a general consensus has been maintained since the earliest attempts at systematic informal pedagogy (and that is no contradiction in terms), namely, that primary education remains its stronghold.

Informality in Curriculum

The earlier reformers, the first to experiment with informal pedagogy, were also concerned with broadening the curriculum. They mostly favoured the inclusion of what would now be termed mathematics broadly conceived, science, modern languages, humanities, and possibly some practical and creative studies, alongside the traditional classical culture; but this was mainly within the secondary curriculum. The emphasis at the primary stage was still distinctly preparatory, and the subject-matter mainly that of basic literacy, itself still a distant dream for many children, together with religious knowledge. It was with Rousseau and his successors that a genuinely new conception of the nature of curriculum began to emerge, one in which the various components were justified not so much for their tool value as for their significance in the formation of intellect and personality, a purpose envisaged long before and in a different way by Plato. Rousseau himself sketched this possibility in a brilliant but unsubstantiated fashion. Pestalozzi and then Froebel groped a little farther on the same road, but it was J.F. Herbart, armed with a pedagogy that was humane but explicitly formal, who first gave a systematic basis to curriculum as *Bildung* or formation in modern terms. Even then he used established subject-matters as the raw materials for his purpose; but the aim was different and he tried to implement it, though sketchily, in primary, as well as secondary, education.

Thus, by the early nineteenth century the way had been opened for a more radical reconsideration of the structure of knowledge and experience as young children encounter it. Froebel, by his emphasis on active learning and on the nature and significance of play, took a further step. For play is not a 'subject' at all. It is itself a form of activity. To regard play as curriculum is to assert that the terminology of curricular discourse is transposed from the object of the verb 'to learn' to its (grammatical) subject. This gives early childhood its own stake in curriculum and its claim that every age has a claim uniquely important to itself, as opposed to the established view that the most important learning must belong to the older pupils who come nearest to the frontiers of human intellectual advance.

Hand in hand with this change in curricular perspectives there developed a further characteristic emphasis, that of valuing childhood and its life for its own sake. It was Rousseau who said that 'children should be children before they are men' (and though rather sexist, he was no ageist) and similar sentiments were expressed by his successors. One reason for this trend was emphasized by Rousseau himself, namely that a sizeable proportion of children in his century would not live to see adulthood, an argument that many in Africa would understand in ours.

So, gradually, there developed a radically different way of looking at the primary curriculum, one that came gradually and irregularly to affect the practice of primary education in the new systems of national education that were established during the nineteenth century. For the most part that effect was confined to the youngest age-levels for whom the actual term Kindergarten, or some other appealing metaphor, was often reserved, Here, at least, the informal curriculum could enjoy formal protection.

Later, with the increasing prestige of positivist and instrumentalist philosophies, the traditional basis of curriculum for older children was also challenged. The culture from which curriculum has to be selected (Lawton, 1975) or in Stenhouse's more graphic phrase 'hewn' (Stenhouse, 1967) was seen as undergoing accelerating transformation. Dewey envisaged a primary curriculum appropriate to a society in continuous evolution, that would emerge naturally from young children's selected experiences and would at first display no subject differentiation, though it could lead towards subject disciplines as human achievements. This could be regarded as a socialized and demystified development of Froebel's approach, though it was far from being irresponsible or extreme. By comparison, Montessori was conservative in matters of curriculum, though her programme of sensory training almost constituted an additional subjective curriculum in itself. Other innovators in the early twentieth century adopted various stances on curriculum, from cross-curricular project work dependent on children's interests to the idiosyncratic procedure at A.S. Neill's Summerhill, where subject-matters were relatively traditional but where the children's engagement with aspects of the curriculum was voluntary and unpredictable, being subordinated to personal needs and growth.

The First World War, and the subsequent revolutions, rocked traditional education, so that post-war reconstruction, especially by self-consciously progressive regimes, looked more favourably on informality in curriculum, almost as though it contributed to national regeneration. So the earlier and concurrent work of educational innovators was studied with renewed interest. It is significant that the now trite quotation from the first official twentieth-century report on primary education in England, the Hadow Report of 1931 (CCBE, 1931), claimed that the *curriculum*, and not just the pedagogy, of primary education should be conceived 'in terms of activity and experience rather than of knowledge to be acquired and facts to be stored', though the report itself, like many of its counterparts, was inconsistent in its elaboration of that principle. Since then informality in curriculum, as in pedagogy, has permeated thinking in teacher education and in the system of education generally, though not so completely as some people hoped or feared. An impression has been formed that informality in curriculum has been almost surreptitiously fostered, and this may be because primary education itself has been largely withdrawn from the public gaze, in maintained schools through the jealously-guarded principle of curricular autonomy which is almost unique to England, and in independent schools through the discreet veil of privacy. Determined parents and others could penetrate both barriers; society as a whole could not.

More recently, informality in curriculum has been subjected to the same kinds of scrutiny as informality in pedagogy, reinforced by the growth of curriculum study as a specific form of educational scholarship. At the same time, cross-curricular issues such as multicultural education have clamoured for inclusion in a manner that challenges any purely subject-based approach, but yet posits claims that are quite formal and objective in nature. It is scarcely surprising that informality in curriculum, more than any other aspect of informality, has aroused controversy for, as Kelly indicates later, it constitutes a potential challenge to the very basis of objective knowledge itself.

Informality in Organization

In the historical record, informality in pedagogy and curriculum preceded informality in its other three aspects. Yet with the passage of time it became clear that those other aspects would also become implied. The first to be considered is organization. If direct instruction in formal subject-matter, of children from a narrow age-range and arrayed in rows of desks facing the teacher, is replaced by informal learning situations involving cross-curricular evolving problem-solving experiences (or whatever terminology is preferred) then it is not surprising that the seating and the classification also come under review.

At first even pioneers such as Pestalozzi and Froebel relegated informality in organization to the margins of education, taking groups of children on nature walks or gathering them at their feet for personal understanding, while the main curriculum was still conducted in schoolrooms. Maybe this was necessary because of the prestige attaching to formal education itself and its hard-won separateness, so that it was only in those marginal aspects, and in what is now termed the hidden curriculum, that informality could be tolerated. For schools, whether formal or informal in character, were generally regarded as oases of promise in an imperfect world, irrespective of their gaze: upward in the older traditions, forward in the newer, and sometimes both. Characteristically, Dewey still saw his ideal elementary school as the secular apotheosis of the little red schoolhouse, riding above the tide of everyday life with its age-old informal practices. Emile Durkheim held a similar view of the elementary schools that were to unite the new secular French Republic.

Yet towards the end of the nineteenth century the rigid didactic patterns of seating and age-grading and 'standards' underwent steady attrition. Children came to be given much more choice about where and when to learn. Once the notion of independent discovery learning became established, the need arose for different forms of organization among children for different kinds of activity. In small schools with inspired teachers, such adaptability had always been in evidence, as was indeed natural in such extended educational families. On the other hand, developments in secondary education in the later nineteenth century and after had rendered customary the introduction of specialist accommodation. Increasing awareness of the possibilities of adaptability and curriculum differentiation (not necessarily for subject instruction) led to changes in the use of existing primary schools and, in an age of architectural innovation, in the design of new schools. First health, then curriculum and pedagogy, influenced building. In its later phases, the development of open-plan schools and the 'integrated day' emerged to impel both the breakdown of age, ability and teacher-centred patterns of organization and at the same time the elaboration of groupings dependent on joint informal activities in bays, 'wet areas' and other arrangements designed to promote informality.

Yet there were other trends running in a different direction. In the large urban primary schools in industrial societies, the model of the extended family was remote and the model of the differentiated secondary school unrealistic. Some kind of formal organization appeared imperative. In some ways it was even intensified while other aspects of informality were growing. Even the Hadow Report of 1931, despite its slogan of 'activity and experience' to which reference has been made, advocated streaming by ability in junior schools in order to secure the homogeneity required for class teaching. Gradually, and in part in response to the contribution of Dewey and his successors, it became more usual to break down that homogeneity by dividing classes into groups, by one means or another, in accordance with the needs of informal pedagogy, and then to substitute such grouping for the more divisive practice of streaming.

Thus informality in organization arose piecemeal and in contradictory ways. The outcome was patchy. Here and there, whole schools adopted informal patterns, though even these could differ from those emphasizing social cooperation to those with wholly individualized procedures such as the Dalton Plan, which occasionally touched primary education. More usually, teachers were able to adopt informal organization within their own classrooms — a 'weak' rather than a 'strong' kind of informality — coming to terms with the ensuing frontier disputes and with their pupils' experience when entering, and more significantly when leaving, their satrapy. For the most part, informal organization was absent, and indeed suspect of being subversive of learning, whereas it had been devised precisely with the intention of promoting learning. Organization was, in effect, evaluated in terms of pedagogy and curriculum.

As for the wider organizational question, that of the appropriateness of the age-structure of educational systems as a whole to promote informality in learning, each society decided what was best for itself; and informality was rarely a major factor in the decision. For many reasons, England decided on boundary ages of 5, 7 and 11, after some experimentation with other possibilities. Most other countries came to a different conclusion. Those independent schools that were committed to an informal approach, and were able to decide these matters for themselves, sometimes chose other boundaries and sometimes none at all. They remained as a permanent question mark over their national systems; but they were among the extended families, and most others were unable to consider that question mark. In England, the 5-7-11 pattern acquired something of an accolade of Nature, and few people noticed that lesser breeds ordered things differently.

Informality in Evaluation

Initially, the advocates of informality tended to look for indications of their success to established criteria. Success in public examinations, at the secondary level, and relatively favourable reports from official inspections, were valued by innovators from Pestalozzi to Neill, even when they were regarded as concessions to a defective society. Alongside these indices of public approval, another kind of evaluation began to appear. It was almost a form of self-justification; what might be termed 'proof by the light in their eyes'. It sustained many innovators in dark hours; but it was hardly calculated to convince their critics.

So, by the twentieth century, some informalists came to consider that their pedagogy, curriculum and organization could neither claim virtual exemption from evaluation, nor could it be entirely subject to procedures evolved for a different kind of education. It required, in fact, its own style of evaluation; rigorous, but different. For example, the competitiveness implicit in examinations and testing, especially of a norm-referenced kind, might be replaced by criterion-referenced markers, each indicating a specific piece of mastery. Montessori's didactic apparatus was a case in point. A further development could be that of self-referenced appraisal, competing against one's own previous best, which involves also learning self-direction and self-assessment. Of course, any such procedure implies a valuing of cooperation and a scepticism about competition that characterizes the social attitudes of many supporters of informality, but by no means all, for 'emulation' enjoys a wide spectrum of support as a pedagogic device, if no more than that. Yet the fostering of criterion-referenced and self-referenced procedures can be said to be consonant with much informal primary education. Incidentally, it was often seen as compatible with the participation of teams and choirs and orchestras in corporate celebrations rather than in exclusively competitive festivals.

Where pedagogy and curriculum are genuinely informal, to the extent of permitting each child to pace and even to select his or her own learning experiences, the demands of evaluation become much more complex. They require something like the trained observation of the Montessorian directress, but also much more. Susan Isaacs, and after her Dorothy Gardner, exemplify in England the initiatives taken in the twentieth century to evolve procedures for the monitoring and assessment of children's progress that would allow for an alternation of diagnosis, matching and learning for each child, within an informal curricular structure that nevertheless takes full account of the progression in skills and concepts that appear necessary to that child's growing personal and social competence. Such informal evaluation is a demanding task, and it is not surprising that this aspect of informality in primary education has been one of the last to emerge.

Evaluation, however, involves more than pupil assessment. It also includes standing back and considering, critically, the whole informal programme itself. For two centuries, attempts have been made to carry out holistic evaluations of this kind against criteria such as nature, reason, progress, democracy, liberalism or socialism, all of which could in different ways be held to justify informality, or against a different array of emblems at whose hands informality would be likely to fare less well. Yet such holistic evaluations have done little more than confirm the initial impressions and attitudes held by those who embarked upon them. Occasionally, as if to escape from this dead end, informal procedures have been introduced into the process of global evaluation itself, but this approach was always in danger of sliding into self-justification rather akin to the proof by the light in their eyes that has already been mentioned. Perhaps the most promising development along these lines is by way of the illuminative approaches to evaluation that have been recently developed; but these approaches belong to the years beyond the scope of this historical account.

Informality in Personal Style

This last aspect of informality, though it has recently become much more prominent, has quite a long ancestry. Where organisation was modified on the margins of education, as in the case of the nineteenth-century pioneers, teachers would mix freely with their pupils rather than maintaining what was then considered a normal social distance from them. Often that implied crossing boundaries of social status as well as of age and sex, and it may have been the implications of such stances that earned Froebel and others a part of their reputation for social subversion. Others such as Wilderspin found the abandonment of personal dignity a virtual necessity if they were to make any impression on large numbers of unruly children.

It was rather later that the modification of personal style came to be associated systematically with what might be termed a political philosophy of informal education. Dewey's transformation of the little red schoolhouse, already mentioned, was also an attempt to perpetuate the American frontier and its spirit of Jacksonian democracy and to carry forward its necessary equalities into industrial society. Proponents of other styles of informality, such as Montessori, held back from that egalitarianism, as indeed they did from the radically different challenge of psychoanalysis; but others who self-consciously adopted a form of socialism and humanism, such as

Bertrand Russell and his wife Dora, and in his own idiosyncratic way A.S. Neill, pursued a personal style less embedded in their society, but more intentionally shocking, than Dewey's.

So one of the marks of informal primary education came to be the unceremonious sincerity of staff and children alike, combined occasionally with a smug assumption that all formal schools were starchy, repressive and antediluvian. Formal schools and their adherents often replied with exaggerated and eponymous accounts of impertinent excesses of every kind; not surprisingly perhaps, since informality in personal style can be particularly symbolic of professional and individual threat.

As time passed, it became more apparent that there were two informal types of personal styles, rather than one. The first could be termed the libertarian style. It laid particular stress on interpersonal equality and on freedom of thought and expression, and belonged in particular to the flowering of independent progressive schools across the Western world in the early twentieth century. The second style was much more closely linked to social and political ideals of the Left, and regards informality of personal style in schools as a means of developing, through teacher–pupil relationships, a confident alternative collectivist culture more congenial to working-class pupils, one which might eventually grow into the culture of a more socialist society. Opponents of informality have not always distinguished adequately between these two styles, whereas their adherents are usually very conscious of their mutual differences[3]. To the libertarian, the collectivist style seems linked with a hankering after a new kind of formality, certainly in curriculum and organization. To the collectivist, libertarian informality in pedagogy, curriculum and organization appears little more than anarchism and at worst a deliberate failure to confront the hegemonic structures of capitalism, thus preserving a haven in which the unconventional middle class can flourish just as much at the expense of the real proletariat as do their fellow-bourgeois who make no bones about their espousal of formal education as a class weapon.

These differences in personal style have become salient only in more recent years. Down to the mid-twentieth century, in the years before jeans, this aspect of informality stood for some kind of progress and emancipation, irrespective of disputes about its more distant goals, while to its opponents it symbolized a gesture of defiance and irreverence towards decent standards of behaviour.

※　　※　　※　　※　　※　　※　　※

During the past two centuries, all five aspects of informality have taken shape and have, to some extent, coalesced into a set of attitudes and procedures that are widely associated with the expression 'informal primary education'. Perhaps the first time when they made a collective impact, as an organized series of educational ideas, on world opinion was in that remarkable period between about 1915 and 1925, when, under the shadow of the First World War and its dark sequel, all the leaders of educational reform appeared to come together, first through the Conference on New Ideals in Education and then, from 1921, in the New Education Fellowship. Governments throughout the world, including briefly that of the Soviet Union, felt obliged to listen to their collective message. Writers such as Selleck in his consideration of the English scene (Selleck, 1972) suggest a permeation of the world of educationists and practitioners by a new orthodoxy in which progressivism and informality flourished. That view can well be substantiated from official documentation, including the Hadow Report of 1931 and its less remembered but no less important sequel concerned with nursery-infant education. (CCBE, 1933). Yet studies based on the actual process of education in the schools indicate that in many cases informality had scarcely scratched the surface between the world wars, or indeed for some time afterwards. Where educational and social conditions favoured the development of informality, there were sometimes quite striking developments; but in general the new orthodoxy met with the resistance of inertia rather than the acclaim of liberation.

After 1945, encouraged by a new generation of HMI such as Christian Schiller, and favoured by the spirit of post-war reconstruction once more, there emerged a second flowering time of informality, this time with England actually as its global focus. The new orthodoxy began to seem more convincing as a majority view. Policies developed under visionary chief education officers, notably in Leicestershire, Oxfordshire and the (then) West Riding of Yorkshire became nationally and even internationally renowned, and some of their primary schools received visitors regularly from the six continents.

Yet, in retrospect, this heyday of informality appears only somewhat more substantial than its pre-war predecessor. Many schools, and many areas, were still almost untouched by it. Meanwhile, informal education itself met the necessity to change and adjust to changing circumstances in schools and in the economic, social and political conditions of the 1950s and 1960s. Pedagogy responded to technological changes; curriculum encountered new demands; organization met with new challenges and new opportunities in response to demographic and architectural trends; the decline of 11+ selection posed new demands on evaluation; and personal styles responded, sometimes abrasively, to cultural change. The accelerating changes of those decades indeed led some adherents of informality to look back to earlier times nostalgically, asking bewildered questions such as 'Who are the progressives now?' (Ash, 1969).

It was in this climate that the Central Advisory Council for Education (England) issued the Plowden Report: *Children and Their Primary Schools* (CACE, 1967): the successor to the Hadow Reports that, in the public mind, epitomizes the high water mark of informal primary education in England. Actually, the Report itself did not extend conceptions of informality very much. Informal pedagogy was approved in the amiable descriptions of practice that adorn the central part of the Report. Hadow's proclamation of informality in the curriculum was endorsed, but again it was individual subjects that figured in the detailed sections. There was a distinct advance in respect of organization, for the Hadow recommendations about streaming were directly opposed, and grouping and team teaching positively encouraged. It was also in this Report that the revision of 'ages and stages' through the introduction of first and middle schools, and the whole issue of continuity between stages, was suggested; yet these suggestions were tentative and have never been made mandatory. The question of evaluation was in general coyly skirted, though the Central Council did in fact use a kind of leisurely, informal procedure in its own evaluation of good practice in primary schools. As for informality in personal style, it was never actually mentioned, though it might be inferred that the members of the Council were probably, if a trifle nervously, in favour.

In sum, the Report identified (para. 505) 'a recognizable philosophy of education' which, though maybe it was a set of assumptions and procedures rather than a philosophy, clearly embraced most of what has been described in this chapter as informal primary education. For that stand the Report has been criticized and challenged, both at the time (for example, Peters, 1969) and subsequently. Yet by common consent it ushered in the latest era in English primary education.

It is with that post-Plowden era that this book is mainly concerned. At this point the other contributors take up the theme of informal primary education, in their own distinctive ways.

Notes

1   The account that follows is based on so many sources, including the works of various educational innovators themselves, that detailed referencing would swamp the narrative and would still, probably, be somewhat inadequate and unrepresentative. So, very few references are included in the text, and those only for specific reasons. For the rest, the most relevant sources are James Scotland's revision of Rusk's *Doctrines of the Great Educators* (Rusk, 1979) and the masterly second volume of Bantock's *Studies in the History of Educational Theory* (Bantock, 1984). Some interesting light is thrown on the early nineteenth century by an older work, Hugh Pollard's *Pioneers of Popular Education* (Pollard, 1956). Among substantial recent biographical studies that extend our knowledge of some significant figures are those by McCann and Young on Samuel Wilderspin (McCann and Young, 1982), Jonathan Croall on A.S. Neill (Croall, 1983) and Elizabeth Bradburn's recently-completed study of Margaret McMillan (Bradburn, 1988). Some useful introductory ideas about pioneers of informal education are included in the early chapters of Rachel Pinder's contribution to current debates, *Why Don't Teachers Teach Like They Used To?* (Pinder, 1987).

General historical and comparative studies of primary education are too numerous to list, though they include a number of important recent works that are germane to any substantial study of informal primary education. Mention must at least be made of Selleck's study of the progressive movement (Selleck, 1972) which is referenced in the chapter itself, and of Campbell Stewart's major work on *Progressives and Radicals in English Education* (Stewart, 1972). The historical chapters of the two Hadow Reports (CCBE, 1931 and 1933) are doubly interesting, as useful sources of information and as themselves embodied in formative instruments of change. (Plowden, unfortunately, dispensed with any historical introduction.) My own earlier study of three traditions in English primary education, including the developmental tradition within which informality took root (Blyth, 1965, vol. 2) may still be of some interest: incidentally, the paperback edition of this book (Blyth, 1967, vol. 1) concludes with my own first reactions to the Plowden Report. Finally, brief but relevant observations about historical trends can be found scattered through Jan Stewart's *The Making of the Primary School* (Stewart, 1986), an absorbing set of reflections, but not the historical account that the title might suggest.

A glance at these references, or even at a few of them, will act as a salutary reminder that a great deal must necessarily be omitted from a chapter designated as 'an historical sketch'. Such omissions can lead to oversimplification and even distortion in places. A chapter of this kind can serve as an introductory overview, but for the serious student it should be little more than a provocation to reveal a little more of the story, a little more fully and accurately.

2   The ages of 7 'or thereabouts', and 11 (apparently with no nonsense about thereabouts), are to be reinforced once again as boundaries in the

structures of assessment associated with the forthcoming national curriculum (DES, 1987).

3　This point can be illustrated by contrasting the loud disagreements that can be heard between some Young Socialists and some Young Liberals with the undiscriminating distaste shown towards both by some Young Conservatives. There is in fact some reflection of these attitudes within the world of schooling.

Primary School Practice Beyond Plowden[1]

Philip Gammage

The Plowden Report

In the *Hadow Report* (The Education of the Adolescent, 1926) there is much advice that educational 'progressives' would find meaningful. For instance,

> Self-education should be the keynote of the older children's curriculum, just as free expression is of the youngest children's, but in neither case is it expected that the teacher will abdicate. (quoted in Selleck, 1972, p. 24).

Thirty years later, the *Plowden Report* (CACE, 1967) affirmed for primary children the Hadow viewpoint that the curriculum was to be thought of as 'activity and experience' rather than 'knowledge to be acquired and facts to be stored'. Thus, in a period since the end of the First World War, two of our major educational policy documents (and there are others in similar vein) have directed British attention to the need for starting from where the children are, for shaping curriculum content such that it fits the entering characteristics of the learners and is not seen as some external 'package' simply to be presented to the children by their elders. Why is it, then, that reality and rhetoric are so often far apart? Is it that self-responsibility as a major principle of 'progressive' education has been systematically tried and found wanting? Is it merely that politicians, as opposed to practitioners, have allied themselves to somewhat meaningless terms like 'standards' (as did the Conservative Party in the mid-1970s)? However it is described, it is clear that the language of British education has changed more this last decade or so than in, perhaps, some forty years previously. It is equally clear, too, that much contained in the *Plowden Report* and said to ensue from it has been misunderstood, mistakenly interpreted, or, worse, misrepresented.

A party game which is beloved of old and young alike is called 'Chinese Whispers'. The rules, as we all know, are simple. One starts the sequence by being given a message to pass on ...

> 'Finding out' has proved to be better for children than 'being told'. Children's capacity to create in words, pictorially and through many other forms of expression, is astonishing. The third of the three R's is no longer mere mechanical arithmetic, French has made its way into the primary school, nature study is becoming science. There has been dramatic and continuing advance in the standards of reading. The gloomy forebodings of the decline of knowledge which would follow progressive methods have been discredited. (*Ibid*, pp. 460–1)

... and as it is passed from neighbour to neighbour it becomes distorted, perhaps ending ...

> I believe the pundits have been trying so hard to dissolve early difficulties that they have emasculated primary education and given the child a completely false impression (if a very cosy one) of what lies ahead. Much of this nebulous teaching is carried out under a plea for 'self-expression' in the mistaken idea that children should not be compelled to learn anything unless they are ready and willing to do so.
>
> This pernicious doctrine leads to 'group activities' with the teacher acting as a kind of peripatetic adviser.
>
> At a later stage we hear and read statements that 'Mathematics can be fun', 'Art is fun', and so on. (Hardie, 1969, pp. 57–8)

'Reality' depends upon which end of the sequence of beliefs you endorse. Clients and workers often differ. As Katz (1977) once remarked,

> One of the most salient aspects of the field of early childhood education is the sharp divergence of views among workers and clients concerning what young children 'need' as well as how and when these 'needs' should be satisfied. (p. 69)

English primary education is no different from early childhood education in general. Moreover, as Katz also has said, in education, ideology is frequently employed as a substitute for theory, such that beliefs, misrepresentations and 'oughts' are frequently taken as indicators of what is actually *there*. This would certainly seem to have been the case in England since the late 1960s. The rhetoric of politicians and the conventional wisdom of the journalist's 'man in the street' seem to have combined in an act of faith which avows that schools have failed; moreover, that, in the case of primary schools, they have failed because they were too 'sloppy', 'progressive', 'child-centred', 'ill-disciplined', and so on. The facts, like those in Chinese Whispers, have become thoroughly distorted.

But, what are the facts — and how might one represent some 23,000 primary schools in England and Wales (working in our devolved, somewhat idiosyncratic system of 105 different LEAs) as though they were some single, uni-dimensional force? The broad issues may be fairly easily identified. But how one describes them, how one interprets, has much more to do with one's own values.

In 1956, as a trainee primary teacher at Goldsmiths' College, I ventured on my first school practice in SE London. I was to be sent, my tutor said, to a 'fairly straightforward' streamed primary school of about 300 children. From notes, I saw that the school was basically an 1880s School Board Elementary Building, with various additions, including a modern annexe (hut). The children sat at individual wooden desks — which, incidentally, are becoming fashionable again. I was to have the 'B' stream, a group of thirty-six 9-year-olds. This was about the average size for a primary class in those days. Most of my work, as befitted a first practice, consisted of taking small groups for basics, of occasional stories with the whole class, and one or two complete class lessons whilst supervised by the teacher. For both the group and whole-class work, I was to set out a fresh sheet in my school practice file. On this sheet were to be recorded details of the lesson plan, namely:- context, aims, methods, materials, resources, apparent results and subsequent reflection and criticism. The last was often augmented by detailed and percipient comment by the visiting tutor from the college. In those days third-year children were beginning to work up to the 11+ 'scholarship' and their school work came increasingly under the shadow of the need for test facility and practice. I was instructed not to disturb this routine.

Thirty years later, in 1986, I carried out certain external examining duties, in the course of which I visited some twelve or so primary schools; six in inner London, six in South Devon. In the former case the students were postgraduate primary course students;

in the latter BEd students. Both groups were on final practice. In all cases the student presented me with lesson plans in almost identical format to those prepared by me some thirty years earlier. The children, however, were not streamed in any of the schools visited. Moreover, only one class was as large as thirty-six children and most were thirty or a little under. I saw no desks, only tables, with shelves beneath, from which the contents spilled regularly. I saw somewhat less whole-class teaching. I *think* I detected generally less formal an atmosphere — a greater warmth, perhaps, in teacher–pupil interaction. But I saw the same friezes on the walls, the same projects on water or flight, the same examples of stories about 'my family'. True the obligatory 1950s nature tables had given way, as a rule, to a 'science/technology-cum-how-does-it-work' corner. There were brighter, more cheerful reading books available, most usually coded for ease of self-selection by the children. But buildings seemed to have deteriorated, to be in generally urgent need of decoration. Textbooks looked more imaginative, perhaps more carefully matched to presumed levels of child ability. Writing was normally with ball-point pen or pencil, usually in some semi-cursive or modified Marion Richardson style. I saw nothing of the italic writing which had become such a vogue when I started teaching.

These early and late impressions, from the 1950s and 1980s, represent for me personally a very considerable transition, from the role of student being examined to that of examiner appraising students. Between these two there took place two other intermediate transitions, from student to teacher and then from teacher to trainer of teachers. But alongside that purely personal sequence came the landmark that is widely assumed to have affected English primary education as a whole, for better or worse: the Plowden Report. I should like to look a little more closely at those intervening Plowden years.

In the late 1960s I became a lecturer in education in a now defunct college of education. As a tutor I visited many schools in Kent, London and Norfolk (school practice pressures were so great in those days that several London colleges were allocated rural areas for certain periods of school practice). During my visits I observed

(a) the gradual disappearance of whole-class streaming and its replacement by within-class grouping (often a disguised form of streaming by ability).

(b) the near demise of the 11+ examination. Apart from these features and the increasing use of grouped tables, rather than desks, there didn't seem much change. Projects still worked their way sporadically and almost seasonally across the curriculum. Occasionally, NFER, Carlton or Moray House standardized tests were administered. The 1936 Burt Gross Word Recognition Test (plus, perhaps, Holborn or Schonell tests) were used for the occasional forays into the reading levels of the class. The 'integrated day' was sometimes in use, usually meaning something very different in each school, and rarely representing a fully integrated curriculum. Overall, the headteacher seemed more in command of the curriculum, and any particular idiosyncracies reflected his or her beliefs, always a strong feature of the English primary curriculum. For the most part the buildings looked the same, give or take the odd visit to a 'progressive' LEA (Leicestershire, Oxfordshire, perhaps Bristol). Overall the children seemed to spend something approaching three-quarters of their week on the three Rs. Apart from the influence of the media, of the depressing lack of singing games and 'nursery' rhymes, there was much that would have seemed familiar to Matthew Arnold a century or so earlier!

I clearly remember the publication of the *Plowden Report* itself. It was, of course, my professional obligation to study it, but I regarded it as more than an obligation. I recall the excitement I felt on obtaining my first copy; I had queued at HMSO to get it. Here it was; the distilled deliberations of a Council that had spent over three years collating and reflecting on primary practice. The blueprint for primary education for all (or of the 95 per cent or so in state schools) had arrived.

Yet even then, and especially as we discussed its content with teachers and lecturers, there was some sense of *déjà vu* as regards the curriculum, organisation and practice. It is common-place nowadays to say that Plowden legitimated 'good' practice where it had been found. Apparently the Council couldn't find that much. It still wouldn't. Some 10 per cent of schools may, by the early 1970s, be taken to have been substantially Plowden-oriented. But, almost by the time of publication of the Report, there was much to counter any 'heady' child-centred or overly process-oriented approach to childhood education. A year earlier, in the USA, the Coleman Report (1966) had already provided considerable challenge to any beliefs that schools really mattered; and only six years after the

Plowden Report, the effects of recession, the decline in the birth-rate and the criticisms of the Black Paper writers were strong.

That having been said, it is clear that Plowden has been an important *lode-star*. It has been a principal aid of navigation for heads, advisers and teacher-trainers alike. It epitomized much that seemed desirable; it focussed, often in near-clichés, on the values that a significant number of early childhood educators seemed to hold. It had somehow clarified the ideas of the 1940s that primary education really did differ from its charity status and from its elementary roots. It neatly echoed Dewey, even Froebel. It had come at a time when LEAs were changing the titles of inspectorial services to advisory ones. It took advantage of the longer, more rigorous three-year training of primary teachers (post 1963). It even expanded some school architects' horizons so that imaginative, attractive work-spaces might become a reality[2]; though one should, in the UK, in *no* way confuse the architecture of open-plan schools with the central values of Plowden style teaching and learning. Such confusions are part of the North American scene, not ours.

That decade of the 1960s was not merely fashioned by belief, changed titles, or declining streaming. Very significant proportions of the educational service's finance were being directed towards primary schools, 'with ten-fold increases in money terms occurring between 1960 and 1974' (Cohen and Cohen, 1986, p. vii). But hard on the heels of optimism came criticism, then retrenchment. The tone of the 1978 HMI survey of primary education (HMI, 1978) is quite unlike that of the Plowden Report a mere decade or so earlier. Moreover, it is clear that despite the widely-held beliefs of a 'revolution' in primary practice, no major improvement was apparent to HMI. The picture is rather confusing in that the popular press and some of the Black Paper writers bemoaned the lack of attention to the basics, whilst the reality was of a usually conventional, probably competent addressing of the basic subjects, with, on the whole, relatively small attempts at imagination, width, and integration (that key-word for Plowden's followers) affecting the rest of the curriculum.

Thus, so far, one might safely say, over thirty years or so primary classrooms have looked remarkably the same. There is still much 'straightforward' class teaching. The Black Paper writers should be delighted. Perhaps a paper on the consistent conservatism of our schools and their laudable attention to 'telling children what to do' is now called for? Of course there are changes; not least, that calculators, microprocessors and small pieces of 'scientific' equipment are much in evidence. But Headington primary school's 'free discipline' of the 1930s (Bent, 1966) was probably considerably more adventurous than that evident in the London schools I visited this year; and, if Plowden gave birth to a child, perhaps it was not so much the monster depicted by some, but simply an ill-nourished waif, an orphan left too long in the cold, a child maltreated, then banished. Certainly, I suspect that is how many primary heads would see it, for not only could they not always get staff to follow Plowden practice; they suffered ill-informed criticism and abuse for implementing things which they hadn't, and which lay outside their power to deliver! Some might also aver that the 'Plowden is a failure; let's move back to the basics' cries came from politicians and others and were merely convenient euphemisms for 'do it cheaper', as Morrell of ILEA has suggested. There are others, also, for whom Plowden has not failed.

> Only when the attitudes and relationships are right within the school and within the larger community will we achieve our educational goals. There has been no rise and fall of the open school in the correct sense, nor has there been a 'back to the basics' effect in our schools (How could there be when the vast majority of schools have never left the basics?) Rather there has been, as happens always in change, a small movement forward followed by a consolidation period that only the foolish would call a regression. (Bond, 1986, p. 11)

There is, too, much in Plowden that has been all too conveniently forgotten. It was the *Plowden Report* which recommended many of those basic changes in record keeping which have quietly taken place during the 1970s (see paras. 435, 448 and 451, CACE, 1967). It was the *Plowden Report* which outlined the dangers in teacher trainers having too little recent and relevant school experience (paras. 973, 976 and 977). It was Plowden which emphasized the desperate need for developments in maths teaching and maths teacher training (paras. 647 to 662). Recent government pronouncements make the shortage of maths teachers sound like a new phenomenon! Indeed, returning to the actual *Plowden Report*, rather than to writers on it, is remarkably refreshing and one is struck by two main features:

(i) the wealth of good, wide-ranging advice (and assertion) from all sections of the education service and from the community;

(ii) how much of its contextual material, and concomitant criticism, would be apposite today.

In the latter respect alone, it provides a sad indictment of government after government. It argued for nursery provision — yet we know that in 1986 nursery school provision for our 3-year olds was below 25 per cent. It criticizes the poor state of buildings and resources — yet the HMI could talk of a 'grim environment' in many schools in 1985 (HMI, 1985a, p. 29). It reminds us that,

> outstanding primary school buildings can support teachers in their use of modern methods, raise the standards of children's behaviour and change their attitude to school and win the enthusiasm of parents. (CACE, 1967, p. 391)

It recommended the abolition of corporal punishment, focussed on the need for a combination of individual, group *and* class teaching, insisted that graduate entrants to the profession should be trained, emphasized the importance of and the right to continued in-service training for all teachers. It also called for a reconsideration of the ages and stages of primary education, recommending a three-tier system as more appropriate to the development of children. There seems so much sanity in the *Plowden Report*; no simplistic 'contingent' view of education is expressed therein. Plowden is not just about education 'getting the country somewhere'; it is about the quality of life-enhancing experiences for all young children. Its weaknesses, though, are self-evident. Whilst there is much in it of optimistic assertion, of what *should* happen, rather than what did, there is also much 'woolliness'. The results of the survey to categorize English schools undertaken by HMI on behalf of the committee hardly bear critical scrutiny. As Simon (1986) has pointed out, they are 'vague categories' and definitions, 'that it is difficult to make much sense of' (p. 13). Nevertheless, the *Plowden Report*, for all its infelicities, its looseness, its minor internal conflicts, was visionary and cohesive to some clear purpose in that it took the ideology of 'being on the child's side', of child-centred approaches, as central to the purpose of good education. It was not the Committee's fault that they were overtaken by economic, political and social events almost before they had published. Perhaps one should recall, as Simon does, the swift demise of streaming, *not* predicted by Plowden, quite the contrary, but certainly hoped for and extolled. In that respect alone, and perhaps aided by demographic circumstances, the Report was the flag-bearer of real change.

Others have written on how well the myth of a 'primary revolution' was created and perpetuated, of the unfortunate coincidence of student unrest, of the publication of the Black Papers, the subsequent devastating impact of the Tyndale Affair in 1974, and of Callaghan's Ruskin College speech of 1976, how the subtle and seeming congruence of these events has been melded into an image of primary school failure. Yet, today, judging from the growing support for the National Association for Primary Education (NAPE), which seems to espouse broadly Plowden principles; judging from my own personal experience of examining primary teacher-training courses throughout the country, there are still many who see *Children and Their Primary Schools* as a broadly valid statement of how things should go on. It is remarkable how the *Plowden Report* is clung to. Despite a period of almost continuous change for the teacher training institutions, massive closures, plummetting morale, constant criticism of their curriculum, continued and major resubmissions for validation by CNAA or university, one notes that the *Plowden Report* has remained a powerful force in prescribed student reading.

Of course, time has passed, and with the benefits of hindsight we are wiser. We know, too, that education is particularly prone to swings of the pendulum, that it is essentially political, that movements grow and die in relatively short periods of time, that terminology is especially slippery and that the right well-turned phrase, like 'management by objectives', or 'computer literacy' can attract vast resources by encapsulating the mood of the time. We know also that, in primary and early childhood education much damage has been done by careless labelling, by the use of such terms as 'formal' or 'informal'. Yet I suspect that, whatever else Plowden has done it has, over the years reminded primary teachers that at best education is (a) not merely instruction, but is an interactive process, a case of 'doing' and 'undergoing' as Dewey would have it; and (b) a continuous, growing, dynamic process. Neither of these two is surprising. Writers from Whitehead to Piaget have constantly referred to them. They are essential features of real education. They rely, not as they are sometimes represented, on simplistic notions that each child is fully equipped to unfold into staggering genius if only we wait, but on views of experience and responsibility as the keys to effective learning. As Helen Parkhurst stated in her original 'Dalton Plan' approaches, responsibility for learning is both the child's and the teacher's. This is what Plowden was all about; good education is essentially experiential. As Dewey (1938) puts it,

> When *preparation* is made the controlling end, then the
> potentialities of the present are sacrificed to a suppositious
> future. (p. 50)

Dewey's is not, therefore a simply, 'contingent' view of education,
though neither is it one which underplays the reality of content
matter in the curriculum. But it is a view which stresses the central
importance of processes of learning. It is a striving to express and
articulate the relation between that 'doing' and 'undergoing'.

The British Psychological Society submission, *Achievement in
the Primary School: Evidence to the Education, Science and Arts
Committee of the House of Commons*, states that certain clear trends
in the 'application of psychology to primary education' have
emerged over the last twenty years.

1 Children are more able intellectually than previously
   acknowledged and this ability develops by actively interacting with the world;
2 limits to children's abilities are located in the day-to-day
   interactions in the classroom, the family and society at
   large;
3 achievement in school can be improved by more flexible
   and appropriate classroom organisation, by more positive
   teaching, by more cooperative relationships with parents
   and by pre-school education;
4 competency in a range of skills can be promoted by a
   broad-based curriculum;
5 some handicapped children can be successfully integrated
   into normal schools. (BPS, 1986, p. 124)

It would be churlish to point out that such 1986 'trends' had been
mentioned (though not quite in that form) in the 1967 Plowden
Report. But, whilst the Plowden Report exhorted primary educators
to make more contact with parents and peers, it did not have the
benefit of knowing quite how such features might work. Whilst it
might aver the benefits of nursery education, the actual advantages
anticipated were, in those days, less well documented. Even that
massive American conglomerate exercise 'Head Start' was only into
its third year. Nowadays, we know that there is evidence to show
that appropriate pre-school experience can have a powerful and
pervasive effect upon child achievement in subsequent stages of
schooling. Turner (1980), and many others, have claimed that the
child's abilities to capitalize on primary schooling depend as much

on self-confidence as on 'intellect', that such self-confidence is itself the result of interactions with a sympathetic and helpfully exploratory environment, one which confirms the child in seeing his own causality as an essential feature in it all.

Thus far I have tried to set out some of the context of Plowden, some of its weaknesses, some of its vision. I have emphasized that it has been a convenient scapegoat, a 'catch-all' for often ill-informed criticism and abuse of English primary education, yet an important beacon for many in the profession. Its philosophy was not new; it overemphasized what Eisner has called the fallacy of process, perhaps to the detriment of content (Eisner, 1974, p. 78). It echoed Dewey and our own pioneers of the early thirties such as Susan Isaacs. Its research bases leave much to be desired. But, withal, it remains read by many, is still inspirational and encapsulates what seems to many as the fundamental logic of starting from the child.

The Primary Curriculum Since 1967

Currently the primary curriculum covers a range of children aged from a little under 5 years to marginally under 12. Two stages of education, therefore, are embraced by the term 'primary'; and many would point out that the Plowden ideology, if such a one can be identified, took root more firmly in the infant curriculum stage than in the junior one. As Davis testifies (and there are many other examples which go back to the early 1900s) teachers, especially infant teachers, experimented with the curriculum well before Plowden. One such teacher

> developed a 'free day' from her frustration with time constraints which limited the exploitation of interest-based methods. Her children did not appear to be taught to read, but she read with them a great deal, and her class became more successful on the reading tests regularly administered by the head than those in parallel classes (Davis *et al.*, 1986, p. 11).

Certainly Piaget's view that play is a primary means of learning (Piaget, 1951) was a well-established feature of much Froebelian infant teacher training during the last century. It had clearly found its way into the accepted orthodoxy of teacher trainers and heads alike by the time of the 1931 *Hadow Report* (CCBE, 1931). The value of play, of 'free activity', of the 'integrated day' even, were well-known curriculum tenets for many English Infant teachers of the 1950s.

'Curriculum' is itself a generic term. Lawton (1984) points out that it is a metaphor for a 'course to be run' and that in turn it has accrued many metaphors which epitomise particular value orientations and approaches, for example, the balanced curriculum (diet), the core curriculum (plant). Such metaphors also abound in early childhood education. The term 'kindergarten' itself (see chapter 8) conjures images of children in need of tender nurturance. I have come across many infant teachers who maintained, in the best Froebelian tradition, that children grow towards the light of knowledge; though one of the best educational solecisms I have met was a comment by a final year Froebel primary student who wrote in a script: 'Children must be nurtured forcefully'. How true! some might remark.

It is unwise to separate the curriculum from its modes of classroom organization, since the latter tend to have a profound effect on the former and are themselves reflections of beliefs about the desirability of certain approaches to learning, such as individualization or group cooperation or competition. Thus one views the impact of particular systems of organization as major exemplars of curriculum development and change; one such was the apparent popularity of vertical or family grouping. During the late 1960s college of education students were sent to particular LEAs to see how it was done. (I recall two such trips made from my college in 1967, the Plowden year.)

It is commonplace nowadays to say that the 1970s provided a period of unique and concentrated attention, documentation and advice on the primary curriculum as a whole. From the mid-1970s primary schools began to have to respond to a much more 'official' and centralized view of the curriculum. Whilst qualitative differences still abound, one suspects that, by the mid-1980s, primary schools have become more similar than at any time since the late 1940s. It is no longer possible for the primary head to shape and set the curriculum with quite the freedom that he or she could in the past, even with or without the constraints of the 11+ (which, incidentally, still exist in at least four local authorities). The language of the 1960s — and even of the very early 1970s — was one of expansion, of diversity, of optimism and reform.

There seemed to be a mood abroad that suggested that the curriculum, teaching styles, materials and modes of assessment needed to be more flexible, more suited to the individual child. (Gammage, 1986, p. 67)

Since then, as Lawton has put it (1982), the door to the 'secret garden of the curriculum' has been firmly pegged open and at least one result of such exposure has been plethora of curriculum documents from the DES, which has itself created a problem of information overload for many teachers.

Notwithstanding that major interest shown by the DES this last fifteen years or so, the English primary school still at present reflects the freedom congruent with a devolved system of LEA organization; and composition, emphasis on certain forms of graded post or area of responsibility, practice and teaching styles are critically affected by the values held by the headteacher. This freedom to alter organization, though less than in earlier times, is still great in comparison with that obtaining in many other countries. Such differences were clearly indicated in the HMI (1978) primary survey and by the subsequent, now published, HMI reports on individual schools. Indeed, the 1978 survey (which was a sample of 542 schools) revealed marked inconsistencies in the curriculum and argued for greater uniformity and consistency. In 1979 the DES Report *Local Authority Arrangements for the School Curriculum* set out LEA replies on areas of the curriculum considered by the DES as central to greater effectiveness and uniformity. Since then and the Schools Council (1981) survey, the inspectorate has published *Curriculum 5–16* guidelines which made the collective responsibility of LEA and school much clearer in respect of both the curriculum and its assessment. In the last eight years, and particularly since the (then) Secretary of State's Sheffield speech of 1984, the DES has moved towards a broadly agreed national framework of curriculum objectives which are thought desirable. DES papers have exemplified a belief in greater control, uniformity and specialization in the curriculum, even at the primary level. The DES talks of curriculum *delivery* (still thought to be an inappropriate term by many primary educationists) as do HMI in the 1985 Middle School Survey (HMI 1985b, p. 73) while official policy speaks of the necessity, now common practice in primary education, for statements on the school's principles, aims and content to be available to parents. In 1984 the Chief Inspector suggested to a conference of primary teachers that 'ideally every primary school should have nine teachers for the nine subject areas' (areas of experience) (HMI, 1985c) now thought appropriate to the curriculum. This, whilst being perfectly congruent with recent DES preoccupations, is antithetical to the essentially generalistic class-teaching ambience which had dominated primary education since its inception and which was lauded in the *Plowden Report*.

Since the ill-informed 'backlash' criticisms of the *Plowden Report*, that is, from about the early 1970s, assays of primary education have been constant, for the most part detailed, and frequently in considerable agreement. Observations range from those of Eisner in the early 1970s through those of the NFER by Barker-Lunn (spanning twenty years) to the most recent ILEA reports of 1985 and 1986. The last study (ILEA, 1986) details not only cognitive, but non-cognitive outcomes of primary schooling, such as self-perceptions, attitudes, and these, as the British Psychological Society emphasizes, are of concern.

> We are concerned, too, that education should promote the development of social competence and satisfactory personal relationships. Various research reports (cited) from individual case referrals to large-scale analyses of school effects on achievement have shown the importance of taking such a broad view. (BPS, 1986, p. 123)

Central to reports, official surveys and individual research has been the 1978 HMI Primary Survey. In this HMIs observed that primary teachers accorded high priority to literacy and that, overall, national reading standards, though notoriously difficult to assess, appeared to be rising. All classes of 7 and 9-year-olds made use of graded reading schemes, and spelling tests, multiplication tables and comprehension exercises were much in evidence (and still are, Barker-Lunn, 1984). Notably, 85 per cent of schools sampled had schemes of work on language. But matching work to ability was least clear in the case of the more able children. In this respect it is interesting to refer to Bennett *et al.* (1984) some six years later. In their study of the quality of learning environments for a sample of 'top' infants (6 and 7-year-olds) they say,

> In reality therefore high attaining children received less new knowledge and more practice than their low-attaining peers. This is the opposite pattern to what might have been expected with the probable consequence of delays in progress for high attainers and a lack of opportunity for consolidation for low attainers. (pp. 213–4)

The findings of both Boydell (1975) (in her work prior to the Galton *et al.* ORACLE study) and Bassey (1978) confirm the worries originally expressed by Eisner (1974), that group work did not seem to involve much of the interactive planning or focus envisaged in Plowden, and that

> Sustained conversations in which children explain and develop their ideas and arguments may be relatively uncommon. (Boydell, 1975, p. 128)

Such observations are confirmed by the ORACLE study (Galton *et al.*, 1980)[3] and by Mortimore *et al.* in the ILEA study.

> Many teachers used groupings when organising their classrooms, especially in the 'basic' areas of the curriculum. Collaborative work, however, was not frequently seen, although there was a slight increase as pupils moved up the school. (ILEA, 1986, p. 13)

Likewise, individualized learning has presented similar problems of organization for the primary teacher such that,

> The extreme liberal romantic model of children purposefully learning through self-initiated activity breaks down, except, possibly in the hands of the exceptionally talented teacher. It entails a high order of adult-child ratio, and therefore quantity as well as quality of interaction if extension rather than repetition is to be gained from the child. (Golby, 1986, p. 57)

This is not to suggest that many primary teachers do not strive to provide individualized work and the opportunities for group projects and, occasionally, peer-led learning. It is simply to remark that most studies of the last decade emphasize that, whilst group work exists and individually matched assignments are not uncommon, the vast majority of class time (up to 70 per cent) seems to be spent in standard, teacher-originated, whole-class teaching. There are some differences to be observed throughout the primary age range, however. For instance Kutnick (1983) found,

> Teachers in the middle and later years of the primary school maintained several behaviours similar to teachers of younger pupils. But they also became more formal and more subject-oriented ... Coincidentally, the children started speaking and interacting more spontaneously with one another ... (and thus brought) a drastic increase in warnings and directions by the teacher. (p. 95)

Despite the general congruence of viewpoints there are some minor conflicts and paradoxes in what is said to exist or said to be desirable. From HMI and other sources there have been suggestions that a certain narrowness pervades the primary curriculum and its organization. Yet at the same time as lauding width and integration (a dominant theme in the *Plowden Report*), many, especially HMI, see forms of 'specialization' as leading to more consistent child achievement prior to the age of transfer at 11. In 1981 the DES wrote that there was no evidence that concentrating only on the basic skills would raise attainment, rather that HMI's observations suggested that such improvements more often took place in wide programmes of work whereby language and maths skills could be applied in various contexts. (DES, 1981, p. 10) The 8–12 Middle School Survey (HMI, 1985b) commented that both specialization and 'the carrying over the certain skills' were important. Significantly, too, it noted that material resources did seem to affect the quality of school work (p. 75). It is perhaps from Barker-Lunn (1984) that we get the clearest picture of what actually goes on in primary schools. She notes that a large proportion of time was spent on very 'traditional' basic subject work, the rules of number, computation, the use of money. This chimes well with the ILEA report of 1986 and tends to confirm the view that what goes on hasn't really changed that much since 1967. There is no shortage of documentation to confirm such an overall view (see especially Cohen and Cohen, 1986; and Richards *et al.*, 1985 vols. 2 and 3). Any amalgamation leads one inescapably to make the following broad generalizations for the period 1967 to 1986:

(a) Despite Plowden's recommendations on group work, interaction within groups is much less marked than the mere physical/spatial disposition in the classroom might indicate.

(b) Individualized work, though observable, is in the minority and is not usually well-matched to developing the abilities of the high-attaining child.

(c) Examination/reinterpretation of the 'formal' or 'informal' methods debate suggests a less clear-cut picture than Bennett's original 1976 position outlined — and one which only serves to emphasise the weakness of such classifications of teaching style (see especially Gray and Satterly, 1981).

Thus, overall the current state of English primary education would seem to be as follows:-

1   Little evidence of declining standards; if anything a rise in reading standards.
2   No evidence of substantial use of progressive, child-centred methods; one suspects that a smaller percentage than that identified by Plowden might be found today.
3   Clear attention to basics. Perhaps a slight increase in attention to English comprehension and formal grammar may be detected.
4   More systematic record keeping, with evidence that LEAs have formulated guidelines; clearer diagnostic and assessment procedures in oracy and literacy. Greater homogeneity across LEAs.
5   Substantial class teaching (approaching 70 per cent of the week), but significant amounts of group work of a (possibly) ineffective kind.
6   A not very broad, nor overly text-book oriented, curriculum. Topics and themes commonly though sporadically employed.
7   DES pressure for more 'specialist' curriculum leadership in those areas deemed critical (maths, language, science).
8   Insufficient attention to science, despite increase in posts of responsibility. Discovery methods not much in evidence.
9   Fairly wide use of microprocessors, clearly not simply allied to maths.
10 Weaknesses in provision of match or 'differential access' in the curriculum, especially for children at the extremes of ability.
11 Decline in specialist music approaches; *slight* increase in attention to health education; virtual demise of French language in the primary curriculum.
12 A major increase in split-age, vertically grouped forms of classroom organisation throughout the primary school. (A consequence of falling rolls not necessarily of educational belief.)

The Future

The late 1980s is a period of high unemployment, surplus school places even at primary level, deteriorating buildings, more voluntary finance around the 'edges' of the state system (and consequent inequalities of provision) and of a fairly demoralized teaching profession. But it is also a period of a slightly increasing output of primary teachers (yet again), a period when primary school rolls have temporarily stabilized, a time when all new primary teachers are graduates and a period when home and school links have never been as strong. For the foreseeable future the benefits of good nursery education will be denied to three-quarters of our children, despite the fact that the impact of nursery schooling on subsequent primary education has been well demonstrated. (In 1986 we had 22 per cent of our 3 and 4-year-olds in school, with such variations as approximately 1 per cent in attendance in Wiltshire and 48 per cent in Cleveland.) In a continued period of high unemployment, the teacher may well benefit from the increased availability of parent time and a renewed awareness of the actual benefits of parent and 'lay' adult involvement in class and school activities. Such involvement has been shown to be particularly efficacious, especially in the helping of low-progress readers. Particularly serious attempts will be made to involve more parents from minority groups.

Despite closures of surplus schools, an especially feared and damaging enterprise for local politicians, it seems likely that British primary schools will remain relatively small on average (about six to seven staff covering both infant and junior stages.) The birthrate and social/economic features are such that primary schools will have to continue to employ some form of mixed-age cohorts in the majority of cases. The covert effects of grouping by ability, often a disguised form of streaming within the class, are likely to persist, however. Primary schools are now required to state explicitly what they are about and the 1980 and 1986 Education Acts enabled governors and parents to be involved in the oversight of the curriculum. Thus the marked improvement in parent-school/community interchange seems ensured.

Curriculum leadership, the current 'flavour' of DES preference, is likely to be encouraged, and the change in in-service patterns from 1987 has undoubtedly led to increasing focus on school-related, 'problem-solving' courses for LEA selected staff, rather than past patterns of choice which were dominated by individual teacher perceptions of need or of career enhancement.

> I do not want a 'paper' qualification but need courses which would improve my performance in the classroom. (Atkin and Houlton, 1986, p. 21)

There seems little likelihood of any major change in the curriculum or in its 'delivery' (current DES term). Individual, class-set, basic in-seat work, often from work cards, will persist as the staple diet of the day, though it is clear that many teachers will continue to operate a range of organizational practices within their one class. But the research messages of the last decade or so do seem to have made an impact, and many primary heads seem well aware that, whilst Plowden advocated group work and interaction, there are limits to its effectiveness. The BPS, referring to the work of Bennett and Desforges (1985), said,

> Experimental evaluations have shown that more time is spent working and more work is completed when children sit in rows than when seated round tables. Certain forms of work, in particular the acquisition of literacy and numeracy skills, require more individualised organisation, whilst work involving communication skills requires group organisation. Thus achievement in basic skills is more likely to be promoted within formal classrooms. (British Psychological Society, 1986, p. 122)

Planning the curriculum in terms of its implied *conceptual development* for children, rather than in terms of 'house-keeping' (low noise, cleanliness, etc.), is another aspect of classroom organization and style which certainly has been advocated by teacher-trainers of recent years. There is greater awareness, too, that, whilst flexible, vertical grouping has its problems in terms of the range of work provision necessary, the competence of the top infant is greater than had perhaps been previously assumed. Several good software programmes which take this factor into account and which actively expand conceptual understanding (for example, which allow children to compose their own music, complete with elaborate harmonies, and to recognize the processes involved) are available and are likely amongst other things slightly to ameliorate the general shortage of musical expertise in the classroom. Evidence suggests very active use of microprocessors in areas of language, geography, history, music, maths, science and technology, and whilst the 'delivery' in science remains fairly low (as opposed to official emphasis), modest computer literacy and minor technological understanding are likely to continue as fairly secure features of both infant and junior departments.

    Fundamental lessons have been learned since Plowden, many of them related to concerns discussed by that Committee itself.

Techniques of class-recording have been thought through more thoroughly and have been aided by the published reports of the Assessment of Performance Unit. Articulation between age groups and the planning of progression are much more to the fore and more likely to be high on the agenda of staff discussions. The HMI curriculum guidelines, for all their weaknesses, have proved useful debating ground and have signalled sharper attention to areas considered fundamental in the curriculum. Staff appraisal is now well-established in some LEAs and is gathering strength. The roles of graded post-holders as essential curriculum leaders is now commonly established (Campbell 1985). Primary teachers have a longer initial training; also they have significantly higher 'A' level scores on entry to college. All this would suggest that the profession of primary teaching is in relatively good shape for the 1990s. Certain external factors, however, may give rise to alarm; low investment in building maintenance; relatively low cost per child in comparison with our neighbours in Europe. On the other hand, we may be getting excellent value for money. 'British teachers cost the tax-payer very much less than those of our major European neighbours.' (Williams, 1986, p. 4)

My own opinion, after some thirty years associated with primary education, is that primary schools benefitted enormously from the inspiration of Plowden, have suffered from grandiose claims and equally wilfully inaccurate criticism, but are, withal, entering these latter years of the century as a trifle dull, yet more humane, more cohesive, more aware that process and content need carefully relating, yet still providing integration through topics and projects and still concerned to commit the child to perspectives of learning which admit the importance of enthusiasm and enjoyment.

Notes

1 This chapter is based upon a paper published in the *Oxford Review of Education*, 13, 1, 1987.
2 In the late 1960s and early 1970s architecture students at the University of Bristol carried out many exercises in 'progressive' school design. I attended meetings with the students at which I and various local head-teachers expounded Plowden 'principles' in respect of the school and class environment.
3 See also chapter 4 below.

Education and Development: Some Implications for the Curriculum in the Early Years

Geva Blenkin

> That the child is endowed with an authentic activity of its own and that education cannot succeed without truly employing this activity and extending it is something everyone has been repeating ever since Rousseau ... But to provide a positive interpretation of mental development and psychic activity was a task reserved for the psychology of this century and for the educational science that has stemmed from it ... Let there be no misunderstanding, however. Modern educational science has not emerged from child psychology in the same way that advances in industrial technique have developed, step by step, from the discoveries of exact sciences. It is rather the general spirit of psychological research, and often, too, the very methods of observation employed, that have energized educational science in their passage from the field of pure science to that of scholastic experimentation. (Piaget, 1969, p. 145)

It is clear from the above passage that Jean Piaget viewed as crucial the contribution that psychology can make to education theory and practice. Indeed, at the time that the paper from which this extract was taken was written, his general thesis had been accepted for some years. It had long been recognized that it is important for teachers, certainly those of young children, to have a deep understanding of how children develop — not just cognitively, but physically, affectively and socially. It had become traditional, therefore, that the main emphasis of courses in initial training for teachers preparing to work in early childhood education, and subsequently the main focus of attention of the teachers themselves, was the study of child development. The findings of researchers in psychology — and in particular those of developmental psychologists — provided the basis of their preparation for work with young children.

A major weakness of this important emphasis, and one that has persisted in teacher education, is that this study has been purely psychological in nature and has seldom been translated into coherent curricular terms. This has meant that the teacher's observations of the child's development have been undertaken in a manner that has been unrelated to his or her theory of education. They have often made no impact, therefore, on the curriculum that the teacher has planned.

Very little time has been devoted, for example, to studying development as an educational concept or to highlighting the significance that the insights offered by research in child development might have for this concept. Instead, teachers have been introduced to the research studies and have been expected to translate the findings into educational practice for themselves. And this is by no means an easy task.

It is not surprising, therefore, that very few teachers have taken on the challenge of 'scholastic experimentation' as a result of their study of psychology. Nor is it surprising that the response of most teachers has been to seek a direct application of research findings to practice in the manner that Piaget considered to be so inappropriate. This, in turn, has led to a negative effect on their practice for it has created several problems for them.

One problem that teachers face is that if the research is studied in purely psychological terms they will be reading the reports of those (including Piaget himself) who have attempted to function as disinterested observers and who offer descriptive accounts of their activities as they pursue the scientific procedures for finding out about human learning. These reports will show that a main aim of the researcher has been to be as dispassionate and objective as possible. Indeed, convincing teachers of the worth of this kind of research is, as a result, a major problem, not least because psychology is not education. The research conditions set up by the psychologist, therefore, which are in some instances laboratory conditions, rarely mirror the realities of a busy classroom.

This problem is discussed by researchers in the Oxford Preschool Research Project who argue that 'any "suggestions" from science that dictate an adult to every child, quiet throughout the day, or expensive materials, will be the butt of practitioners' ironic laughter' (Sylva et al., 1980, p. 16). The findings of such research, if taken on face value, will seem to teachers to be either too obvious or too unrealistic. If such work is rejected by teachers as irrelevant, however, many informed insights into human development will be missed and curriculum theory based on the principle of development will be, as a consequence, impoverished.

A complete rejection of theory and research findings by some teachers is not the only distorting factor that can be seen in professional practice. In other instances there are teachers who have accepted the force of developmental theories, but have interpreted research findings and the theories on which they are based in an oversimplified manner and, it must be said, have often been encouraged to do so in their professional training. The effect of this has led to inconsistencies in their practice. For example, Brown and Desforges (1979) have shown how many teachers of young children express a concern to promote every child's unique development. These same teachers, however, are distracted from considering each child's uniqueness because they evaluate the children's performances by reference to a crude notion of Piagetian stages of human development. Brown and Desforges go on to argue that this inconsistency of approach results in a situation where not only is a genuine concern and support for the individual child lost but also the under-achievement of many children in school is accounted for by the dubious claim on the part of some teachers that these children have not reached the stage in their development which will enable them to learn from the experiences offered.

A third problem in practice — and perhaps the most serious one of all — occurs when it is assumed by teachers that, as psychology is a scientific study of individual development, all psychological research will be value neutral. This has led some teachers to treat the findings of research with equal validity, regardless of the branch of psychology from which these findings have emerged. They have approached research findings with an eclectic attitude, adopting the advice offered if its practical application is obvious and ignoring the assumptions that underlie this advice. And they have been encouraged to be eclectic by those who claim that it is a virtue in practice to find a compromise between any ideas that have a practical application or who assert that to argue for a consistency in approach is an undesirable form of idealism. This eclecticism, however, has led both to muddled thinking and to serious distortions in practice.

Many examples of such distortions can be found but the one that occurs most frequently, perhaps, relates to how the teacher promotes the individual development of the child. All teachers of young children would consider that promoting the individual development of each child in their care was an important part of their responsibility. If asked to describe how this development occurs, most would have some recourse to the ideas of developmental psychology. They would be likely to refer, for example, to the active nature of the child's learning, to how experience is personal and to how the child's development depends on his or her interaction with both the social and physical environment. It is not unusual, however, for these same teachers to translate this idea into practice by devising individualized programmes of learning for each child, a procedure which is derived from behavioural psychology. And they will do so in spite of the facts that such a procedure implies a passive role for the learner and that individualized learning is both impersonal and solitary.

It seems clear from this brief examination of the difficulties that occur when attempts are made by teachers to translate research findings into educational practice that, far from having energized that practice, their study of psychology is more likely to have had a confusing and negative effect. To claim this, however, is not to discount the view that psychology has an important contribution to make to education. Rather it is to highlight the fact that, if this contribution from psychology is to inform practice, then its significance must be expressed in clearer educational terms and should be related to a coherent view of the curriculum.

Indeed, it is becoming increasingly important to clarify what the curricular implications might be. For recent work in the field of psychology raises issues that challenge many educational ideas. Research has taken thinking beyond the work of Piaget and other pioneering theorists and, although the fieldwork has concentrated on development in infancy and continues, therefore, to be of particular interest to teachers of young children, implications can, and should, be drawn for human learning in general.

This chapter sets out to support teachers in making this crucial translation. My intention is to examine aspects of the recent work in psychology from the perspective of curriculum theory in order to clarify the relation between these two sources of understanding. In doing so, I hope to identify the ways in which psychology can inform the practice of teachers and can provide them with more coherent points of reference for curriculum planning.

The discussion will be based on an important premise — that if psychological research is to inform educational practice, then the principles of the psychological and educational theories must be in tune. This point seems to be self-evident but it is one that is worth emphasizing as, unless the assumptions that underlie both kinds of theories are clearly seen to be complementary, then the muddled practice that was discussed above will continue and incoherence will be perpetuated.

For this reason, the chapter will discuss three major themes which have emerged from the work in one field of psychology, that of developmentalism, and will explore the ways in which these themes have influenced one approach to the curriculum, that which is based on a view of education as process and which has led to the informal style of education that is adopted in the primary school. The views about both the nature of the child and the nature of human learning upon which the work of developmental psychologists is based are, as I have argued elsewhere (Blenkin and Kelly, 1987), in accord with the principles that inform a 'process' approach to the curriculum. Indeed, developmental psychology has played an important part in shaping this kind of approach. The research findings of developmental psychologists, therefore, continue to offer those teachers who adopt this approach to the curriculum a rich source of insights into their work.

When teachers embark upon planning a curriculum, important decisions must be made that will affect how the child's role in learning will be characterized, how that learning will be promoted and how experiences will be selected and presented in order to suppport that learning. My three themes relate to these points of decision and explore how choices can be illuminated by research findings from psychology.

The first theme, which I have called 'the competent newborn', examines some recent research that focusses on the nature of the child as a learner. The second theme, 'the growth of competence', looks briefly at developmental theories of skills learning and at the claims made by such theories about the relationship between skills learning and overall intellectual development. The third and last theme, 'culture and cognition', discusses the help that developmental psychology offers teachers when they are making decisions about the content of the curriculum.

The Competent Newborn

There was an intense excitement abroad in the world of early childhood education during the late 1960s and early 1970s. The source of this excitement was a series of results from research studies which had been designed to investigate the very beginnings of human thinking. Advances in modern technology, notably in video recording, had enabled researchers to study closely the activities of tiny babies within weeks, or even days, of their birth. One such researcher, Tom Bower, in an article published at the time, comments on his findings as follows:

> Perhaps the most shocking thing about results like these is the remarkable capacity displayed by the infant subjects. Problem-solving, hypothesis-testing, learning for its own sake, are not phrases that we associate with infants. Indeed, experiments like these, which were originally undertaken to prove that infants begin life with few capacities, have in fact shown the reverse. (Bower, 1971)

In their experiments, researchers such as Bower had devised ingenious ways of posing problems for the babies that they worked with. From the babies' reactions to these problems, several deductions were made about the beginnings of human thinking.

The first was that humans demonstrate intention-directed behaviour from the start of their life. It was noticed, for example, that babies are interested in watching pictures closely but will turn away from them if the images become blurred. When they were enabled to bring the pictures back into focus themselves, by sucking on a comforter which is connected to a focussing mechanism, for example, they combined the two activities of sucking and looking to good effect and showed, by the manner in which they did this, their interest and involvement in the activity. Bower (1977) describes many other practical settings where infants have shown their capacity for combining actions in this way in order to achieve control over their environment and, in doing so, have demonstrated a capacity for solving problems, an ability to formulate a plan in which ends and means match, and an ability to combine actions, when necessary, to form more complex activities. They were able, in short, to deploy skills which enabled them to act intelligently from the earliest age.

A second deduction that was made from these studies was that the environment that was provided for the infants needed to be sufficiently supportive but also challenging. The babies, of course, had limited means at their disposal for achieving their intentions and would show distress and frustration if they could not formulate a plan of action and were reduced to random responses to the problems posed. They showed the same distress, however, if the environment posed no challenges. This point is illustrated well by Jerome Bruner who describes the reaction of babies to an experimental room which was furnished with cream drapes and designed to be a soft and gentle environment for the newborn child. He comments, 'so soft was the visual environment that there was nowhere for the infant's eye to light! Within thirty seconds, he would be in tears. We shifted to a more burly, cluttered style. The infants were immediately more content.' He goes on to conclude that, 'the world activates him or fails to. There are stimulating and supportive environments, and ones that put him to sleep or bore him beyond limits' (Bruner, 1983, p. 148).

A third observation was that the babies were characteristically playful and it was deduced from this that a disposition on the part of infants to try out a range of actions through play was related to their human urge to plan and control activities. Again it is worth quoting from Bruner who explains this playfulness as follows, 'It is as if the play — usually in the form of performing a wide range of acts on a single object or a single act on a wide range of objects — has the effect of sensitizing them to the combinability of the things of the world for goal-directed action' (*ibid*, p. 150).

A fourth deduction made about the beginnings of human thinking as a result of these studies was that social interactions and social perceptions were very important to the child's learning and development from birth. The researchers discovered, for example, that by two weeks of age the baby was able to distinguish his or her mother's voice and face from those of a stranger (Bower, 1977). In many of the studies the babies demonstrated sensitivity to and interest in their interactions with the adults who were working and playing with them. And they showed clear signs, through their eye movements and gestures, that they were able to share the adults' viewpoints (Bower, 1974; Lewin, 1975). From these social interactions it was deduced that, certainly by the age of one year, the babies were sociocentric and were disposed to participate in and even shape the pre-verbal interactions that they became involved in (Bruner, 1981).

Although it is claimed that, in their enthusiasm and surprise at the results of their fieldwork, psychologists such as Bower may have been too emphatic in some of their interpretations, this research showed that the capacities of tiny babies had been seriously underestimated. It followed, therefore, that older children, too, were more capable than had been assumed and this, in turn, influenced the investigations into early childhood that were underway.

As the findings of these investigations into the development of older children were published, it became clear that they confirmed the deductions that had been made about the nature of the child as learner as a result of earlier studies of infancy. They also, however, caused psychologists to question some of the concepts that are proposed within the Piagetian theory of cognitive development.

In a review of this subsequent research, Donaldson, Grieve and Pratt (1983) argue that a new picture of the young learner and his or her development is emerging which is different in several significant ways from the one originally proposed by Piaget. One change in that picture has resulted from the many re-runs of the Piagetian tests of cognition which were claimed by Piaget to prove that young children were egocentric thinkers because they were unable to perceive and think about situations from another's perspective.

In one such experiment, which used Piaget's classic 'three mountains task' (Piaget, 1955), Helene Borke explains that, 'By replicating Piaget's and Inhelder's basic experimental design but substituting a more age-appropriate task, it was hypothesized that children as young as three and four years of age would demonstrate perceptual role-taking ability' (Borke, 1983, p. 256). In her tasks, therefore, the children worked only with the three-dimensional miniature world layouts and were not expected to select two-dimensional pictures to demonstrate how the view would look from a different perspective. Nor were they expected to reconstruct that other view. They were simply asked to turn an identical display to show the point of view of another person. The results confirmed Borke's hypothesis, for not only did the children show a high level of success in interpreting scenes which contained toy replicas of objects and figures which were moveable and familiar, they were occasionally successful also in communicating how another person's view would look on the more static and less familiar three mountain scene which had been used in the original experiments. If the task was age-appropriate, these very young children completed it in a manner that indicated that their thinking was not constrained by egocentrism.

As was noted above, recent work of this kind has cast doubt on some of the assumptions that have been made about the intellectual limitations of young children. In the same way that the studies of babies showed how surprisingly competent the newborn child is, this work is indicating that the capacities of the young child are more extensive than had been assumed. Such work, therefore, has called for some modification of Piaget's stage theory. It has also highlighted a need for other changes in the picture of the individual's development.

The Piagetian theory of development was derived from evidence which had concentrated on the responses of the individual child to tasks set in the physical environment. Piaget's approach was narrowly focussed and did not take account of the social setting or of how each child interpreted the language of the adult researchers.

More recent studies, however, have recorded the degree of the child's sensitivity to the social or interpersonal context, and have shown how this sensitivity has a powerful influence on the child's response. Because of this sensitivity, researchers have claimed, for example, that the development of language and the development of thought are intimately connected and that both depend on social interaction (Wells, 1981). For meaning is construed by the young child in a social setting and the main focus of the child's attention is on making sense of the complex interplay of the evidence provided by the people as well as the objects and materials in that setting. This evidence includes the status, the purposes, the actions and the language of the persons involved, all of which will influence the child's interpretation. Indeed, it cannot be assumed that children will make sense of a situation if the meaning of that situation is entirely dependent on understanding only one feature of that context — the words that are uttered, for example — and on discounting all other evidence. For children in this situation are likely to misconstrue the meaning, particularly if the words are those of an adult, as they are bound by, and sometimes misled by, all the other contextual clues. They are disposed to make sense of situations but their natural manner of doing so is, in Margaret Donaldson's words, context-dependent (Donaldson, 1978).

This finding has prompted researchers to investigate whether or not question and answer techniques — techniques that are commonly used by teachers as well as researchers — are the most effective means of gauging children's levels of intellectual understanding. In one study (Hughes and Grieve, 1983), for example, children were asked bizarre questions by adults and it was found that they almost invariably provided answers, even though the questions were designed to be unanswerable. The children responded to the total context and assumed, therefore, that, as the questioners were adults, their questions must be meaningful. They rarely paid attention to the one feature — the actual words of the question — that would have indicated to them that the task made no sense. They were ingenious, therefore, in providing the adults with answers. The assumption on the part of the children that a question required an answer overrode the fact that no answers could be given to these particular questions and this led the researchers to conclude that 'Psychologists and linguists — and all others who rely on questioning young children — can no longer treat the child as merely a passive recipient of questions and instructions, but must instead start to view the child as someone who is actively trying to make sense of the situation' (*ibid*, p. 114).

The examples referred to above form a small part of the considerable literature that is now available as a result of recent research into the nature of the child as learner. The daunting though important task for the educator is to draw together these findings so that they can be examined in a form that will provide a more coherent and comprehensive reference point for decisions about the curriculum.

From this work it is clear, for example, that the validity of three elements of Piagetian theory have been subject to some revision. Firstly, as was noted earlier, aspects of Piaget's stage theory, and in particular his notion of the learner's egocentricity in the early stages of cognitive development, have been questioned. The young child is able to appreciate another's viewpoint and seems to be sociocentric rather than egocentric. Secondly, Piaget's explanation that development depends upon the learner's interaction with objects and materials in the physical environment has been shown to be inadequate as it neglects social interaction and ignores the interpersonal dimensions of learning. Thirdly, and also in contrast to Piaget's theory, recent research has shown the importance of symbolization, and in particular the importance of language, in cognitive development.

In addition to extending or modifying some aspects of Piaget's theory, these research findings have also confirmed many of the other key concepts in early developmental theory. They have shown, for example, that the nature of human learning is active from birth. In addition, the infants and young children were observed to be playful and this playfulness was seen as a vital means by which they gained control over both their experiences and their learning. The kinds of experiences offered within the child's environment were also found to be crucial. These needed to be appropriately challenging if they were to prompt a positive interaction which would lead to developments in the child's understanding and ability. The undesirable effects on the learner of inappropriate experiences were shown most dramatically in the studies of babies who in some instances ignored or were bored by such experiences and in other instances showed their frustration and distress.

It is clear from this brief summary that, despite the fact that many details are still subject to investigation, when the findings from these research studies are pieced together, the teacher is provided with a comprehensive picture of the child as a learner. By concentrating on what young children can do and by questioning assumptions that have been made about the limitations of children's thinking, developmental psychologists have shown the child to be surprisingly competent.

This is not to say, of course, that they have found no limitations on children's thinking, for they show, for example, that children are bound by the context of their learning and that experience and skills are limited in early childhood. A more detailed exploration of the nature of these limitations and how they might be overcome will be the subject of the next part of our discussion, for these are certainly crucial factors that must influence the planning of an appropriate curriculum.

Before embarking on an examination of this aspect of development, however, it is important to highlight some of the curricular implications that follow if the picture of the learner that is sketched above is used by teachers as a reference for decisions about how the child's role in learning should be characterized. The first implication that can be identified is that it is essential for teachers to evaluate the materials and teaching techniques that are used with the children. There is a wide range of resources and strategies available to teachers and the experiences that result from using some of these can have a negative and constraining impact on the child's role as learner as characterized above. For, as I have argued elsewhere (Blenkin, 1983) the use of inappropriate teaching styles and materials may lead to three serious pitfalls for teachers who are adopting a developmental approach. Learning can become individualized, learning can be made impersonal and the learner can be made passive. If these three pitfalls occur because the wrong approach is adopted, the possibility of encouraging the learner to be active and to make sense of experience in an interpersonal setting and in the manner described above will be denied.

A second implication is that teachers, like the researchers described above, should focus on what the children can do rather than concentrate on their incapacities or assume that certain aspects of their learning begin only with formal schooling. For it is clear that children are already highly skilled before entering school and continue to be so. The more 'intellectually formal' tasks of school do, admittedly, make different demands on the child than those that are met in everyday situations (Donaldson, 1978) and these more formal tasks may cause stumbling blocks for the learner, a point that we will return to later. However, the curriculum that is prepared by the teacher should extend the existing skills of the child in a way that is meaningful. When this approach is adopted and teachers concentrate on what the child already understands and can do, an approach which has been adopted by some teachers in the teaching of early writing, for example, the development of children has been dramatic (Whitehead, 1985). It has, indeed, given new significance to the phrase 'Start from where the child is'. This leads us to a third implication which is that teachers — not children — must learn to 'decentre'. They must both see experiences from the children's viewpoint and share with children their own viewpoint. They must, in Gordon Wells' terms, negotiate meaning so that meanings can be shared (Wells, 1981). This can best be achieved if relationships are informal so that genuine discussions can occur between teacher and children and the classroom talk is not predominantly that of the teacher. In short, the kind of relationship that is promoted between the teacher and learner is crucial and should, when possible, be interactive and informal.

This informality, of course, should extend to the atmosphere and organization of the classroom. For it is clear that the whole context of learning is vital and the classroom environment, therefore, should be set up in such a way as to encourage action, interest, talk and listening of different kinds. Setting such a context is a complex planning activity for the teacher and one which I have detailed elsewhere (Blenkin and Kelly, 1987). The evidence from research re-emphasizes the importance of the context of learning and suggests that the creation of an educational environment is one of the most important aspects of curriculum planning, although it is an aspect that is often neglected by teachers.

We have seen that the powerful notion of 'the competent newborn' has prompted much empirical research and this research has, in turn, provided teachers with many insights into the child's role in learning. It has also provided teachers with a more detailed picture of how the child's development proceeds and how, therefore, it can be promoted, and these insights also have implications for practice.

One source of such insights is the study of the child's development of skills and this takes us to the second theme of this chapter.

The Growth of Competence

One characteristic of children's thinking is highlighted again and again in the research studies of the past two decades and this is that it is context-dependent. If a task is set or a problem arises in a context which makes sense to the children, and if it is a task which enables them to use their existing intellectual skills, then they show that they are highly competent and can extend these existing skills to meet the challenge.

This has been shown to be true even of their mathematical skills such as performing operations on number. In the past it had been assumed that pre-school children's understanding of number was extremely limited and intuitive. Recent studies, however, have shown that this is not so and that, by the time they start school, most children have considerable ability in the area of simple addition and subtraction, provided that the numbers are small and the operation is related to a meaningful situation (Gelman and Gallistel, 1978; Hughes, 1986).

This finding presents teachers with a problem, as most children experience difficulty in performing these operations on number in school. And their difficulties continue throughout schooling, making the teaching of mathematics a major cause for concern. As Martin Hughes explains, 'We have something of a paradox: young children appear to start school with more mathematical knowledge than has hitherto been thought. In that case, why should they experience such difficulty with school mathematics? (*ibid*, p. 36).

It is a difficulty that is partly explained by the context-dependent nature of the child's thinking. Margaret Donaldson, however, extends this explanation and argues that much of school learning, and certainly that of a mathematical kind, requires what she calls 'disembedded' thinking (Donaldson, 1978). By this she means that tasks that are set in school often require thinking that is independent of context, and that require the child to ignore contextual clues and think about only the language used. We saw earlier how difficult this kind of thinking is for the young child.

Donaldson argues that 'disembedded' thinking is not only very difficult for young children but it also creates difficulties for older children and adults. Thinking in a meaningful context, she argues, is relatively easy, but she goes on to say that, 'When we move beyond the bounds of human sense there is a dramatic difference' (*ibid*, p. 76). It is when this move is made that the learner's difficulties often start.

The means by which the learner becomes able to move from 'embedded' to 'disembedded' thinking, therefore, has become the focus of considerable interest to psychologists. One team of researchers, for example, has proposed that there are two dimensions to this problem. Such a move in thinking depends firstly on the children's ability to develop internal representations of experience and, secondly, on their effectiveness at deploying these in a manner which enables them to distance themselves from the context (Copple *et al.*, 1979). These researchers have developed an educational programme which is based on the view that children do not usually develop these abilities spontaneously, but that they need to be encouraged to make internal representations of experience. In other words, children must be helped to reflect upon the materials that they use, to imagine and to create mental pictures of experience. Such representations can only be promoted, according to this team of researchers, if the child is engaged in practical activities which provoke representation, such as symbolic play or early drawing, or if the child participates in conversations about his or her practical experiences. The use of representations in conversation, for example, will enable a degree of distancing from the immediate context to occur which will, in turn, allow the child to achieve a greater degree of generalization of thought. This will not occur, the team argue, if the child is subjected only to questions about experience, because direct questions tend to focus the attention of the child back to the context. Copple, Sigel and Saunders offer a range of examples which show how teachers can promote such conversations with children and how the children are able, as a result, to move towards more 'disembedded' ways of thinking.

Martin Hughes comes to similar conclusions in his study of why children have so much difficulty with the mathematical tasks that they meet in school. He argues, for example, that, 'the formal code of arithmetic contains a number of features which distinguish it from the informal mathematics which children acquire before school' (Hughes, 1986, p. 168). Among these features is a frequent use of context-free statements such as 'two and two make four'. Hughes demonstrates how such statements mystify many young children, including those who are well able to tell him that 'two bricks and two bricks make four bricks'. Hughes argues that, when such context-free statements are combined with other features of the formal code — a heavy reliance on written symbolism such as 2 + 2 = 4, for example — a situation is created which makes it impossible for most young children to make sense of the task and forces many to resort to meaningless recipes for providing a solution or to wild guesses. He suggests, therefore, that children must be encouraged to build links between their informal and their formal understanding of number and that this will involve them in, 'negotiating a complex of subtle and interrelated transitions' (*ibid*, p. 169).

It is on this process of 'translating' understanding from the informal to the formal and back again that the child's development of understanding depends. It is on finding ways of helping the child to make these translations, therefore, that the teacher must focus attention.

Hughes offers two examples of the ways in which this help can be offered. In the first example he shows how, through a variety of games, children can be introduced to arithmetical symbols in contexts where the meaning is clearly understandable. In his second example, which involves the use of a simplified version of LOGO, (a computer programming language which enables very young children to send mathematical commands to control the floor-Turtle) he shows how working with the Turtle 'allows important links to be forged between the concrete world of the Turtle and the formal language of mathematics, and it provides a clear rationale for making these links' (*ibid*, p. 165).

Recent research has highlighted one further dimension of the development of competence that has important implications for the curriculum. This is that, as children become more competent, they become more able to reflect upon their actions and, as this self-consciousness increases, they are more able also to exercise control over those actions and hence over their learning.

This reflective self-awareness or 'metacognition', as it has come to be termed by psychologists, is of increasing interest in research studies. For it is clear that, although in an every-day setting thinking is goal-directed and related to the immediate purposes of the individual, thinking of a more formal kind which is context-free makes different demands on the child. Formal thought requires that the child should be conscious of, and guided by, the processes of thinking and not by the goal that has been set.

It is for this reason, for example, that Margaret Donaldson (1978) emphasizes the importance of becoming literate. For she argues that learning to read is not just important because it is the learning of a skill that, when acquired, gives the child access to the products of a literate society. Becoming literate is also important because it involves the child in thinking of a kind that is free of context, is more controlled and is less goal-directed. Because it facilitates this kind of thinking, the process of acquiring cognitive skills such as literacy enables the child to become more aware of the processes of his or her thinking. By facilitating metacognition, therefore, cognitive skills make it possible for the child's overall thinking to be of a more formal 'disembedded' kind.

Donaldson argues that this is not only true of the thinking of young children but is also true of the development of human think-ing in general. She asserts that cognitive skills play a crucial role in supporting cognitive development at all stages and should, therefore, be of central concern to all educators. In her view, the intellectual demands which can be made of the child in the process of reading have 'incalculable consequences for the development of the kinds of thinking which are characteristic of logic, mathematics and the sciences' (*ibid*, p. 95).

This work on metacognition, although in its early stages of development, is beginning to emphasize, as has been shown above, the importance of the relationship between skills learning and over-all intellectual development. For if the learning of cognitive skills can support the child's ability to exercise intelligent self-regulation and by doing so can facilitate formal, 'disembedded' and self-conscious thinking, as has been proposed by several researchers (Vygotsky, 1962; Cazden, 1974; Donaldson, 1978; Brown and DeLoache 1983), then skills learning takes on a vital status in educa-tion. For, according to this view, the learning of skills not only leads to a growth in competence and a confidence in performance but also promotes intellectual understanding in its broadest form.

These studies of how cognitive development proceeds make it possible for teachers to elaborate upon the picture of the child as learner which was outlined earlier. They also add a further impor-tant dimension which is of great significance to curriculum planning, for they offer insights into the ways in which development can be promoted and indeed into the nature of development itself. This enables teachers to be clearer about their own role in providing for and advancing the children's development.

The studies confirm that an informal, interactive style is essen-tial if the child's learning is to be meaningful. They show, however, that this is not sufficient in itself, as development also depends upon the child's ability to think meaningfully in more abstract settings which are not bound by contextual clues.

The studies show, for example, that human thinking is more naturally context-dependent but that the higher intellectual functions of the mind require more formal thinking, thinking which does not depend upon contextual clues for its meaning. This kind of thinking is difficult for adults and it is not surprising, therefore, that children find that tasks which require formal thinking can be mystifying.

Children often first face the challenge of this kind of thinking when they begin school. Indeed it could be argued that one of the main purposes of schooling is to promote thinking of a more formal, 'disembedded' kind. It is certainly true that school learning often demands this kind of thought from pupils and this, in turn, places an important responsibility on teachers, and in particular on teachers of young children. For they must find ways of helping learners to make translations from formal to informal thinking and back again.

If teachers do not find ways of helping children to make these translations, then many children are likely to find the tasks that are demanded of them in school more and more alienating and meaningless. Even worse, the development of their ability to think in a more abstract way and one which continues to be meaningful to them will be left to chance and may well, as an adult, not happen at all.

In summary, then, the important message of these studies is that the teacher's role is crucial in promoting thinking which is of a more formal kind but which continues to be meaningful to the children. The findings suggest that there are several ways in which translations of thought might be supported and this, in turn, provides teachers with more detailed guidance for their practice. Studies of the growth of competence offer insights into when it is appropriate for an adult to intervene in a child's learning and also show the kind of intervention that is appropriate. They illuminate, in short, the decisions that teachers make about how children's learning will be promoted.

For it is clear that, in their research studies, these psychologists have explored issues which have taken them beyond a narrow consideration of the nature of the child and the nature of development. It has been shown, for example, that, when they have considered the ways in which children move from thinking that is context-dependent to thinking that is context-free, they have implied that certain experiences will facilitate that move.

Translations depend, for instance, on the children's ability to make internal representations of experience. In addition, it is clear that genuine conversations about their experiences seem to encourage children to achieve a greater degree of generalization of thought. Formal thought can only develop, however, from concrete experience which has obvious meaning, and tasks which demand thinking of a formal kind, therefore, should be made only when the children are able to refer back to this concrete situation, if necessary, to work out or to check their solution. Finally, and, perhaps, most significantly, it was shown that the process of developing cognitive skills such as literacy supports the children's ability to think in a manner which is independent of particular contexts, for such skills make it possible for children to become deliberately conscious of their thinking and in this way enables them to exercise intelligent self-regulation.

Implicit in all of these findings is the view that the nature of experience has a significant role to play in development. Psychologists have argued, therefore, that children should be involved in certain kinds of experiences, and in particular those which facilitate symbolic thought. It is these claims which shape the third and final theme of this chapter.

Culture and Cognition

It was argued at the start of the chapter that one problem that teachers must resolve if they are to translate the research findings of psychology into effective curriculum practice is that much of this research is presented to them in the form of descriptive accounts. In order to plan a curriculum, the teacher must make many prescriptive decisions. The psychologist, however, is mainly concerned to let us see how children think. Psychologists, therefore, have tended to insist that it is beyond the scope of their work to provide teachers with prescriptive suggestions.

Despite this, however, it is clear from the research studies that have been cited in this chapter that the researcher often implies, or, in some instances, makes explicit the kind of curriculum that should be designed if the learner's development is to be promoted. Indeed, it has been claimed by Bruner that this is an important part of the psychologist's responsibility for, unless a theory of development is linked to both a theory of knowledge and a theory of instruction, it will be 'doomed to triviality' (Bruner, 1968, p. 21).

In this last section, therefore, we must discuss briefly some of the elements that have been considered by developmental psychologists to be essential to a theory of instruction. For it is in their consideration of these elements that they offer teachers most help in the decisions that must be made about how experiences will be selected and presented to children; decisions, in short, that are concerned with the content of the curriculum.

The pioneering work on a theory of instruction in the field of developmental psychology was undertaken in the 1960s by Jerome Bruner. His theory was based on the assertion that individual development is dependent on an ability on the part of the learner to create representations of the world. We saw earlier in the chapter why developmental psychologists consider that the development of this ability is crucial to formal, disembedded thinking.

These representations of the world can be accomplished, according to Bruner, in at least three ways; through action, through imagery and through symbols (*ibid,*). This led him to argue that instruction should be classified and planned in accordance with three modes — the enactive, the iconic and the symbolic modes — in order to facilitate the different ways in which representations are made.

In his later work, Bruner also emphasizes the representations that are accomplished by very young children through their interactions with those caregivers, usually their mothers, who are very close to them (Bruner, 1981). It can be deduced from this later work, therefore, that a fourth mode of instruction, the interpersonal mode, could be added to his original three.

Bruner argues that children's ability to make representations is influenced by factors that are both internal and external to them. Internal factors include the children's existing competence at symbolizing experience and their preferred style of making these representations. External factors, on the other hand, include those public modes of symbolizing experience that are in use in the society where the children's learning is taking place. The factors that interact as children make representations are, therefore, according to Bruner, both personal and cultural.

The cultural aspect of experience and development is, of course, of great significance to the teacher. Many teachers would argue, for example, that the content of their curriculum should be based on a judicious selection from society's culture and that a major responsibility of education is to transmit to children the best of that culture. Bruner, however, disagrees with this view of the role of culture in education. Although he sees the relationship between culture and development as a crucial one, his characterization of intellectual activity suggests that the link between the two is not straightforward. The culture of society does not, in other words, have significance only when decisions about curriculum content are being made and culture, therefore, should not be seen as something merely to be transmitted.

For the view of developmental psychology is that culture should be seen as influencing the child's cognitive growth by providing modes of representation in a public form and also by providing cultural amplifiers — amplifiers of action, amplifiers of the senses, amplifiers of thought processes. In this way, culture facilitates both the understanding of experience through these modes of representation and their development within the individual child. It provides a public structure through which the meaning of experience can be shared and can also be internalized.

Bruner argues, therefore, that the teacher must ensure that the child's experience of the public and cultural forms of representation is such that it will support and advance his or her development. He argues, for example, that 'the educational process consists of providing aids and dialogues for translating experience into more powerful systems of notation and ordering' (Bruner, 1968, p. 21). Indeed, this was one of the main reasons why he and other developmental psychologists were led, as we saw earlier, to an increased interest in language. For in all human cultures language is one of the most important forms through which representations of experience can be made public.

In summary, Bruner emphasized in his theory of instruction that it is a function of culture to provide the child with experience of public modes of representation. By providing such experience, culture enables the child to structure his or her personal modes of representation. Thus culture provides a further dimension to the support that the child needs if he or she is to move from context-bound to context-free thinking, for publicly expressed modes facilitate the structuring of internal representations of experience.

The implications for the curriculum of this characterization of the relationship between culture and cognition have been elaborated upon in recent years by Elliot Eisner (1982). He, like Bruner, argues that, although individual learners may favour particular modes of representation, an ability to understand and employ different modes is not something that a child acquires simply through maturation.

Indeed, Eisner's main concern is that the opposite is more likely to be true in Western cultures at present. For he claims that schooling systems, by over-emphasizing experiences which lead to discursive and numerical forms of thinking and knowing, reduce the opportunities for representing a wide range of sensory experience. This, in turn, reduces also the ways in which individuals will be able to conceptualize this experience and thus narrows development (*ibid*).

Eisner argues for a more sophisticated view of human development and one which does not separate the affective from the cognitive. He emphasizes the central role played by the senses in what he calls the twin processes of human conceptualization and expression by asserting that forms of representation are 'the vehicles through which concepts that are visual, auditory, kinesthetic, olfactory, gustatory, and tactile are given public status' (*ibid*, p. 50). Like Bruner, he sees the process as dynamic and therefore argues that 'the choice of a form of representation is a choice in the way the world will be conceived, as well as a choice in the way it will be publicly represented' (*ibid*).

He urges teachers to study the uses that people make of the forms of representation that are employed within a culture. Such a study, he claims, will help them to appreciate that there are many dimensions to experience and many ways in which experience is secured. He suggests, for example, that 'the very existence of such varieties should be clue enough that they perform important functions in helping us grasp aspects of the culture in which we live,' (Eisner, 1985, p. 240).

Eisner goes on to provide us with a more detailed image of how cognitive development proceeds for he argues that the notion of forms of representation is not sufficient in itself to explain development. He is of the view that, in the process of conceptualization of experience, each form can be treated in one of three ways. Experience can be represented as a replica (mimetically), as an expression of the deep structure underlying the experience (expressively) or in a manner which conforms to the meaning assigned within a particular culture (conventionally). Eisner (1982) offers many examples of how culture is shaped by public forms of representation and modes of treatment. In discussing such cultural phenomena, he elaborates upon the developmental theory of instruction in a manner which provides teachers with insights into the kinds of experiences that should be made available in schools if the development of children is to be promoted.

It is through the work on culture and cognition, therefore, that developmental psychology offers the most detailed analysis of the kind of teaching that ought to be promoted. Through this work we see added to the description of the nature of cognitive development a prescriptive theory of instruction which has as a central tenet the view that education is itself a developmental process. And in this process different kinds of thinking are to be seen not only as stages through which children may pass on the road to intellectual maturity but also as modes of handling experience which persist into mature adulthood. In short, modes of representation continue to be available to the educated adult for dealing with subsequent experience and converting it into further knowledge which can be culturally defined.

It is, then, in the third theme of this chapter, the theme of culture and cognition, that there is a fusion of ideas which shows clearly that development is a concept which has psychological, cultural and educational dimensions. And this brings our exploration of the world of psychological research full circle to Piaget's assertion which was quoted at the start of the chapter. For many examples of research have been cited which show that the research and analysis that is undertaken in the field of psychology can energize educational practice.

Such a source of energy, however, is conditional. We have seen, for example, that it depends on whether or not psychologists and educationists are making the same assumptions about the nature of the learner and about the ways in which learning proceeds and can be promoted. This is one of the reasons why the work of developmental psychologists provides those teachers who plan education as process with such a rich source of insights into their work and why the advice which is based on research from other fields of psychology can confuse these same teachers and lead them to muddled practice.

This enrichment is also dependent, however, on the realization on the part of teachers that psychologists cannot provide solutions to the problems that they face in educational practice in any direct or Utopian sense. This is the fundamental message that Piaget was concerned to highlight when he asserted that the insights of psychology could inform and enrich education. It has been the main purpose of this chapter to show that, if this enrichment is to happen in any meaningful and practical sense, then the curricular implications of such insights must be clarified.

The Nature of Learning in the Primary Classroom

Maurice Galton

It is only in the last decade that educational researchers have begun to show a greater interest in the complex ways in which young children attend to and process their classroom experience so that it becomes transformed into useful knowledge and generalized skills. Prior to this period the links between teaching and learning were obscure and, with few exceptions, the study of how children learn was regarded as the province of mainstream psychology rather than of education.

History will show that the division has been a source of loss to both sides. Psychologists have been called into schools, as a last resort, to investigate causes of failure rather than to celebrate success in learning. Generations of student teachers have filed into lecture rooms convinced that a discipline which sets out to understand human behaviour, particularly cognitive development, must have some relevance to their work in the classroom. Inevitably ratings of such courses plummet the longer they go on, with students claiming that there is little in the lectures that is of practical help on entering the classroom.

To the psychologist, for whom the importance of the subject for teachers must be self-evident, this reaction must be frustrating and dispiriting. During the past decade, writers on early child development, in particular, have made every effort to make their books more readable. Consider the contrast, for example, between a standard work issued to student teachers at the beginning of the 1970s, such as Lovell's *Educational Psychology*, and a more recent offering such as Sara Meadows' *Understanding Child Development*. Educational researchers have also provided teachers with a reasonable set of prescriptions, mostly embodied in the direct instruction model (Rosenshine, 1983) reflecting the central concepts which underpin information processing theories (Joyce and Weil, 1982). In the SIMPLE Instruction Cycle, Laslett and Smith (1984), for example, suggest that the teacher makes use of the principles developed for storing and retrieving information efficiently by recapping previously taught work at the start of the lesson followed by repeated practice in the use of new material. This material is introduced through teacher talk or demonstration making use of Ausubel's (1978) notion of 'advanced organizers' to structure the presentation. The initial input is then reinforced through question and answer sessions involving the whole class. Towards the end of the lesson, utilizing findings concerning the human memory span, the new learning is reviewed and linked to previous knowledge so that it can be accommodated within the pupils' existing schema, thus aiding long-term retention. Studies of the effectiveness of direct instruction claim that it brings about improvements in learning and performance although the performance measures have been relatively low level (Brophy, 1979). Similar claims have been made in this country by Wheldall (1982) using methods of behavioural analysis to improve performance, in particular, of poor readers.

Difficulties arise when the teacher attempts to apply the above relatively simple ideas in a class of say thirty lively 8 and 9-year-olds. A student teacher, for example, may have prepared a very clear lesson plan along the following lines,

> Sit children on mat, take register, remind them of work we did last week on our trip to Vernon Woods, ask questions to make certain they understood why we collected samples of leaves and soil from different one square metre areas — explain carefully what we are going to do with the samples today. Organize groups — work in groups for thirty minutes — final ten minutes back on the mat where group show each other their drawings and review their results.

When drawing up this plan, however, the teacher had no foreknowledge that during the lunch hour a fight would break out between two of the children so that when they sit on the mat for the introductory session they are restless and cross. The student consequently finds her train of thought continually broken by having to stop her questioning and sort out minor 'misdemeanours' which have a 'knock on' effect on other pupils. Finally, she is forced to raise her voice and rebuke the whole class so that now, when she presents the 'advanced organizer' outlining the task, the children are sullen and inattentive.

Eventually, the class is sorted into groups, but some children cannot find their samples and quarrels again break out when one group of pupils accuses another of stealing their leaves. In the intervening exchanges the samples are spilt on the floor. Peace is finally restored and twenty minutes of useful work completed by dint of the teacher moving rapidly from group to group ensuring that small disagreements do not flare up into a major disturbance. Back in the staff room at the end of the day, the student teacher can be thankful that whoever controls her destiny arranged matters so that neither the class teacher or the college supervisor came into the lesson that afternoon. Almost certainly, if the student were to be asked whether she had found her psychology course of use to her during the lesson, she would have replied negatively.

One reason for the student teacher's failure to relate theory to her practice is that much psychological research on children's learning has usually taken place outside the classroom either under controlled experimental conditions or using clinical interview methods. Our understanding of memory retention derives from experiments using nonsense syllables and random sequences of numbers, while Piaget's theories were developed from close observation and questioning of individual children under controlled laboratory conditions. Even when experiments have been conducted in schools, the artificiality of the exercise has been such that it appears to bear little relationship to a typical lesson such as the one described in the previous paragraphs.

For example, there is extensive research on discovery learning. In these studies the experimental group was given a series of mathematical problems and asked to work out solutions. The success rate of this experimental group was then compared to a placebo who were asked to solve the same problems but were first given some training, unlike the experimental group. Not surprisingly, the placebo group, who only had to apply the strategy they had learnt during training, did much better than the experimental group who had to 'discover' the strategies for themselves (Anthony, 1973). Few teachers, however, would interpret discovery as leaving children to 'find out for themselves' how to solve mathematical 'closed' problems of this kind (Richards, 1975).

These researchers appear to assume that learning under these experimental conditions closely parallels learning inside the classroom, whereas teachers, because of the experiences described earlier, often find themselves in situations where learning appears to be controlled largely by social rather than cognitive factors. Recently, however, educational psychologists have begun to be more interested in the application of learning theory within the classroom, mainly because of the attention now paid to the problem of matching the tasks set to the needs and abilities of the pupils. Interest in the tasks teachers set and, in particular, the ways in which children interpret the teacher's instructions, has led to a better understanding of these social factors and to the development of new theoretical perspectives which, at least, make existing theories of learning more applicable to everyday classroom circumstances.

Turning Teachers into Teddy Bears

An important example of the social effects of learning can be found in research seeking to reinterpret the work of Piaget as reported by McGarrigle and Donaldson (1975). In one experiment on conservation by McGarrigle, children were given a number task. The investigator showed pupils two rows of equal length containing five buttons. When the adult researcher rearranged the buttons so that one of the rows was either shortened or lengthened and asked the children whether the two rows were still equal in length, using the same form of question as Piaget, then 84 per cent of the children did not understand number conservation. The findings also replicated Piaget's earlier research with respect to the age level at which children mastered this developmental stage. However, when the researcher no longer asked the question directly but instead introduced a small mischievous teddy bear who 'messed things up' by moving the buttons, the children's responses changed. The researcher told the children that 'naughty teddy' tended 'to get things wrong' and 'needed help'. In particular, 'naughty teddy wanted to know whether the two rows of buttons were still the same length?'. Now 63 per cent of the children were able to conserve number. Clearly the children found it easier to deal with naughty teddy than they did with the adult researcher.

Some clues for the success of naughty teddy can be found in the writings of John Holt, who has probed the pupil's thinking during class discussion. In his book, *How Children Fail*, Holt describes a sequence in which he asks the children what it feels like when he asks them a question. He sees suspicion in every child's eyes and the relaxed atmosphere in the class suddenly evaporates. One child responds 'we gulp'. Holt goes on to comment:

ERRATUM

line 18: delete the words 'in length'
line 28: delete the word 'length'

He spoke for everyone. They all began to clamour and all said the same thing, that when the teacher asked them a question and they didn't know the answer they were scared half to death. I was flabbergasted . . . I asked them why they felt gulpish. They said they were afraid of failing, afraid of being kept back, afraid of being called stupid, afraid of feeling themselves stupid.

What is most surprising of all is how much fear there is in school . . . Most children in school are very scared. Like good soldiers, they control their fears, live with them, and adjust to them. But the trouble is, and here is a vital difference between school and war, the adjustments children make to their fears are almost wholly bad, destructive of their intelligence and capacity. (Holt, 1984, pp. 70–1)

Holt suggests, elsewhere in his book, that this incident is the direct result of the highly competitive nature of American education with its emphasis on grades and standards. Similar exchanges with 9-year-old pupils have been obtained in the follow up project of the ORACLE study, *Effective Group Work in the Primary Classroom*. To the query 'What do you feel like when the teacher asks you a question?' the pupils replied,

P1: It's like walking on a tightrope.
P2: We guess.
P1: And then you get found out that you don't know the answer.
P2: Then you wait until the teacher tells you and say 'Oh yes, that's it'.

Other researchers, particularly John Elliott (1976) in earlier work on The Ford Teaching Project, have identified what Measor and Woods (1984) have recently called 'knife edging strategies' during class discussion. In one instance, Elliott and his fellow researchers examined the questioning techniques of a particular teacher during a 'discovery' lesson invesigating the effects of pollution on the environment. A number of these 'knife edging' strategies emerged during the lesson. Pupils raised their hands immediately the teacher asked a question but put them down the second before the teacher picked them to answer, pretending to rethink their response. Children seem to have anticipated the research findings on 'wait-time' (Tobin, 1983) and to realize that, by keeping silent for a few seconds when asked a question, they can ensure that the teacher either passes on to another pupil or gives additional clues. Presumably, the 4-year-olds in the naughty teddy experiment also give the researcher the answer they thought he wanted and, when the line of counters was lengthened, they took that as a clue to what they were expected to say.

In the classroom, the discussion process is thus turned into a bargaining encounter in which the teacher seeks to confirm by questioning that the children have understood what has been taught while the children try to delay answering questions until they are certain they know the answers that the teacher wants. Similar bargaining exchanges were much in evidence during the observation of primary classrooms in the ORACLE project (Observational Research and Classroom Learning Evaluation) which was carried out between 1975 and 1980 and also in the follow up study *Effective Group Work in the Primary Classroom* which has recently been completed.

Pupil Behaviour in the ORACLE Study

The first stage of the ORACLE study (Galton *et al.*, 1980; Galton and Simon, 1980) attempted, as one of its main aims, to examine the pupils' behaviour when subjected to different teaching styles. Although the research identified six different styles, a feature of all of them was the strong relationship between the teaching tactics (the interactions during the lesson) and the organizational strategy employed. For example, when teachers were working with individual children two patterns emerged. The larger proportion of teachers found the situation difficult to manage and tended to engage in brief interactions with pupils, mainly of a didactic or managerial kind. There were low levels of verbal feedback with much marking of work by means of a written rather than a spoken comment. These teachers were characterized, as a result of this marking procedure, as *individual monitors*. Another group of teachers had the second highest proportion of individualized working within the sample. However, they were more successful in extending the range of interactions with the pupils in these individualized settings, being able to give high proportions of feedback and improve the proportion of questioning, particularly questions involving higher order cognitive thinking. This group of teachers was at the time, perhaps misleadingly, called *infrequent changers* on account of their tendency to switch from the individualized setting to whole class teaching in response to the perceived needs of the pupils. For example, in cases where the presence of disruptive pupils lowered the average amounts of feedback and questioning because of the need to engage in disciplinary exchanges, the teacher would revert to whole class teaching to raise the level of pupil involvement. These teachers maintained an exceptionally high workrate, interacting with children for upwards of 90 per cent of the day, over 20 per cent higher than the rest of the sample.

At the other end of the scale there were teachers who engaged in the greatest proportion of whole class teaching. Paradoxically, although it was commonly thought that this type of classroom organization was associated with didactic exchanges between the teacher and pupils, it was found in the ORACLE study that these *class enquirers* frequently engaged pupils in challenging interactions so that they asked more open ended questions and made more statements of ideas.

Two of the remaining styles were variations involving different grouping strategies. *Rotating changers* tended to put children in curriculum groups so that, at certain points in the day, the children moved from the maths table to the art table or else remained at the same table but changed the curriculum activity. These changeover periods involved a considerable hiatus in pupil behaviour so that this style of teaching was characterized by a high incidence of disciplinary interactions. A more successful variant of group teaching was provided by the *group instructors* who used ability groups, in the case of mathematics, to introduce the children to new work but then reverted to individualized attention in subsequent exchanges. Finally, a sixth style, that of the *habitual changers*, appeared to be an amalgam of all three organizational strategies whereby the teacher would change from individual work to class work to group work and back again without, seemingly, any obvious reason. Levels of interaction were low and the style was the least successful of any in terms of pupil performance in basic skills.

Some of the most interesting findings to emerge from the project, however, concerned the relationship between these six teaching styles and the behaviour of the pupils. Initially, from the analysis based upon the first year of classroom data, four types of pupil, each type corresponding to a different pattern of behaviour, were identified. *Attention seekers* consisted of pupils who both sought and received 'above average' levels of the teacher's individual attention. The latter group tended to exert a strong influence on the classroom organization and the curriculum. The type was made up of children who generally attracted the teacher's attention because they appeared to be responsible for patterns of disruption as they moved around the classroom. These pupils were prone to take an interest in other pupils' work but not in their own. When summoned to the teacher they would stand in the queue but move back one pace in order to let another child move in front of them, thus increasing the amount of time when they were not working. The presence of a number of such pupils in the classroom would generally cause the teacher to replace practical activities by routine writing and computation tasks where the children were expected to remain seated in their place. In the latter situation the teacher found it much easier to win the following typical exchange.

> *T:* 'What are you doing?'
> *P:* 'Nothing, Miss'.
> *T:* 'O.K. Bring your book here and let me see.'

If the task consisted of completing a page in a worksheet it was easy for the teacher to check whether in fact it was the case that the child had done nothing? If, however, practical activities were involved then the pupil might make a reply such as, 'Collecting the data, Miss' or 'Measuring' and the teacher would have little chance of confirming her earlier suspicion that the pupil was, in fact, wasting his time. In such cases, she could only reply in an exasperated tone,

> *T:* 'Well! Get on with it then.

It was noticeable that the presence of several disruptive *attention seekers* in the classroom would result in a considerable reduction in practical activity of every kind.

The second type of pupils identified in the study were given the name *intermittent workers*. These pupils, as their name implies, tended to work whenever the teacher's attention was focussed upon them but when the teacher was engaged elsewhere they would resume their interrupted conversation. In most cases these conversations were not about their set tasks. It was estimated that the 'typical' *intermittent worker* spent, on average, one day a week engaged in such conversations. These pupils were in sharp contrast to the *solitary workers* who seemed to avoid conversation with other pupils and also with the teacher. Lastly there were the *quiet collaborators*, who, like the *solitary workers*, rarely engaged in conversations with other remaining children in the class even though they would quietly share materials as part of a working group.

The data in table 1 shows the proportion of different pupil types

Table 1: Distribution of Pupil Types Across Teaching Styles (Taken from Galton et al. (1980)) Inside the Primary Classroom)

Pupil Types	All Classes	Individual Monitors 1	Class Enquirers 2	Group Instructors 3	Infrequent Changers 4a	Rotating Changers 4b	Habitual Changers 4c
1 Attention Seekers	19.5	19.0	18.4	5.4	27.5	21.7	22.8
2 Intermittent Workers	35.7	47.6	9.2	32.1	35.3	44.9	38.6
3 Solitary Workers	32.5	31.4	64.5	25.0	33.3	23.2	21.2
4 Quiet Collaborators	12.3	1.9	7.9	37.5	3.9	10.1	17.5
	100.0	100.0	100.0	100.0	100.0	100.0	100.0
N =	471[a]	105	76	56	51	69	114

associated with the different teaching styles. It can be seen that the *class enquirers* and the *group instructors* tend to have classes dominated by pupils who work independently and silently. As expected, *quiet collaborators* were the largest type in the classes of the *group instructors* whilst *solitary workers* comprised 64.5 per cent of pupils taught by the *class enquirers. Intermittent workers* were more likely to be found in classes with the highest level of individualization (*individual monitors*).

The data in the table was taken from year 1 of the study. One of the most significant findings concerns the replication of these patterns during the second year of observation. Although after the first year it was not possible to separate *habitual changers* from *rotating changers*, the patterns from the first year were repeated in every other case. In the second year nearly three-quarters of pupils moved to a new teacher with a different style and changed their pupil type. The results of the replication exercise show clearly, therefore, that the dominant influence on the pupil's behaviour was the teacher's style. For example, pupils who were *intermittent workers* when taught by an *individual monitor* became *quiet collaborators* when they moved to the classroom of a *group instructor*. This is not to say that the teaching style caused the pupils' behaviour. It is clearly possible to envisage, as in the earlier episode involving the *attention seeker*, how the behaviour of the pupil may cause the teacher to adopt a certain style. In the same way, *solitary workers* may force the teacher to contribute more ideas to the class discussion in order to compensate for the pupils' seeming reluctance to participate, thus emphasising the main characteristics of *class enquirers*. These results, however, provide evidence that it is the pupils who appear to be more flexible in terms of classroom behaviour. As already mentioned, nearly three-quarters of the pupils changed their behaviour when they moved classes at the end of the first year and found themselves with a teacher using a different style. In the smaller group of teachers who were observed in both years (about 12 per cent of the sample) none changed their style over the period (Galton and Willcocks, 1983).

Further observation of pupil behaviour during the transfer from primary to secondary school showed certain variations within some of these pupil types. For example, the sizeable group, known as the *solitary workers*, now appeared to consist of two distinct subgroups. The first of these, the *easy riders*, worked continually but slowly, taking every opportunity to mak routine tasks last as long as possible. When, for example, they were told by a teacher to mark out their book in a certain way with a 2 cm margin, using a sharp pencil, these pupils would take a considerable time to find the ruler, would mark the 2 cms carefully in several places and would, if the opportunity arose, deliberately break the point of the pencil so that they had to get up from their place and re-sharpen it. In stark contrast to this behaviour were the activities of pupils known as the *hard grinders*. They worked quickly and efficiently, so much so that in classes containing both types of pupils, teachers would find it very difficult to manage the range of work. On occasions, some pupils might have completed a full exercise while others had barely written the title. In such cases, teachers would exhort the slower pupils to speed up and try to delay the quicker ones. *Hard grinders* would be told to look over their work and check their mistakes because they 'could not have finished so quickly'. In these classes, therefore, teaching rapidly moved towards the mean with the consequent mismatches at the extreme ends of the ability range, identified by Bennett *et al* (1984). In the secondary and middle school transfer classes, *easy riding* was associated particularly with mathematics. Nearly 80 per cent of the pupils indulged in this kind of behaviour in this curriculum area. In English and in Science there were differences with respect to gender. Nearly two-thirds of the *easy riders* in Science lessons were girls whereas the reverse was true in the case of English (Galton and Willcocks, 1983).

Attention seekers also contained a small sub-group called the *fuss-pots* who took every opportunity to engage the teacher in fairly trivial questions of the kind requiring reassurance, such as asking the teacher whether they should go on to question 3 having finished question 2. Such pupils rarely completed a task without consulting several times with the teacher to make certain they were following the instructions correctly.

Explanations of Pupil Behaviour

An important feature of many of these behaviours was that they concerned task avoidance. In lessons of the *class enquirers*, characterized by discussion with a relatively high proportion of challenging questions and statements, the majority of pupils tended to remain silent. When working on schemes or worksheets, pupils slowed the rate at which they completed their tasks, either by *intermittently working* or by *easy riding*. A small group of disruptive pupils tended to avoid work altogether, preferring to move around the class showing interest in what other children were doing rather than in their own activity. The situation appears not unlike that described by Holt,

> A year ago I was wondering how a child's fears might influence his strategies. This year's work has told me. The strategies of most of these kids have been consistently self-centred, self-protective, aimed above all else at avoiding trouble, embarrassment, punishment, disapproval, or loss of status. . . .
>
> Even . . . when I did all I could to make the work non-threatening, I was continually amazed and appalled to see the children hedging their bets, covering their losses in advance, trying to fix things so that whatever happened they could feel they had been right or, if wrong, no more wrong than anyone else . . . They are fence-straddlers, afraid ever to commit themselves — and at the age of 10. Playing games like Twenty Questions, which one might have expected them to play for fun, many of them were concerned only to put up a good front, to look as if they knew what they were doing, whether they did or not.
>
> These self-limiting and self-defeating strategies are dictated above all else by fear. For many years I have been asking myself why intelligent children act unintelligently at school. (Holt, 1984, p. 91)

One consequence of these behaviours concerns the argument that Direct Instruction is effective because by training teachers to set clear objectives it can provide a secure 'safe' structure where pupils are no longer anxious because they are certain what they have to do to achieve success. The data presented in the ORACLE study seems to suggest that the children may also prefer this kind of structure, not because it is safe but because it enables them to manipulate it to their advantage in order to avoid the possibility of failure. Several of the 'impressionistic' accounts which all observers were required to complete when the lesson ended, describe situations where pupils began to cause disruption in the classroom as soon as the teacher set more difficult and demanding tasks.

In one case, for example, the children quietly, and apparently happily, carried out the first stage of a task in which they were to solve mathematical problems which were presented as the clues to a crossword. First, however, the pupils were told to draw the crossword in their exercise books and shade in the black squares with a felt tip pen. Once this task was completed and the more difficult activity of working out the computations began, the children increased their demands on the teacher, calling out and complaining that they did not understand or they could not solve a particular clue. At one time, nearly a third of the class was queuing around the teacher's desk until eventually he was forced to shout and tell them to go back to their places and that only one pupil was to come out when he called 'next'. At the back of the class three boys were to be found as if in their starting blocks for the 100 yards race, and on the command 'next' they rose and ran up the classroom.

The contrast between the first and the second half of this lesson could not have failed to produce different impressions of the teacher, if by chance, a visitor had been passing by the window of the classroom. For the first half of the lesson, the visitor would have seen a classroom with many of the characteristics which define effective teaching in the eyes of a teacher's colleagues — a classroom full of well behaved, hard working children — while in the second half of the lesson there was 'loss of control'. which is a pre-occupation of great importance in teaching (Nias, 1986). Given a similar experience on other occasions, a teacher is unlikely to depart, to any great extent, from safe, relatively undemanding lessons.

The above description of the exchanges between teacher and pupils is a good example of what, two decades earlier, Howard Becker and his colleagues observed in an American Liberal Arts College, which they described as 'exchanging performance for grades' (Becker *et al.*, 1968). In these colleges, freshman classes were more likely to be taken by newly-appointed instructors on temporary contracts. Hope of a permanent appointment largely depended upon their ability to gain a reputation as an effective lecturer. One manifestation of this success would clearly be the students' reaction to their courses. Ineffective instructors would find that students didn't turn up in large numbers to the lectures, complained to their personal tutors that they could not understand the content and gave in their written assignments late.

The students, too, had problems. To remain in college they had to maintain a certain grade average throughout their first year and this partly depended on the difficulty of the assignments, since the more challenging these were, the more difficult it was to get a good grade. Becker and his colleagues described the subtle, subconscious negotiation that went on between the students and the instructors. Early in the course, work that was perceived by the freshmen to be difficult would be met with complaints and a certain degree of restlessness during the lecture or tutorial. The anxious instructor would attribute this response to his lack of experience, simplify the assignments and thereby set lower grade standards. The students' response would improve and more satisfaction would be expressed about the course. The instructor, noting this improved behaviour, would conclude that his lectures were now 'pitched' at the appropriate level.

Becker, like John Holt in the passages quoted earlier, which is an example of similar bargaining at a primary level, puts the blame for this pattern of interaction on the highly competitive nature of the American education system, of which the emphasis on attaining good grades is one manifestation. For the American freshman, or for that matter the American primary pupil 'above average' grades are one of the main ways of establishing a 'good self image' with one's parents, teachers and peers. While it may be true that, in terms of formal assessments, English primary education is relatively free from this pressure (although according to Barker Lunn (1984), the emphasis on assessment has again increased) there are more subtle ways in which teachers 'test out' children in their classrooms. Reading aloud, answering the teacher's questions, gaining the teacher's approval for a piece of work, are all ways in which pupils can establish themselves in the eyes of their peers and the teacher.

Within this class climate, a pupil's dilemma, when faced with a new and challenging situation, is how to seek appropriate ways of dealing with the situation so that, at a minimum, it does no harm to this individual's self-esteem. One to one private negotiations with the teacher are therefore preferred because there is less risk in such a situation of a public demonstration of incompetence. Class discussion is the next best alternative, first because in the typical primary classroom there is a one in thirty chance that the teacher will pick a particular child, and second because there are well tried strategies, as described earlier by Holt and Elliott, for saving face if, by an unfortunate chance, the teacher actually picks a particular individual. Group work presents the greatest threat to a pupil's self-esteem, not only because when the teacher joins the group there is less chance of avoiding exposure, but also because the task will often be organized in ways which require individuals within the group to make a particular contribution. Any failure to make an effective contribution may result in public exposure at the synthesis stage, when the pupil may be blamed by the other children, in front of the whole class, for their collective failure.

> *P1:* 'John was supposed to work out the distance, Miss, but he got it wrong.'

In groups, therefore, children attempt to bargain for safer patterns of work, by appointing a leader who does most of the talking or by drawing the teacher into the discussions and trying to renegotiate work on an individual basis. When, in the follow up ORACLE study *Effective Group Work in the Primary Classroom*, children were shown cartoon pictures of different classroom activities and asked for their preferences, they rated individual work highest, class work next and group work lowest. Within the group work category they differentiated clearly between group work involving a practical activity, which was rated more highly than group tasks involving discussion.

Using Doyle's (1979) terminology, most group tasks have high 'ambiguity' and 'high risk'. From numerous transcripts, collected during the group work study, it seemed that in many classrooms this ambiguity increased during group work because teachers, although very good at providing 'advanced organizers' concerned with what children had to do, were extremely bad at providing explanations of why children were required to work in this particular way. During interview, children regularly responded to questions about working in groups with the reply, 'I don't see the point of it'. Greater ambiguity was created because of the emphasis placed by teachers on being 'in control' of the social interactions within the classroom while, at the same time, they encouraged children to think independently within such groups. For example, the status of questions was never quite clear. Was it, for example, part of the enquiry process — a response to the teacher's oft quoted remark, 'I want you to learn from your mistakes', or was it a check on the pupils' attentiveness — a wrong answer bringing a reproof for not paying attention? Faced with this uncertainly, most pupils bargained for 'safer' ways of working, leaving the teacher to determine the appropriate cognitive and social outcomes.

Bringing this bargaining into the open can, for the teacher, be a risky and therefore stressful business. But to create the kind of classroom climate where children do not maintain a total dependency on the teacher, where they are prepared to risk wrong answers and respond to challenges, requires these risks to be undertaken. In the process we, as teachers, will have to expose our feelings of uncertainty to our colleagues and in some cases to our pupils.

On a personal note, my own short return to the classroom

reinforced my view of the importance of this approach, while at the same time bringing home to me the stress involved. In one instance, I attempted to negotiate with the children an arrangement whereby, in return for allowing them to spread themselves around the library area and read in comfortable chairs, they would agree to behave reasonably since I could no longer keep all of them in my sight. Inevitably, I found myself facing the usual challenges from these pupils because, presented with what appeared to be a new bargain, they needed to test out its limits. There are no adequate words to describe my feelings when, for example, the deputy head arrived with prospective parents to find two pupils fighting over the right to sit in a particular chair. Even pupils who I felt I could trust in any circumstance began to react and fool about. By the end of the session, the children were all back at one end of the library where I could see them and constantly control their misdemeanours. I had shouted and they were satisfied they had found out I was like all teachers who offered bargains of this kind.

However, there is always another day and with the support of colleagues I was determined to try again. Next morning, some pupils were clearly discomforted by a teacher who tried to explain how he had felt during yesterday's session — how he wanted a classroom where he, as well as they, could be happy and relaxed. The children were generous in their response and out of these small beginnings came lengthy discussions about one's feelings when asked a question or when asked to read aloud or how it felt when one had an idea and the teacher came and interfered. Discussing such incidents from my point of view as well as theirs made it possible for some children to realize that my 'interference' was really a clumsy attempt to help. This led to further discussions about ways in which they might signal to me when they wanted help, when they thought I was taking over and so on.

The above account is not presented as an example of good practice, although in the hands of more experienced teachers, with better craft knowledge, I am sure it could have been. The incident is included to illustrate the point that learning is an important social activity as well as a cognitive one, and that we have concentrated too much on the developmental stages in the child's thinking while paying too little attention to similar development in the growth of the child's social awareness when working with adults and peers. To give one further example, children often say that one of the main qualities of a 'good' teacher is fairness. It needs, however, the kinds of negotiation previously described for children to appreciate that the concept of fairness is not measured on a uni-dimensional scale. A pupil may say,

> It's not fair. I talked once and got done but she talked several times and didn't.

Looking at this incident from the teacher's point of view, the pupil's intervention may have occurred at a crucial moment during the lesson, when the rest of the class had finally settled or when an important piece of information, necessary for completing the task, was being explained.

For some teachers, opening up a debate of this kind, which appears to allow children to challenge one's decision and therefore one's authority, is to run grave risks of 'losing control'. Recent research, including that of the ORACLE studies, however, suggests that unless there is continuity between a teacher's approach to the management of learning and the management of behaviour then attempts to develop strategies for independent learning in children are doomed to failure. This is because of the exchange bargains, based on risk avoidance, which take place in a classroom climate controlled by the teacher. In such a climate it is arguable, as those in favour of direct instruction do (Gage, 1981; Brophy and Good, 1986), that teachers should increase the amount of whole class teaching and concentrate on talking 'at' rather than talking 'with' children more effectively.

There are, however, many primary school teachers who reject this view and who continue to seek ways in which they can maintain classroom control without adopting what Sieber (1972) describes as power-coercive strategies of leadership. In the past such teachers, when putting this case to colleagues, have had to argue on the basis of conviction rather than from empirical evidence. Thankfully, psychologists and researchers in education are now beginning to provide the evidence to reinforce these convictions.

Informality, Ideology and Infants' Schooling

Ronald King

What is usually called informal education is probably characteristic of most British infants' schools. The caution of this statement is due to the vagueness of the term 'informal education', and the absence of any research about the incidence and distribution of the use of different approaches. 'Progressive', 'child-centred', 'open' (used particularly by American commentators) and perhaps even 'exploratory' (of the HMI survey of 1978) are near synonyms for informal.[1] Robin Alexander (1984) considers such terms are 'too vague to be useful' and to have 'strong evaluative overtones'. However, their vagueness and emotional charge are part of their social strength. Galton *et al.* (1980) have similar reservations to Alexander's, but their typology of teaching styles, individual monitors, class enquirers etc, has little currency among teachers. The major research into teaching methods, although sometimes claiming to be of 'primary schools', have been of junior or middle schools and departments (Bennett *et al.* 1976; Galton *et al.*, 1980).

Comparing this research with my own of infants' schools (King, 1978) and junior schools (as yet unpublished), it is clear that whatever is meant precisely by informal methods, they are more common in infants' than junior schools. Neville Bennett's (1976) typology of junior teachers was produced by a cluster-analysis of teachers' self-reported practices. The ideal typical most 'progressive' teacher favoured integration of subject matter, allowed children choice of work, whether in groups or individually, choice of seating, some freedom of movement and talk, used little assessment by testing, and favoured 'intrinsic motivation' — in my research experience, a typical infants' teacher. In my research, both infants' and junior teachers have expressed what is special and different about themselves and the other group, and although the terms are not commonly used, the former think of themselves as informal and are thought to be so by the latter. Michael Bassey's (1978) survey of 900 primary school teachers, implicitly accepted that those of infants' and junior were different by asking each mainly different questions about their approaches.

Ideology and Informality

Infants' (and nursery) education has a different and separate history and ideology to that of junior education. Nanette Whitbread's (1972) chronicle of the 'evolution of the infant–nursery school' is marked by the names of famous educator-ideologues: Fredrick Froebel, Maria Montessori, Susan Isaacs, Rachel and Margaret McMillan. The term 'primary education' and the existence of schools for the 5 to 11 or 12 age-range often obscures these infant–junior differences.

Educational ideologies exist at a number of different levels. Most were originally articulated by the ideologues whose names are usually only remembered when their ideas become accepted and institutionalized in practice. Those of infant education have been perpetuated through the teachers' colleges they or their followers founded, that may still bear their names. Unlike many countries, the central authority of state education in Britain has not usually made explicit ideological formulations or prescriptions (although this may be changing with what seems to be the demise of consensus politics). However, the Central Advisory Council (1967) chaired by Lady Plowden clearly endorsed informal education, glossed by developmental psychology, as shown in their rather sentimental vignettes of composite schools in their 'outstanding' or 'good' categories, based upon unexplicated criteria in surveys by HMI. (The more recent survey of primary education (HMI, 1978) says, despite its title, little about the education of under-7s who figure only once in all the subsequent series, namely in *Education 5–9* (HMI, 1982) which considers only the minority case of first schools as distinct from infants' schools). The official ideology of the Plowden Report is essentially one of child-centredness:

> At the heart of the education process lies the child. No advance in policy, no acquisitions of new equipment have their desired effect unless they are in harmony with the nature of the child, unless they are fundamentally acceptable to him (sic). (CACE, 1967, p. 7)

Children are seen as passing through a naturally ordered sequence of physical, physiological, psychological and social development, although each child possesses a unique individuality. Young children are viewed as naturally curious, exploring and discovering things around them, learning best through their play when they are happy and busy, and free to choose to do what is of interest to them. Education is seen as creating conditions which acknowledge these properties and allow the full development of individual potential — the horticulture model as Bernstein and Davies (1969) have called it.

Ideologies have real consequences when they are taken for granted as the truth or the 'way things are'. Infants' teachers (and others) internalize their recipe ideologies (Schutz, 1954) through their professional education (they follow separate and different courses to other students), and confirm them or attempt to confirm them, in their teaching. It is possible to distinguish a number of important elements that comprise infants' teachers' child-centred ideology; developmentalism, individualism, play as learning, and childhood innocence (King, 1978).

The first three of these elements were explicitly endorsed by the Plowden Committee (1967).

> Knowledge of the manner in which children develop, therefore, is of prime importance in avoiding educationally harmful practices and in introducing new ones. (p. 7)

> Individual differences between children of the same age are so great that any class, however homogeneous it seems, must always be treated as a body of children needing individual attention. (p. 25)

> Adults who criticise teachers for allowing children to play are unaware that play is the principal means of learning in early childhood. (p. 193)

The idea of childhood innocence was not explicitly expressed by the committee, perhaps because it was so widely accepted as to be unremarkable. However, I would argue that childhood innocence has a special status in the ideology of infants' teachers. It is not the case that they regard young children as being incapable of doing things that they, the teachers, define as being naughty, but that the children could not be blamed for these things, because they had not yet developed the capacity to control themselves. This state of innocence also required young children to be protected from what were thought to be unpleasant aspects of the outside world — an attempt to preserve a world of childhood in the face of adult reality.

This child-centred ideology not only defines the nature of children and their learning but also that of their teachers' teaching. Since children learn best when they are happy, and are innocent in their intent, their teachers show professional pleasantness, affection and equanimity, the latter being most remarkable. When the paints are spilt for the fourth time, when someone has let the hamster out or wet his pants, their teacher stays calm with little emotional response, privately rebuking herself when this equanimity is momentarily disturbed (King, 1978).

Informality and Social Class

Informal approaches may be typical of infants' teachers but not universal, as the controversy over a Surrey headteacher showed[2]. Her introduction of such standard infants' practices as sand and water play, lego construction and dressing up, led to some parents protesting. The social distribution of different teaching styles is not at all clear[3]. Bennett's (1976) junior school study showed that the children in his sample taught by teachers he defined as progressive, had lower average measured ability than those taught by formal methods. Given the statistical association between social class and measured intelligence, this suggests they were more commonly working rather than middle class in origin. Are informal methods introduced as a solution to a defined problem of underachievement or behaviour? The McMillan sisters introduced their new approach for the slum children of Deptford and Bradford, but Isaacs catered for what were ironically called 'Kensington cripples' (Whitbread, 1972). The class origins of the use of informality are mixed, although the originators were mainly middle class women.

Informal methods might be thought to correspond to Basil Bernstein's (1975) 'invisible pedagogy', a 'particular form of pre-school/infant school pedagogy'. Unfortunately, we are not told what other forms there are. Bernstein regards the invisible pedagogy as being particularly advantageous for the children of what he admits is an ill-defined 'new middle class'. Karabel and Halsey (1977) are wrong in referring to this paper as being based on re-search. A secondary analysis of my own empirical data led to the conclusion that the invisible pedagogy could not be found (King,

1979). According to Bernstein the pedagogy is predicated upon a particular 'knowledge code'. This theory of codes is a self-sustained academic conceit, which may in time be regarded as being as quaint as MacDougall's (1908) hormic theory of human behaviour. Both theories purport to explain much but explain nothing, there being little or no empirical evidence for the real existence of either instincts or codes.

Whatever the social distribution of informal approaches, Bernstein, in his earlier work, thought them inappropriate for lower working class children, who would benefit most from formal methods. 'The passivity of the working class pupil makes him (sic) peculiarly receptive of drill methods, but resistant to active participation and co-operation' (Bernstein, 1961). No observer of reception class children in schools serving working class catchments is likely to regard them as 'passive'. Their teachers do rate them (especially the boys) slower at settling in than middle class children (Davie *et al.*, 1972), and rate them less favourably for behaviour and school work (again, especially the boys) (King, 1978; Brandis and Bernstein, 1974). We do not have the information to know if they are more favourably assessed when they are treated more formally. In America, compensatory education programmes for young children have typically used 'drill' techniques (for example, Bereiter and Engelmann, 1966), some of them using Bernstein's early work as their justification.

Middle class mothers interviewed by Julia Jones (1966) were more likely to report that they had prepared their children for the prospect of school than working class mothers. They point to the similarities between home and reception class, such cultural continuities as the kind of play activities (the actual toys may have been bought from the same catalogue), and encourage their children to be active pupils, to take part in things. Working class mothers were more likely to pose school as being different to home ('you won't be able to do that when you go to school') and encourage their children to be more passive ('do what the teacher tells you'). It's by no means sure that these reported practices have the consequences the mothers intended (as the teachers' class-differential ratings of children show). Reception class activities are probably more familiar to middle class children, who John and Elizabeth Newson (1977) have shown are more likely than working class children to paint, draw, write and read for pleasure at home. These homes and gardens children have access to private spaces, single bedrooms, designated play and storage spaces. Not only are the material conditions of their homes similar to those of school, but also the quality (I write non-evaluatively) of their relationships with significant adults. The middle class mothers' propagation of principles of behaviour that prevail independently of their feelings or emotional state (Newsons, 1977) is matched by the professional equanimity of infants' teachers (many of whom are middle class mothers). Working class mothers are more likely to smack their children and respond to their behaviour according to their own moods. Working class children are more commonly street children, playing with other children, not as host or guests in homes and gardens, but in public places, sorting out their own quarrels and differences and subject to the arbitrary authority of any adult, ('go and play somewhere else').

It is often assumed that young children feel reassured by familiarity in times of transition. However, the familiarity of the activities of the infants' reception class may be boring to some middle class children. They are certainly exciting in their novelty to some working class children, for whom the play facilities are an Aladdin's Cave. I have observed such children rushing from one toy to another in a near frenzy of new experiences. They quickly find that their usual methods of negotiation, grabbing, pulling and fighting, lead to the intervention of their teacher, not with a smack or rebuke, but with distraction ('Why don't you play with this lovely engine?') and enunciation of principles ('Toys are to share. Let Kevin have his turn. You can have yours later') The remarkable growth of forms of confusingly called pre-school education (reviewed by Jean Northam, 1983) has introduced many children to some elements of the materials and methods of the infants' reception classes. Pre-school playgroups were originally the initiative of middle class mothers, but they are spreading to working class areas, so that more children may be finding the reception class activities all too familiar. Some teachers regard an adequate experience of classroom play as a prerequisite for further learning. It could be that this earlier experience of adult organized play may lead to the earlier introduction of more formal learning in school.

Informality and Social Background

The social class distribution of informal methods may be unclear, but such methods allow, indeed encourage, children's presentation of their class-based (and sometimes ethnically-based) cultures. The origins of these cultures are highly visible when parents are allowed and encouraged to come into classrooms to be seen and to talk about their children. Newstime ('who did something exciting over the weekend?'), pictures ('draw me a picture of your house') and discussions ('what shall we talk about — our favourite things?'), all present teachers with information about children's home-lives.

Playing in what was known, in more sexist days, as the Wendy house allows children to act out extra-school experiences. *Child Education* (1986) invited infants' teachers to draw on their own experiences in commenting on ten invented classroom incidents (For example: 'A group a children are overheard playing in the hospital created from house play provision in the nursery. Tracey: 'I'll be the doctor', Sean: 'No you can't, only boys can be the doctor. Not girls. You be the nurse.'). The teachers reported children simulating sexual intercourse, expressing racist and sexist sentiments, and dis-valuing school work in conditions of high unemployment.

Such incidents, and others (as in my research of 1978) such as stealing and swearing, are a challenge to the ideology of childhood innocence, and show how although their teachers may attempt to protect them from what they (the teachers) may define as unpleasant and upsetting things, they are part of the extra-school experiences of some children. The response to these events may be to ignore them (as in my research, when a boy caused much amusement among other children with a plasticine penis), or distraction. In the Child Development investigation, sex-play was interrupted by Postman Pat delivering a letter.

Teachers use such experiences in their typifying of individual children (King, 1978). Childhood innocence is preserved by attri-buting unacceptable behaviour to the children's family-home background, which also preserved the teachers' faith in their in-formal pedagogy. However, these methods and the associated classroom material provision allow the legitimate expression of such experiences.

Informality and Material Conditions

The social structure of an informal infants' classroom consists of repeated patterns of behaviour between teacher and pupils. To be in a classroom before school started (as my research of 1978) and to observe (in time) the familiar patterns of social relationships as the teacher and children arrived, was to see the creation of a social structure; also, as the day continued, to see how this structure was not static but a process — the continued interaction of the participants. None of them were 'inside' the classroom social structure; what they repetitively did *was* the structure. All social structures are created in material conditions, such as classrooms and playgrounds (indeed, the participants creating these structures, the teachers and children, are themselves material objects). Clearly, the nature of social relationships and the subjectivities that are part of the participants' actions are related in some way to the material conditions. What are the material conditions required for informal infants' education? Bernstein (1975) hints that his elusive invisible pedagogy requires generous material provision. Westbury (1973), in a prescriptive and evaluative article, assumes that the teachers' limited material resources prevent their engaging in an ill-defined 'open-education'. (Westbury could have tested this hypothesis from a survey of provision and pedagogical practices in Canadian schools. It would have been simple to have correlated the incidence of 'chalk and talk' with, for example, class size.)

Sharp and Green (1976) give a similar importance to the supposed consequences of material conditions for pedagogical practice, proposing that infants' teachers use of 'busyness' was a response to their having to teach large classes of children, and not a consequence of their professed 'progressive' (Sharp and Green's term) ideology. Sharp and Green's research was of three (of four) teachers in the infants' department of a 5–11 school, and of the headteacher. Their main method was the use of 'probing' interviews, and although observations (by three different observers using three different methods) were used, they report few descriptions of classroom events. Their study has all the elements of neo-Marxist theory which, David Hargreaves (1978) has suggested, did not arise from the research but were applied retrospectively.

In the absence of the once-predicted revolution, neo-Marxists pose a basically functionalist explanation of structures in capitalist societies, as perpetuating those societies. Hence Sharp and Green's conclusion that progressive infants' education is conservative in perpetuating the existing capitalist order. The continued existence of capitalism is also explained by false consciousness — that workers do not know their 'true' interests, the overthrow of capitalism. Thus Sharp and Green largely ignore the explanations the teachers give of their practices. The material determinism of their Marxism is shown in their proposal that the teachers' practices were not an expression of their ideology (false consciousness) but of the material conditions of overcrowded classes.

In my research (King, 1978) a few teachers were defined by their headmistresses as not being 'proper infants' teachers'. They did do things differently to their colleagues, for example, using direct control of children ('don't do that') rather than oblique control ('someone's being silly'). They were aware of their being different, and they and their headmistresses attributed this to their not being 'infant trained'. This contradicts Sharp and Green's view that the constraints of material conditions, rather than ideology, accounts for infants' teachers' practices. These teachers worked in the same material conditions as their colleagues, but taught differently because of their non-acceptance of elements of the ideology of informal infants' teaching. Sharp and Green's analysis of Mapledene Lane School traduces infant education. Their conclusions were reached independently of the research, and could be applied to any form of education (including those in non-capitalist societies). They explain nothing that is special about infants' education, or of the particular school they studied.

To repeat my question: what are the material conditions for informal infants' practice? We know little about the relationships between class size and teaching methods. Neither Galton *et al.* (1980) nor Bennett *et al.* (1976) seem to have investigated this in junior and middle schools. Is the embarrassing relationship between class size and reading attainment (as in Little *et al.*, 1971) due to the use of more effective practices in larger classes? Bennett *et al.* (1980) have shown that different pedagogies may be practised in the same design of open-plan primary school. Material conditions do not determine practice in any simple way.

Infants' teachers in my research (King, 1978) were adept at defining many things as educational resources. Their use of egg boxes, cans and many other cheap and easily available objects was extensive and imaginative. Coping with shortages could be a test of resourcefulness, a matter of pride and congratulation among colleagues. However, the lack of some material resources could limit practices. Lack of space could make playing and working on the floor difficult. Painting and other activities were not easily arranged without a classroom tap and sink. There are limits to the inventiveness and ingenuity of any teacher.

At least one clear example of the relationship between ideology, material provision and pedagogical practice concerns play in infants' classrooms. The play-as-learning ideological element is related to the developmentalism element, in that older children are defined as having developed to need less play. This definition is made to have real consequences by providing these children with fewer play materials and possibilities. The classrooms of 7-year-olds have no Wendy houses (or their unisex equivalents) (*ibid*).

Informality and First Schools

The age-structure of educational institutions is becoming more diverse. Children may be changing schools at 7, 8, 9, 10, 11, 12, 13 or 16. This diversity is a consequence of the introduction of many kinds of comprehensive secondary schools. Of the new forms of primary education, middle schools for 8–12 or 9–13-year-olds have attracted more attention than first schools for 5–8 or 5–9-year-olds (see King, 1983). The 5–8 version was endorsed by the Plowden Committee (CACE, 1967) as an extension of the infants' school, a view shared by the headteachers in my study (King, 1978). In discussing the prospect of reorganisation into 5–8 schools they rejected the local authority advisors' invitation to discuss the first school philosophy since they saw Plowden's recommendation to set up such schools as an endorsement of the 'philosophy' and methods of infants' schools. Subsequently, the middle school teachers in the area have expressed the view that their former first year juniors were getting another year's infants' schooling.

How do the three types of school differ, other than in age-range? Her Majesty's Inspectors (1982) take the view that, 'There are marginal differences between these two kinds of first school and others with the more traditional age ranges'. This may be so in terms of the limited and often unexplicated criteria used by HMI's in their evaluations, but their own survey results do show differences that may be significant. The 'main phase experience' of teachers in 5–8 schools was mainly (63 per cent) in infants' schools, only 10 per cent in junior schools, compared with 46 and 23 per cent, respectively, in 5–9 schools. This may have followed from the origins of the schools, most 5–8 schools having been formerly infants' schools (73 per cent), but most 5–9 schools having been junior with infants' (5–11) schools (68 per cent). This may explain why 46 per cent of the headteachers of 5–8 schools were formerly infants' heads and 30 per cent formerly combined school heads, compared with 13 and 40 per cent, respectively, for 5–9 schools.

In my own study the view of the planning committee was that it would be a 'good thing' if more staff in the new 5–8 schools were men, usually with reference to boys playing football (*ibid*). The

DES statistics show this to have been fulfilled nationally. Men form 1.5 per cent of infants' school teachers, but 12.2 per cent of first school teachers (the statistics do not distinguish between 5–8 and 5–9 schools, but we might expect the proportions to be higher in the latter). The headships of infants' schools are very much the preserve of women, with men holding only 2.3 per cent of posts. However, 33.5 per cent of first school headships are held by men. Just as the declining number of girls' secondary schools brought about by comprehensive reorganization is associated with reduced chances of headships for women, so also has the reorganisation of infants' to first schools.

Have differences in staff sex and experience had consequences for educational practices, including informal approaches? I have already referred to those few teachers who in my study (*ibid*) were defined by their headmistresses, as not being 'proper infants' teachers' on account of their not using what the heads saw as acceptable methods, explained (by the heads themselves) by their not being infant trained; they had not accepted the ideology of informal infants' practice, particularly the element of childhood innocence and play as learning.

It could be that first schools, especially those for 5–9-year-olds, are the sites of ideological tension between infant and junior school factions. Not that this is necessarily new. Similar tensions may exist between the infants' and junior departments of 5–11 schools, and between the first and middle departments of 5–12 and 5–13 schools, where, since the headteachers are predominantly male (5–11, 74.1 per cent; 5–12, 84.1; and 5–13, 88.3), they are also likely to be junior trained. A (male) junior trained headteacher said of his infants' department, 'It's all play down (sic) there. It's only a matter of getting them used to school. All the learning takes place in the juniors' (*ibid*). My current research shows this to be a common view among junior teachers. For their part infants' teachers view their contribution to children's education to be the most important; the foundation for what was to come. 'We have done the best by these children. Let them (the middle school teachers) do their worst' (*ibid*). (It would be wrong to infer that these possible ideological tensions might be sex-based conflicts. The few men trained infants' teachers I observed, worked in ways similar to their women colleagues, the only conspicuous difference was a deliberate restraint in physical contact with the children, for what one called 'obvious reasons'.)

The ideology of junior school practice includes an element of ability differentiation; what has been called the psychometric paradigm (Esland, 1971). Children's rates of cognitive development are assumed to be finite; some will never be as able as others. This is made real in the creation of ability groups for teaching/learning purposes (see Barker Lunn, 1982). This kind of thinking is not common among infants' teachers who have a more open-ended view of children's capacities; informal methods are believed to be best for revealing potentialities. However, differential ability thinking may be entering first schools; I have a number of unofficial reports of separate maths groups in the final year of such schools. Mixed ability groups (even where 'ability' cannot be precisely defined) are the structural basis of informal education.

Informal Infants' Education in Prospect

Informality has a long history in infants' education and is widely honoured. As the Plowden Committee reported. 'We heard repeatedly that English infants' schools are the admiration of the world.' It may seem pointless to speculate whether informality is on the wane, but there are changes occurring which suggest this could be so. What has been the response to post-Plowden Black Paper criticisms? As previously discussed, the spread of pre-school education and of first schools may be leading to the introduction of more junior school thinking, especially ability differentiation. This may also be encouraged by the diagnosis of 'special educational needs' of individual children, through the use of standardized tests following the 1981 Education Act. Lack of resources may sometimes exhaust teachers' inventiveness. The general trend towards accountability, the explication of aims and the judgement of outcomes, are pressures towards formality.

That young children should be happy, helpful, quiet, tidy and kind, with some choice in their learning to read, write and do sums, and in experiencing painting, drawing, craft work, singing and dancing, are thought to be intrinsically worthwhile by infants' teachers, of importance to the children in the here and now. Such a view is, unfortunately, politically rather weak.

Notes

1   Another near synonym is Alan Blyth's (1965) 'developmental tradition'.
2   Reported in *The Observer*, 31 August 1986, 'Heads roll in parent revolt'.

3   Galton and Simon (1980) claim that 'socio-economic status (of pupils) ... did not seem to vary in any systematic fashion between teaching styles'. However, an inspection of their reported results shows that the group instructor style was used almost twice as often as the individual monitor style with children of semi- and unskilled manual workers, whilst the individual monitor style was used three times more often than the infrequent changer style with children of professional and managerial workers. Galton and Simon are reluctant to relate their styles to any dimension of formality/informality, but there is at least a hint that what others think of as informality is a more common experience for middle class children.

4   Sharp and Green's 'busyness' refers to a range of activities going on at the same time, where the teacher attends to small groups or individual children.

The Middle Years of Schooling

Vic Kelly

The most superficial glance at the current educational scene will immediately reveal an escalation of the traditional conflict of ideologies between what used to be rather loosely described as the formal and informal approaches to teaching but which can now be seen in more specific terms to be, on the one hand, the view that education is no more than the teaching and learning of clearly defined subject-content or skills, the transmission of knowledge from teacher to pupil, and/or a form of training for the attainment of clearly defined objectives, and, on the other hand, the view of education as a process by which the development of children is promoted, by which they are helped to extend their many capabilities and fulfil their potential. The conflict of those two views has been with us at least since the publication of Rousseau's 'Emile'. They meet head to head in the current scene, not least (in fact primarily) because of the increase of political interest in the school curriculum, all such political interest being almost by definition naive, and unavoidably seeing education from the outside and thus in terms of its content and/or products rather than its processes.

It is perhaps a caricature (though only slight) or an over-simplification (though again not a great one) to see this as to a large degree a conflict between the traditional, subject-based approaches of the secondary school, especially apparent in its upper reaches, and the less formal process-based approaches adopted (perhaps more often in theory than in practice) by many primary teachers and encapsulated, albeit with less conceptual clarity than one would like to see, in most of the literature on primary education, including the two major government reports in this field, those of the Hadow (CCBE, 1931) and Plowden (CACE, 1967) committees.

It is thus not difficult to understand why the focal point of this conflict is currently the interface between primary and secondary schooling, the upper classes of the junior or primary school and the lower forms of secondary schools or, where they still exist, those middle schools which, let us remember, were created, on the recommendation of the Plowden Report itself, to straddle the primary/secondary divide, to minimize the effects on children of too dramatic a transfer from one ideology to the other and, indeed, to act as a buffer and to protect the 'progressive' ideology itself.

It is thus in the junior and middle section of schooling that the battle is currently joined. The advocates of process-based approaches have lost most of the, always rather tenuous, footholds they have had in the upper secondary curriculum mainly through the arrival on the scene of the Department of Trade and Industry (DTI), the Manpower Services Commission (MSC), the associated initiatives, such as the Technical and Vocational Education Initiative (TVEI), its related developments under the TVEI Related In-Service Training (TRIST) schemes, and the Certificate of Pre-Vocational Education (CPVE) and, not least, the quite significant additional resources that have been made available for these developments. Attempts are now increasingly being made to extend these initiatives downwards and to press the curriculum in the junior and/or middle years towards a 'preparatory' role, an emphasis on 'basic skills' and the laying of the foundations for what secondary education for most pupils has now become. Or, what is perhaps worse, the concern seems to be to force the curriculum at this stage into an 'elementary' role, to restrict it to the offering of what, for many pupils, especially those from working-class and/or non-white cultural backgrounds, must always be an inferior diet of subject-content. And so, if one can pursue the rather bellicose metaphor that has been adopted so far, if the war is not to be lost entirely, there is an immediate need to face up to the battle of the junior and middle sector.

In this context it becomes especially important to understand the major features of the terrain which is to be defended and the main points of thrust, not to mention the major weaponry, that will be the enemy's concern. In short, to abandon the war games metaphor, those who would advocate a developmental or process-based approach to education need now more than ever to be very clear what that entails, what the central issues are, and to be capable of articulating their views in a way that our predecessors, at all levels, have sadly failed to do. It is the purpose of this chapter to attempt to do that and to do it by identifying the points of conflict between this and other views and the particular implications of these for the curriculum in the junior and/or middle years.

It will, first, attempt to set out briefly the main characteristics of the developmental approach, second, to identify what are consequentially the main points of conflict and friction with the other kinds of educational ideology, third, it will stress the incompatibility of these approaches and the resultant impossibility of compromise solutions and, finally, it will offer some concrete examples of this conflict in the current educational scene.

First, however, it has to be said that the kind of approach to education which is the concern here has never been as well established in junior and middle schools as it has in those concerned with the early years of schooling. The evidence of the primary survey (HMI, 1978) and of the ORACLE research in particular has indicated that what the Plowden Report (CACE, 1967) once described as a 'quickening trend' has fallen some way short of meeting this description in terms of classroom realities. Both of these studies were of course concentrated on the education of children from 7+; other studies of the younger age-ranges, such as the HMI survey of first schools (HMI, 1982) have revealed both a better understanding and a greater commitment to the practice of this form of education in the early years.

It would be interesting to speculate on some of the possible explanations of this difference, but this is not the place in which to do that. One possible explanation needs to be mentioned, however, since it is a basic theme of this chapter. It is quite clear that one reason for the lack of development in this area has been a lack of conceptual clarity which has led to muddle at the level both of theory and of practice and has offered far more scope to its critics than they should have been given. This conceptual confusion can be seen in the Plowden Report itself (Blenkin and Kelly, 1987) and it can certainly be identified in most discussions of primary education both by 'experts' and by the ordinary classroom teachers and, consequently, in many practical situations. It is my view that most teachers at primary level would prefer to embrace some form of 'progressive' or child-centred' or 'informal' or 'developmental' philosophy of education, but that their practice too often falls short of what such a philosophy would dictate because of a lack of clarity over its theoretical and practical implications. It is a main purpose of this chapter to identify and clarify some of these, since it is only from a clear view of what one believes in that one can understand and resist pressures to settle for something less.

The Main Features of a Developmental Approach to Education and Curriculum

The developmental approach has been the subject of a chapter in this book written by Geva Blenkin (Chapter 3). For this reason, and also because the coincidence of her views and mine have already been fully exposed by several joint publications, it should not be necessary for me to spend too much time here reiterating what will already have been said. It is important, however, if only in the interests of coherence, that my main concerns or emphases be made plain at the outset so that the reader has a clear view of the perspective from which I am viewing the conflict I wish to describe.

The developmental approach stems first from a completely different concept of education from that which seems to underpin other alternative ideologies of education and curriculum, even though the rhetoric of those alternatives often lays claim to a similar concept of education and would often suggest greater similarities than is borne out by any careful analysis. The major element in that difference is that it views education as a process of individual growth and development and insists that all other considerations must be subservient to that. Put simply, it sees education as the process by which the powers of the individual are extended in every way that seems possible in the course of extending his/her scope for gaining the most from life's experiences, what is often called the 'growth of competence'. It sees education as the process by which children learn to think, to understand, to appreciate, to value and to do all those other things which most people would argue constitute what it means to be educated in the full and proper sense of that term. Conversely, therefore, it does not see it as the central concern to engage in behaviour modification, to offer a diet of experiences justified only in instrumental terms, whether narrowly vocational or more broadly and subtly political, or to transmit subject/knowledge-content for its own sake.

It can take this stance, and justify it, primarily because it is built on an epistemological base that is equally distinctive and, again, quite different and completely incompatible with that upon which knowledge-based approaches to education and curriculum are predicated (Kelly, 1986). It sees all knowledge as transient, as shifting, as evolutionary and thus argues for an approach to education which not only recognizes these characteristics of knowledge but also acknowledges the need for education to take full account of them and to facilitate the continuous development of knowledge which this view entails. Thus knowledge becomes almost synonymous with understanding and is something to be developed by each child (and, indeed, adult too) rather than acquired by him/her in some ossified form.

It follows again from this that the engagement of the pupil with the knowledge-content of his/her education must be an active rather than a passive engagement. Education does not consist of the acquisition of inert pieces of knowledge — indeed on this view such learning cannot be productive of knowledge as such at all. It consists rather of active involvement, of experience, through which real learning, learning which is conducive to intellectual development in the full sense, is promoted. In short, it claims that education is a good deal more than mere learning.

It is for this reason that the proponents of this view of education have eschewed the version of 'educational' psychology offered them from the behaviourist tradition. What they have found unacceptable in that tradition is not merely the assumption that human learning is in essence indistinguishable from animal learning, but, also, and more crucially, the resultant view that the role of psychology in education is to advise on methods of teaching and learning only, to offer advice on how we might most effectively teach or transmit those bodies of knowledge we have decided ought, for their own sakes or for utilitarian reasons, to be transmitted. It has, conversely, embraced warmly the developmental tradition in psychology which has set out to offer interesting perspectives not only on how children learn but also on what the learning process itself is.

Those perspectives have of late increasingly pointed us towards the importance of dimensions of development other than the cognitive/intellectual dimension (Eisner, 1982; Donaldson, Grieve and Pratt, 1983). And this too has helped to strengthen the view which has been adopted by proponents of developmentalism almost from the outset, that education must be seen as a process of development on many fronts. Moral and aesthetic development have always been the concern even of the proponents of other theories of education, but too often they have been interpreted in terms of moral or aesthetic knowledge and there has been a failure to acknowledge the important place of feeling in both. Attempts have been made to reduce development and learning in these areas to some form of cognition (Kelly, 1986) and these have ignored that affective dimension which is crucial to both. The developmental view has long tried to acknowledge that aesthetic, moral, and also social and emotional, development are equally, if not more, important than the merely cognitive, and, further, that all of these forms of development are inextricably interwoven in the developing experience of the individual. Indeed, it is difficult to know what education is — or even, for that matter, what human existence is — if it is defined in, or reduced to, purely cognitive/intellectual terms.

Finally, all these considerations have led to a recognition that education is an individual matter, that what will promote one child's development may be quite unsuited to that of another, that, as with the food with which we promote physical growth, the diet which will lead most effectively to educational growth must be very much a matter of individual tastes and needs, It is quite bizarre to claim, as, for example, the proponents of a common curriculum would have it, that, whereas children need different sizes in shoes and clothes (one manufacturer of shoes has recently been claiming in a television advertisement that children's shoes need to be individually fitted), and different nutritional diets, they must all be given exactly the same diet of educational offerings, designed not, like their clothes and their food, by reference to their own characteristics and needs, but by reference to someone else's notion of what constitutes an acceptable uniformity.

The view of education that emerges from the coherent application of all these basic principles is one in which, above all else, the role of subject-content is very different from that allocated to it in those theories which see it either as having some life of its own, and thus some consequent entitlement to inclusion in the curriculum regardless of children's responses to it, or as instrumental to some other purpose. It is thus a view of education that is totally at odds with that which sees it as a matter of initiation into certain pre-specified 'intrinsically worthwhile activities' (Peters, 1965 and 1966), and to that which sees it as instrumental to the attainment of goals extrinsic to it. It is thus incompatible, within the context of the junior or middle school, with views of schooling at that level as being concerned essentially with academic content, or as 'preparatory' for what is — perhaps — to come, or as 'elementary' in the sense of providing a vocationally oriented grounding in the 'basic skills' along with a 'gentling' of those masses who will not — for whatever reasons — pursue their academic learning very far.

In essence, its concern is with the quality of the child's learning, and consequential development, here and now and with whatever will contribute to that. And it is that concern that many advocates of this view, from Rousseau to the Plowden Report, have been attempting to express and to forward.

It is this, then, that is the main source of that conflict with other approaches to education which are currently being pressed upon teachers and which we must now attempt to identify.

Points of Conflict with Other Views

What I have attempted to define in the last section is what might be called the developmental tradition or ideology of education and curriculum. It is what Alan Blyth (1965) once identified as the developmental influence on the growth of the primary curriculum. There are at least three other traditions and/or ideologies with which it is in conflict. First, there are those other two influences Blyth drew our attention to — the 'preparatory' and the 'elementary', then there is what I shall call the 'academic', the view of education which is as old as Plato but which, in more recent debates, stems from Richard Peters' (1965 and 1966) view of the concept of education as initiation into certain identifiable intrinsically worthwhile activities. The developmental view is at odds with all three of these views and I want now to try to show why — not just because this is theoretically interesting, but, more importantly, because it is my view that all of these other ideologies, and, worse, a hybrid of them, are currently laying claim to, and rapidly gaining ground in, the curriculum of junior and middle schools.

The 'Preparatory' Ideology

There are a number of reasons why it is unsatisfactory to see education in the early or middle years merely as a preparation for what is to follow. First, what is to follow for many pupils is not so attractive as to warrant spending what may be the best years of one's life preparing for it. Second, to adopt this approach is to lose all those advantages which can accrue, and often have accrued, from the fact that this sector of education has been, until recently, largely free of external constraints. More importantly, however, this approach reflects a caricature of learning and certainly of education.

It is this kind of thinking that lies behind the demands of those (some of them within the profession — secondary colleagues and HMI, for example) who would have primary schools concentrating on something they call 'the basic skills'. These are seldom defined, except in the broadest terms as 'literacy' 'numeracy' 'oracy' etc., and one reason for this is that they defy any further definition — even by people far better endowed intellectually than most of those who use the term. They cannot be satisfactorily defined primarily because they cannot be effectively isolated. And even if this could be done in theoretical terms, in educational terms it will always be an impossibility.

For real learning is just not like this. It is only the kind of convoluted theory which too often in education is allowed to get in the way of plain common sense that suggests that it is. We do not learn the basic skills even of something as mundane as tennis *before* we actually indulge in playing tennis. Even in a field like this, we acquire skills by using them rather than in a decontextualized disembodied manner. I seem to remember that a soccer coach some time ago made a reputation for himself in that field by the discovery that soccer players improved their skills faster by using them than by practising them in isolation — I even seem to remember that his major breakthrough was to let them practise with a ball!

In exactly the same way, other more complex intellectual skills are learnt by using them. We learn to read effectively by reading, we learn to calculate by calculating, we learn craft skills by creating things. In no sphere of human activity has it been shown that the most effective way of learning is to acquire the skills first and then to use them later. Yet this is what many people seem to expect of primary schools.

Furthermore, there is evidence that this latter approach is counterproductive to the very learning we are endeavouring to bring about, that children are actually put off reading, calculating, craftwork, even tennis, by approaches which require of them endless practice or repetition of 'basic skills' in a decontextualized form. Yet this is what many people seem to expect of primary schools.

This latter point leads one to claim that whether this is a justifiable model of learning or not (and there is no evidence that it is), it can never be a justifiable approach to education, at least as we have seen developmentalism defines it. And it is at this point that the incompatibility of this 'preparatory' ideology with that of developmentalism becomes apparent. If children are to grow and develop through the experiences they are offered in schools, then those experiences must have a value for them in their own right and not as merely instrumental to something which is to follow. To approach the teaching of them in any other way is to embrace a content-based view of education or an instrumental view; it is to seize on that behavioural psychology that tells us that all learning is linear and that we must set out the 'aims and objectives' of our teaching in this linear fashion, the fundamental fallacy of Bloom's taxonomy (1956). It is thus to adopt a far too simplistic view of something which is a highly complex process, and by doing so to put that process very much at risk.

If education is indeed growth and development – as on our earlier characterization of it it is — then we must be looking for growth or development at every point; we must see it as a continuous process. And at no stage can we say we are merely laying the foundations for the education, or even for the development, that is to come. If we believe that literary appreciation is important and hope to help our pupils towards it, we must encourage them to appreciate the literature we offer them from day one. If we attempt to teach them the 'basic skills' of reading first so that they might come to appreciate literature later, we are almost certainly putting the whole process at great, and unnecessary, risk. And we are concentrating on 'mere learning' at the expense of proper educational development. Development is just not like that; nor is education; it is a model of teaching that fits only the most simplistic and low-level forms of learning. This is the real 'crime' of the 'preparatory' approach and this is why it is incompatible with any view of education as a process of development.

The 'Elementary' Ideology

The incompatibility of the 'elementary' ideology with the developmental approach is even easier to recognise. For this is the view of schooling which sees it, especially in the early years, as being a preparation not for the education that is to come but for something far more mundane and even, on closer analysis, sinister.

In essence this is the view of that group of people Raymond Williams (1961) once described as 'the industrial trainers', the people whose view of schooling, and especially of the purposes of making it available to the masses, is two-fold. First, it is provided in order to produce what others have called 'fodder for industry', a trained work-force to ensure the industrial and economic health and viability of society and, second (the sinister bit), to assist in the creation of a well-behaved and orderly society by the process some have called 'gentling the masses' (Gordon and Lawton, 1978).

Within this philosophy of schooling (it is difficult to call it a philosophy of education, since it would seem to be opposed to education in any sense one could thoughtfully give that term), there is no room for anything whose prime concern or purpose is to be defined in terms of the advantage to the individual recipient (except in so far as the securing of a job may be seen as such). Its main, indeed, its only, focus is the health of society, defined in industrial/economic and narrowly social terms.

The main concern of this approach, then, is not with *what education is* but with *what schooling is for*. It is thus essentially instrumental in its thrust. It advises forms of planning which are product-based in that they start from the 'aims and objectives' to be attained. There is again a major interest in the teaching and learning of skills, although these are conceived differently and their justification is to be found in economic, industrial or vocational terms rather than as preparatory to the later achievement of educational goals. The same is true of the role of knowledge-content in this kind of schooling. The transmission of knowledge is regarded as of the essence, but the knowledge to be transmitted is selected and justified in economic or utilitarian terms, in extrinsic terms, rather than on any view of knowledge as being in some sense intrinsically worthwhile. Finally, more readily, and indeed more logically and coherently, than most ideologies, this lends itself to planning by 'aims and objectives'. For its aims are quite clear-cut and the exercise of breaking these down into step-by-step, linear, short-term objectives (the 'Thirty Nine Steps' model of teaching) is both easier and more consistent with its basic tenets. For it is readily possible to view this kind of teaching as a linear process and the approach is not complicated by any concern with the impact it is having on the child beyond the effectiveness of the learning or the behaviour modification that is intended.

It is not hard to identify, therefore, the many reasons why this approach to schooling is incompatible with developmentalism. Again, as with the 'preparatory' ideology, there is the view of learning as a linear process, the basis of which can be handled separately and in advance of anything more sophisticated which might come later. Further, however, it offers little that is sophisticated at any stage. It is, as was suggested above, an approach to schooling rather than a theory or ideology of education. It is thus incompatible with the developmental or process approach from its very first principles.

The 'elementary' view is also a view which is essentially élitist and anti-egalitarian. It was this feature of it that Raymond Williams had in mind when he coined the term 'industrial trainers', since he wished to draw attention to the thinking of those whose central concern was that the masses should not be educated 'beyond their station', who wished them to be given enough learning to make them useful workers and, at the same time, to keep them passive. Real education was to be reserved for the élite, those who would govern and manage. This clearly continues to be the view (although it is now much less fashionable, and, indeed, much less safe to utter it publicly) of those who are still advocating the use of schooling to provide a basic vocational training for pupils today.

It is also the result, if not the purpose, of that third ideology we identified earlier, the 'academic'. For that derives from the Platonic tradition in educational theory, which, while, on the one hand, offering us what has been called a noble view of the potential of education (Nettleship, 1935), also, and inevitably, went on to say that this potential does not exist in, and cannot be attained by, any but a few gifted people, so that the others must be satisfied with something far less noble, a form of schooling whose two main purposes were the vocationalism and social control of the 'elementary' tradition. Plus ça change . . .

It is to a consideration of the incompatibility of developmentalism with this 'academic' ideology that we must now turn.

The 'Academic' Ideology

There is an ideology which is in a sense more honourable (in that its concern is with the promotion of what it sees as education) and which is certainly more clearly argued than those we have explored so far and that is the ideology which sees education as primarily concerned to offer access to all that is best in human life and achievement — what Matthew Arnold once called 'the best that has been thought and said', what some would call our cultural heritage or 'high culture' (Bantock, 1968; Lawton, 1975) what, as we saw just now, Richard Peters (1965 and 1966) once called 'intrinsically worthwhile activities'. Its advocates are those whom Raymond Williams (1961) in that analysis of influences on the development of mass education to which we have already referred characterized as 'the old humanists'.

The main features of this view are, first, that it eschews all suggestion that education is to be viewed or planned in instrumental, product-based terms. Education is to provide access to those human activities which are worth engaging in for their own sake, activities which are worthwhile intrinsically, by reference to what they *are*, rather than extrinsically, by reference to what they may be thought or expected to lead to.

Secondly, a major concern of the proponents of this view is that education should offer children the opportunity for initiation into the high culture of their society. The view is that there is much there that is valuable and that children are entitled to be offered access to this. What is more it is a fundamental tenet of this view that they must be pressed — if necessary, very hard (spare the rod etc.) — into accepting this offer of access to what is claimed to be a superior form of human existence. For, by inference, if we define some activities as especially valuable, we must be claiming that there are others which are relatively worthless. It is precisely this point that John Stuart Mill is making when he tells us that 'it is better to be a human being dissatisfied than a pig satisfied; better to be a Socrates dissatisfied than a fool satisfied'.

Thirdly, and crucially for our discussion here, this kind of stance can only be taken, or at least can only be justified, on the prior assumption that it can be demonstrated in some indisputable way that those activities so designated as 'the best of what has been thought and said', as 'intrinsically worthwhile', as superior, as 'high culture', do in fact, objectively and absolutely, enjoy the status that is claimed for them.

It will be plain from this that one concern of the proponents of this view is with the development of this 'high culture', this superior knowledge, these intrinsically worthwhile activities themselves. Certainly, it is with these that their educational planning begins. The first consideration is the value of the knowledge which is to be transmitted and to which children are to be exposed or given access. If children reject what is thus offered them, it is because they are perverse, bearers of 'original sin', victims of depraved social backgrounds, 'deficit systems'. The fault is to be found in the child, not in the diet s/he is offered nor in the ideology by which this diet is justified. Such children must be coerced, 'compensated' or, in the last resort, offered something different, something which then by definition cannot be education. It is this that renders this view fundamentally élitist. For, the planning of education in terms of its knowledge-content, however one views that, must lead to a situation in which many pupils cannot, because of intellectual limitations, or will not, because of their social and/or ethnic origins, respond to it or take advantage of it. Plato was very honest in recognizing and accepting this. For him, education, in his full sense of access to superior forms of intellectual activity, was possible only for the few, those who were to be the 'rulers'; for the rest, as we saw just now, there was to be a vocational training and a form of what John White (1968) once called 'education in obedience'. This is the view propounded more recently by Bantock (1968) whose view of education as access to 'high culture' includes the notion that for some the concern must always be with some form of inferior 'folk culture'. It leads to what Marten Shipman (1971) once called 'a curriculum for inequality'.

It is this élitism that is the prime source of conflict, and indeed incompatibility, with the developmental view, whose concerns are that the growth of all pupils should be attended to with the greatest possible care, that opportunities should be provided for every child to achieve the highest possible level of development in all of its dimensions, and that all children should be helped towards the attainment of personal automony and responsibility for their own lives. The claims of some of the proponents of this 'academic' view, such as Richard Peters (1965 and 1966) and Paul Hirst (1965; Hirst and Peters, 1970), that personal autonomy is the aim but that this will be attained by exposure to those activities identified as intrinsically worthwhile, or viewed as the repositories of the seven forms of rationality, is fundamentally muddled and reveals precisely where this approach goes wrong and why it is at odds with what the developmentalists are claiming.

For, firstly, in an odd way, it is human development that is the prime concern of the 'academic' ideology. Although there clearly is a concern with the intrinsic value and merits of certain kinds of knowledge and of certain subjects, so that clear hierarchies of human activities and school subjects (not always the same hierarchies) can be discerned in their claims, and although there is an undue emphasis resulting from this on cognitive content, on intellectual activities, and thus on cognitive or intellectual development — the development of rationality — nevertheless it is development which is the concern. Plato's prime intent is that his élite should develop to the point where they have complete understanding or knowledge and can thus make autonomous judgements (although how autonomous such judgements could be within his theory of knowledge is a moot point). And more recent advocates of this view, as we have just suggested, have also been concerned with the development of such qualities as understanding, rationality, the ability to care for and value certain activities for their own sake, autonomous thinking and so on. All of these seem to be better characterized as aspects of development than in terms of subject-content.

Thus, the muddle, the inner inconsistency, of this view comes from the confidence with which it claims to be able to identify the kinds of knowledge which enjoy this kind of superior, timeless, eternal status and its consequent assumption that, for all children who are capable of the kind of development it envisages, that development will occur only by exposure to that kind of knowledge.

It is this, as we have just seen, that leads to its inevitable élitism. And it is this that is the focal point of its conflict with the developmental view. For, as was noted earlier, that view is based on a totally different theory of knowledge, a theory which sees knowledge not in the timeless forms of the 'academic' ideology but as shifting, transient, evolutionary, and which cannot, as a consequence, confidently claim that only some kinds of knowledge may act as a vehicle for educational development. It thus is also not constrained to argue that only one kind of culture can be accommodated in its educational planning. Potentially all kinds of knowledge are grist to its mill, and all forms of culture, including working-class and all ethnic cultures, can be used as sources from which to enrich the experience and promote the development of individual children (Kelly, 1986). It believes, with Jeremy Bentham, that 'quality of pleasure being equal [it would say "educational effectiveness being equal"], push-pin is as good as poetry'.

It is this that is crucial in the claim that considerations of knowledge-content are secondary in the developmentalist's educational planning. Of prime concern is the development of the individual and if that can best be promoted in some cases by explorations of Mogul India, as has been demonstrated by the Schools Council's Language and the Multicultural Primary Classroom project, then why should children in all cases be required to study Tudor England? If it can be promoted through black American jazz music, then why should the curriculum be confined to music from the Western European tradition? If children's language development can best be promoted by the use of their native language or through the advantages of bilingualism, then why should this development be placed at risk by requiring them to satisfy the standards of basic English? In short, if development is our concern then we must recognize that that concern is not compatible with a prior, or even parallel, concern for certain kinds of knowledge, certain forms of culture or certain aesthetic, cultural or social values. We must use whatever is at our disposal to promote the development of individual children and not allow ourselves to be held within the confines of traditional views of what constitutes appropriate subject-matter. For to do this is not only to put at risk those acknowledged goals and principles that are our central concern, it is also to introduce into the curriculum a major source of social and ethnic divisiveness.

If product-based, instrumental planning is incompatible with our developmental theory, then so too is content-based planning, whether its concern be with utility or with some notion of intrinsic, superior value.

The Fundamental Incompatibility of These Approaches With Developmentalism

Enough has probably been said already to highlight the incompatibilities of these approaches with the 'developmental' ideology. It may be worth picking them up here, however, before we move on to look at the present scene in the junior/middle sector against the backcloth of this analysis.

We must briefly note first the root differences in the epistemological assumptions from which they begin, the fundamentally distinct views of what knowledge is, what constitute its grounds and what status it consequently has in discussion of curriculum. Secondly, we must note the two largely discrete psychological traditions that these views appeal to, the one looking to behaviourist theories for help merely with methodology, — and sometimes looking for no more than this in such elements of developmental psychology as its, now hugely modified, 'stage theory' (Lawton, 1973) — while the other looks to the essential insights of developmental psychology for assistance with the issue of what human development and learning actually are. And thirdly, we must note again that what these basic distinctions lead to is to theories of education which differ not merely in their methodologies but, much more crucially, in the very view they take of what education is, the one seeing it as concerned primarily with the transmission of knowledge, of whatever kind and for whatever reasons, the other as a device for promoting children's development.

As a result, the major points of conflict are to be found, first, in the opposing views of the role of knowledge-content in education, whether it is the central concern or whether, as the developmentalists would claim, it is merely the vehicle for growth and development. And, secondly, there is the question of whether education is to be planned in terms of goals extrinsic to it, the product-based, instrumental, 'aims and objectives' model of curriculum planning, or whether it has to be conceived, planned and executed in terms of what it is, the developmental processes of which it consists, the procedural principles upon which all educational decisions, at whatever level, including those of the humble teacher in his/her humble classroom, must be based.

One final point must be added, before we turn to the current scene in junior/middle schools. The incompatibilities which we have just noted are absolutely basic and central, so that compromise solutions are not possible; they are oil and water or chalk and cheese. If the differences go as deep as the fundamental views adopted of knowledge, of human development and of education, then any attempt to conflate them must lead to illogicality and incoherence of both theory and practice. It is this that is the underlying weakness of many of those attempts to criticize 'informal methods' or 'progressive education' from the perspective of one or more of these different ideologies. Some of the criticisms of 'discovery methods' (Dearden, 1967 and 1968) are good examples of this.

To argue (and this is not an unfair paraphrase or simplification of some of the arguments) that children cannot learn by discovery all that they must be taught in schools is to miss the point of developmental or process approaches altogether; it is, as I have suggested elsewhere (Kelly, 1986), to attempt to criticize poetry by the rules of prose.

Thus, too, all those suggestions, that we can plan our curriculum by the use of 'process objectives' (Barnes, 1982; Skilbeck, 1984) reflect a failure to understand how deeply the ideological differences go, or at the very least a use of the term 'process' that no developmentalist would accept (Blenkin and Kelly, 1987). They lead to self-contradiction and incoherence, and, while this would not matter too much if it were confined to debates between theorists in ivory towers, when they reach the consciousness of teachers and others in the field, they lead to similar contradictions and incoherences at the level of practice and thus to unsatisfactory experiences for children.

There is every temptation for teachers now to seek such compromises. And most of those with whom I have talked in the junior/middle sector readily acknowledge that it is this kind of compromise they are seeking. 'We see all the attractions of the developmental approach but we have also to respond to external pressures, so that our approach is a compromise, an attempt to respond to those outside pressures while preserving our own educational ideals'. This dilemma is easy to understand and to appreciate. What must be made clear, however, is the dangers of attempting to offer children experiences which in themselves are intended to satisfy both these criteria. It may be possible to do one in the morning and the other in the afternoon; it is not possible, logically as well as practically, to set out to satisfy both at the same time. This too, then, we must bear in mind as we now turn to consider aspects of the current scene against this theoretical backcloth which I have endeavoured to paint.

Aspects of the Current Scene

What are the main points of conflict in the current scene for education in the middle years?

It was suggested at the beginning of this chapter that the influence of the styles of curriculum, both old and new, adopted by most secondary schools have been in recent times bringing increasing influences to bear on the curriculum of the middle years. It was also suggested that these influences would need to be resisted by those who wished to retain a developmental stance and that, in order to do this, we need a clearer view of what these influences are and what are their main manifestations.

It should now be clear, from our earlier discussion, that these influences reflect all of those incompatible and alternative ideologies we have identified. It should also be apparent that the two major points of conflict are their subject base and their product orientation, their concern with subject-content and their, often related but sometimes inconsistent, concern with the instrumental functions of schooling. It is at these two points that the conflict with developmentalism is at its greatest and it is also there that the need to resist these influences in the interests of developmentalism is most crucial.

It may be worthwhile first, however, considering some of the evidence for claiming that these are the flavours of current influences on junior and middle schools. First of all we must note the tone and tenor of the current pronouncements on curriculum emerging from Elizabeth House and especially the 'Curriculum Matters' series. It is worth noting that since the demise of the Schools Council, these, along with the publications emerging from the Assessment of Performance Unit (another branch of the DES) are the only kinds of documentation on curriculum that are being made readily available to teachers. This is the documentation that now fuels (or perhaps dampens) the fires of the curriculum debate. The tone and tenor of these documents is essentially both subject-based and product-oriented. The 'Curriculum Matters' series itself is planned by subjects. And the documents list both what is felt to be appropriate content for the curriculum in these subjects at various ages and stages, and the objectives to be set, attained and assessed at these various ages and stages. It is difficult to find within the documentation any reference to the development of the children or to the capacities it is intended that education might foster within them. The Introduction to the mathematics offering, for example, (HMI, 1985d, p. 1) tells us that its purpose is 'to focus attention on the *aims* and *objectives* for the teaching of mathematics from 5 to 16 and to consider their implications for the choice of *content*, the *approaches* to be used in the classroom and the *assessment* of pupil's performance' and this is asserted also in the Preface by the Senior Chief Inspector himself, Eric Bolton. There is not a developmental or procedural principle in sight. The concern is with *what* and *how*, but not *why*.

The Preface also invites comments on this document, and, indeed, the covering letters which have accompanied all the documents I have received in the series have reiterated this invitation. I have met many primary teachers, however, who — quite reasonably — tell me that they do not know where to begin to make their comments, the whole tone of these documents being so foreign to their perceptions of education and of their role as teachers within it. The only comment one can make is to say that one's ideology is totally at odds with that of the authors. But then it does seem that these authors do not recognize, or at least do not acknowledge, that the position from which they address these issues is in any sense ideological. That this is so is borne out by the response that has been elicited by those who did comment in these terms on the English document (HMI, 1984), since that response revealed a complete failure to understand the points of criticism that were being made (HMI, 1986).

For these documents, while purporting to be concerned with the curriculum from 5 to 16 — and few of us would object to any attempt to suggest that the curriculum should be seen as a single entity whatever the age of the pupils concerned — have been written for the most part by people whose background is predominately that of the secondary school (often selective) and whose ideology is thus essentially subject-based if not also product-based.

In this connection it is also worth noting that the ambivalence declared by those HMI who were responsible for the 1978 survey of primary schools (HMI, 1978) concerning whether subject specialism or the 'one-class-one-teacher' system were the better has now disappeared. It is unusual to meet an HMI nowadays who is not an advocate of increased subject specialism in the junior and middle schools if not in the primary school as a whole.

This is perhaps at its most obvious in what is currently happening within teacher education, as will emerge in Robin Alexander's contribution to this volume (Chapter 8). For the emphasis there is now, *perforce*, very much on the subject-specialisms of teachers whatever level or age-range they are preparing to teach. An increasing number of primary teachers are now being prepared by the 3 + 1 route, three years of subject study followed by one year of training; they can only be admitted to this one year of training if the subject(s) of the first degree is/are cognate to the school curriculum, i.e. if it has provided them with appropriate subject-content to transmit; and those who continue to take the four-year BEd course must now devote at least two of these four years to the study of a subject or subjects at a proper undergraduate level and of a kind that will equip them for the role of subject transmitters that is envisaged for them in schools. Again the emphasis is on the *what* and the *how*, and the *why* is a question to be largely ignored, mainly, and sadly, one feels because its significance completely escapes the political authors of these requirements — or perhaps, even more sadly, because it does not.

Finally, it is interesting to look at what is happening within the junior and middle schools themselves in respect of their curricula. Reference has already been made to the partial disappearance of the middle schools with all that they stand for or endeavoured to stand for. Institutions of teacher education were forbidden to prepare teachers for them several years ago. And within those that remain as well as within the junior schools and departments, curriculum guidelines are regularly and increasingly being demanded in subject terms and/or in statements of 'aims and objectives', often expressed in 'checklists'. This reflects the predominantly subject-base, even secondary base, of the local advisory service in many authorities. Governing bodies too can often best understand the curriculum in subject or product terms and thus expect schools to be able to express their curricula in these ways. And the trend over the last few years has been increasingly to use scale posts for subject specialisms. As Campbell (1985) puts it, 'in recent years changes both in the criteria for allocating posts of special responsibility, and, more importantly, in what is expected of postholders have been proposed' (p. 48). Nor have they merely been proposed; they have been acted on and insisted on in many authorities.

The main thrust of these changes has been away from the practice of using scale posts to reward long and valuable service by allocating them to such teachers for responsibilities in which they had no special expertise, and occasionally no interest (*ibid*) — Campbell records one post of responsibility for stuffed toys and another, which he concedes may be apocryphal, for the school lavatories. And perhaps one could not complain too much at this development. However, it is clearly also the case that the trend has been not only away from this kind of practice but towards the use of these posts increasingly for the appointment of subject-specialists and this has often been at the cost not merely of the stuffed toys but also of aspects of education such as home-school liaison and, most importantly in the context of this chapter, curriculum development of a holistic, cross-curricular and non-subject-based kind. Again, therefore, we can see the move against the developmental ideology.

It should be made clear, if it has not emerged already, that the criticism I am offering is not of subject-specialism in itself, it is of the prime place that these developments would give it in the hierarchy of curriculum planning considerations. Content is essential to education — only a fool would argue with that — but it is not the whole of education nor is it the prime concern and, if, as at present, it bids fair to become so, then the notion of education as a process of development is not only placed at risk, it is lost altogether.

If we seek for the reasons for these trends, they are not difficult to find but they are somewhat depressing to contemplate.

For the first of these would seem to be a disturbing level of professional ignorance at the highest levels in our profession. There is no doubt that it is ignorance of the developmental approach — what it is, what it stands for, what its theoretical bases are, what it entails in practical terms — that is the root cause of its being either ignored or completely misunderstood in the official literature from DES/HMI and in many other contributions to the curriculum debate. And the quality and level of discussions of the curriculum, especially in those official documents but elsewhere too, is often convincing only in relation to what it says about particular subjects; it is too often 'Mickey Mouse' in its professional understanding of curriculum issues of a broader kind. Some of the statements about technology and education, for example, such as those concerning the use of microcomputers in education (Kelly, 1984) are technologically impressive but educationally barren.

A good general example of this is the failure to recognize that educational 'standards' might mean something other than academic standards, the assumption that we should evaluate standards by reference to the amount of knowledge children possess rather than by reference to the developmental changes, the growth of their capacities that education has been able to bring about. I have even been 'assured' by more than one HMI that the requirement that all BEd students should spend two of their four years studying a subject or subjects is mainly to ensure that they achieve proper 'standards' of intellectual attainment and thus to help to raise the intellectual status of the teaching profession — a clear indication that such HMI are unaware of the possibility of intellectual standards of other kinds and, most sadly, of the possibility of standards of professional understanding which might satisfy whatever demands they might like to make of intellectual quality or rigour. If standards of professional understanding are so low at the higher levels of the education service, among those with most power to control or shape things, there is little hope for the rank and file teacher.

A second, and equally depressing, reason for these new trends and influences is the emphasis that is increasingly being placed on value for money, in economic terms. It is becoming increasingly plain that the money that is being allocated or made available to education cannot sustain a system of schooling which will at the same time meet both the economic needs of society and the personal, educational needs of the individual. That dilemma, identified by the Crowther Committee (CACE, 1959), between education as a national investment and education as the right of every child 're-gardless of whether, in each individual case, there will be any return' (p. 54), education as 'one of the Social Services of the welfare state' (*ibid*), is a dilemma no more. The school system is now a national investment and all or most expenditure within it must be justified in economic or social terms. It is for this reason that much of the funding of secondary schooling is now controlled through the Department of Trade and Industry and/or the Department of Employment. It is for this reason that money is more readily available for overtly vocational initiatives than for anything else. And it is for this reason that science and technology are better funded in higher education than the humanities. This, after all, was the central thrust of James Callaghan's famous speech at Ruskin College in 1976, which began the 'Great Debate' on education.

And this brings us to the third reason for these recent trends and pressures on the curriculum in the middle years — the rapidity of technological development.

There is no doubt that rapid technological advance is having a major impact on the school curriculum. It is creating the growing unemployment which, with typical politician's logic, has led, and continues to lead, to increased vocationalism in the curriculum of the secondary school, the effects of which are already having their impact on the middle years. And it has brought about those increasingly insistent demands for an increased emphasis on technology in the school curriculum at all levels.

Nor is this latter a development that is necessarily to be resisted. Much depends, as always, on how technological education is conceived. And it is true to say that what has been happening in this area in secondary schools for almost two decades now, reflected most notably in the move from 'handicraft' to 'craft, design and technology' (CDT), has come closer to evincing the basic principles of our developmental ideology than anything else to be seen there.

For the advocates of that move to CDT have consistently resisted the pressures either to conceive of that subject in terms of its knowledge-content or to view it vocationally or instrumentally. They have for a long time insisted that it is a procedural activity and thus to be planned, practised and evaluated in terms of the processes it consists of, and that its major justification in the school curriculum is to be sought in what it can contribute to the development of the individual and expressly not in economic terms.

Furthermore, they would claim too that, conceived in this way, its potential contribution to the economic health of society, although a subsidiary consideration, is likely to be enhanced. For it should be productive of people who are not merely knowledgeable technologists but also innovative, creative and imaginative, since their experience of technological education in schools will have encouraged them to think and to develop their potential in these directions, not merely to acquire and/or use whatever technological information someone has decided should be transmitted to them. And it is creative technologists society needs, not mere tradespersons.

It is interesting to remember that when attention was first turned on the school curriculum in the post-Sputnik era as a potential source of technological expertise, the concern then was as much with the development of creativity as with technology itself. And, at the same time, the Crowther Report (CACE, 1959) was quite properly drawing our attention to the impossibility, indeed illogicality, of attempting to purvey technological knowledge and/or skills when we have no way of knowing what knowledge or skills industry will need within the lifetime of any of our pupils. That report coined the phrase 'general mechanical ability' and it is still a useful concept for summing up what is needed.

Our concentration, however, must be on what it has to offer towards the development of the individual. And this has been the focus of developments in CDT, so that here, for once, an extension of secondary philosophy and practice back into the middle years would reinforce our intention to plan the curriculum there along developmental lines.

Perversely, however, that is not what is currently happening. There is increasing pressure on the secondary curriculum to adopt a more subject-based and/or product-oriented approach — developments in TVEI are one example of this but some of the newer technology courses reflect this too. And the form in which technological education is currently being offered to, and indeed pressed upon, junior and middle schools is similarly subject- and/or product-based. Too often we hear not of craft, design and technology or even of design and technology but of technology pure and simple; and it is the loss of that element of design that reflects also the loss of the developmental advantages that experience of working with materials can offer many, perhaps all, pupils.

And those advantages are potentially legion. The scope for development on many fronts which is offered by opportunities for children to engage in activities involving not merely scientific and technological exploration but also, allied to that, productive design activities is enormous. Certainly from this will come an understanding of materials, of scientific principles, of mechanics and so on. But there is also enormous scope for the development of creativity, of imagination, of spacial awareness, and of a recognition of the importance of aesthetic, social and even moral considerations. It is the emphasis on this developmental potential that was the major contribution of the Schools Councils' 'Learning Through Science' project to the primary school curriculum; the extension of its basic principles into the area of design and technology must offer even greater educational advantages. It is not without reason that some enthusiasts from this field have been known to claim that it can provide a complete educational diet in itself. It would be difficult to argue with that claim.

Yet, again, all of that educational potential is at risk because of the form in which technological education is currently being advocated for the middle years of schooling. Again, the concern is too often with the transmission of knowledge, with the development of 'basic skills', with instruction, with teaching rather than with learning in the full sense that developmentalism would give it. Foundation courses in CDT, in middle schools or the early years of the secondary schools, are increasingly reflecting this kind of didacticism, and it is to technology in this form that junior schools are being asked to respond.

A good example of this is to be found in the most recent offering by the Lego company to schools and teachers. Many teachers, especially in junior and middle schools, but even in infant schools and departments, have found the Lego kits hitherto offered to schools ideal for providing children with opportunities to explore, to experience, to create and thus to develop potential of many kinds. This has been true not only of the basic kits but also of the Lego Technic kits more recently produced for the pupils in the middle years. Quite properly these have now been developed into the field of control technology and especially of computer technology. This development, however, has been accompanied by what appears to be a reversal of educational philosophy, although this may well be another example of the educational theory, as always, lagging well behind the technology. For the new offerings are highly prescriptive — knowledge-based, skills-based and product-oriented. Teachers and pupils are offered set lessons by which they can develop skills which they *may* later use more creatively. The materials, we are assured, do lend themselves to more creative use, but it will take a very determined teacher — or pupil — to transcend the step-by-step instructions by which they are accompanied. And it is clear that the main concern is with technological skills and knowledge rather than with educational development. One can see these kits being accepted by Secondary teachers, especially within the context of some CDT Foundation courses, and TVEI programmes, and used as aids to basic instruction. One can see them also being pressed upon teachers in the middle years (they are specifically beamed at the 11–14 age group). They can only be accepted and implemented there at the direct risk of that developmental tradition which is our main concern.

Summary and Conclusions

The middle years of schooling, then, are currently the warring ground. It is here that we can still see vestiges of concern for the processes of education and for the development of a wide range of capacities in children. In spite of the evidence of the ORACLE study and others that this is not as widespread in practice as we once thought, or hoped, it is still prevalent in the attitude of teachers to their work at that level. And this is more than mere rhetoric; in my experience it represents an approach to education that many teachers would like to be able to adopt but which they find it difficult to implement, partly because of inadequate appreciation of what it entails, but mainly because of external pressures such as those we have just briefly explored. It is both of these factors, in my view, which explain why, as Robin Alexander (1984) has claimed, 'the primary curriculum is an epistemological muddle, whose justificatory face is empiricist but whose practice is dominated by, if anything, an overt *a priori* epistemology' (p. 66). The way out of that muddle has to be by increased conceptual clarity and consequent practical coherence. For the alternative is to be led tamely up whatever garden path our political masters or mistresses have in mind for us (and we must remember that some of those paths necessitate a trampling on the flower beds of the curriculum's 'secret garden'.) Such increased clarity of thinking and of articulation, will, in my view, lead most teachers in an opposite direction and encourage them to reassert those educational, and indeed human, values that Hadow and Plowden encapsulated and which most of the primary teachers I have met would wish to lay claim to.

Whether we call this approach 'informal education' or 'progressivism' or 'child-centredness' or, as I have done, 'developmentalism', it needs to be protected against the inroads of other, educationally less satisfactory, ideologies. For what it has that they do not have is a central concern with the welfare of the individual child and a desire to help him/her to develop to the full whatever potential or capacities s/he is blessed with. If I did not believe that that was my prime purpose and justification, then I would not be a teacher. And nor would many of those I most respect in my chosen profession.

I make no apology for ending by quoting yet again the words of the Hadow Report (CCBE, 1931, p. xxv). 'The primary school has its own canons of excellence and criteria of success; it must have the courage to stand by them'.

Informal Primary Education in Action: Teachers' Accounts

Jennifer Nias

'But what *is* "informal education?"' they all replied, when I told them I had been asked to write this chapter. Their response confirmed my doubts. Could anyone, least of all one who now taught adults not children, present an accurate, up-to-date picture of 'informal education in action', when its putative practitioners — primary and middle school teachers — had no clear understanding of the term? So I changed the question and over a period of some months asked experienced teachers if they could describe 'formal teaching'. With hesitations and qualifications most of them could: 'to teach formally' was to show, tell, instruct, direct, with a view to controlling what their pupils learnt; it was often, but not always, directed at a large group of children, with the intention that they should all learn the same things at the same time; it therefore involved teacher control of social interaction as well as learning (for example, to restrict pupil-initiated talking and movement); it was often associated with testing or some other form of assessment of a learning outcome or product against externally derived criteria. A 'good' formal teacher could command the attention of learners, present information or instructions clearly and reinforce correct learning swiftly and encouragingly. There was also general agreement that 'formal teaching' was logically independent of numbers of pupils; it described a set of assumptions about the nature of knowledge, of learning (and therefore of teaching) which could be brought to bear upon one pupil or many.

All of the teachers to whom I spoke felt that they used 'formal teaching' at some time, often when dealing with curriculum areas (such as spelling or computational skills) for which there were accepted 'right answers'. Almost all of them felt that it was a useful component of their repertoire of teaching skills and was sometimes a highly effective way of ensuring that children acquired a particular skill or piece of information. However, many said they used it more often than they wanted to, as a control device, as an expedient to help them cope with large pupil numbers and inadequate resources or because they felt compelled to concentrate on their classes' attainment of pre-defined learning outcomes.

But a fair degree of consensus about the nature of 'formal teaching' did not help them to define 'informal teaching'. I therefore approached six experienced teachers of children from 6 to 12 years old, working in very different types of primary or middle school in various parts of England, and asked them if they could let me have a brief description of a situation in which they felt they had not been teaching formally. They did not know one another and all they had in common was that, in one context or another, I knew them all. Five wrote their accounts; one gave hers orally.

To my surprise there was substantial agreement within these teachers' accounts, despite the personal differences between them, the variety of contexts in which they taught and the ages of their pupils. Their descriptions suggest that they hold similar views about the conditions under which children learn, the classroom relationships which make these conditions possible, the role of the teacher and the nature of the curriculum. In the rest of this chapter I have attempted to present these common themes which, I suggest, encompass a coherent, if largely tacit, view of 'informal education in action'.

Ann was deputy head of a group 4 infant school in a large village. She had been teaching for nine years, for all of that time in infant schools. She had a two-year Certificate from a college of education, as a mature student. Her account describes work with twenty-eight 6 and 7-year-olds.

Lynne taught twenty-two 7, 8 and 9-year-olds in a group 4 multi-ethnic, inner city school. She had been teaching for eight years, one of them in this school where she held a scale 2 post for science. She had a first degree (in art) and a PGCE.

Roger was deputy head of a group 4 primary school in a new town. He had been teaching for eleven years, and had a three-year Certificate from a college of education. His account describes work with thirty-five 8 and 9-year-olds.

Chris held a scale 2 post for language in a group 4 rural primary school, having been deputy head of another primary school before taking time out to raise a family. She had a three-year Certificate from a college of education and had taught for fifteen years. She describes work with her class of twenty-five 9-year-olds.

Gill was in her second deputy headship, this time of a group 5 primary school in a small town. Her class consisted of thirty-one 9 and 10-year-olds, and she chose to describe work with a self-designated 'non-reader' of nearly 10. She had been teaching for twenty years, following two years at a college of education. She taught in a secondary modern school before moving, early in her career, into primary education.

Rob was in his first year as deputy head of a group 6 8–12 middle school in an overspill estate. He also held the post of science coordinator and taught craft, science and maths throughout the school. He had been teaching for fourteen years, for much of that time as a class teacher. He had a first degree (in engineering) and a PGCE. He was the only one of the six not to have a class; instead he worked throughout the school as a specialist teacher.

The following table summarizes the examples of informal teaching discussed in this chapter:

Teacher	Age Group	Number in Group	Focus
Ann	6–7	28	Hatching eggs
Lynne	7, 8, 9	22	'Where do we come from?' in the context of general classwork
Roger	8–9	35	Television and radio sets
Chris	9–10	25	Dramatization of a sixteenth century farm treatise
Gill	9–10	31	Helping John to read
Rob	11–12	17	Designing a folding chair

They have all read this chapter and agreed that it accurately reflects their understanding of what is going on in their classrooms when they are not teaching formally. Of course, there is no guarantee that they actually did what they believed they were doing. In the past decade studies of teaching have revealed all too clearly the gap which often exists between the rhetoric of the practitioner and the reality of his/her classroom practice. Ideally, therefore these descriptions would have been triangulated with observers' accounts, or have been subjected to analysis by the teachers themselves. However, even in the absence of such corroborative evidence, the accounts of experienced teachers provide insights into their professional thinking, documenting at the least what they would like to be doing and suggesting that their practice is informed by common perspectives.

All of these teachers set out to create situations in which their classes could undertake purposeful learning. They endeavoured to set up for their pupils or to encourage the latter to devise for themselves activities for which, as learners, they could see a reason. 'Purposeful' in this context appears to have three possible meanings. It describes an activity which contributes to the fulfilment of an end desired by individual pupils (for example, finding the answer to their own questions; making something they want or need) or which contributes to fulfilment of a goal set by the teacher (or other children or adults) but accepted by the learners as interesting and/or worthwhile (for example, learning to read; taking part in a group project). Frequently, it also refers to situations in which pupils have initially accepted their teacher's aims or suggestions out of habit or goodwill but have developed or converted them into activities which they themselves wish to pursue.

Pupils from these classes were involved in all three types of purposeful learning. Sometimes they suggested activities themselves:

> One of the books also described how to make a crystal radio set and Helen suggested that we made one, since we had already pulled most of the required items out of the now prostrate receiver — copper wire, tuners, nuts and bolts, capacitors, transistors and coils. (Roger)

> At the end of the session, John demanded paper to take home so he could finish the story. Next day he handed it to me. I read it to him because he wouldn't read it to me. Then, with his encouragement, I shared it with everyone. He was obviously satisfied with the applause and got started on the further adventures of Commander Bone. This was also taken home to finish and was brought back after the weekend. So the excitement of authorship sustained his attention for two non-school days. (Gill)

Sometimes they were prepared to fall in with their teachers' initiatives. Rob wanted his pupils to do some thinking for themselves rather than simply learning by following instructions, so he created the opportunity for them to design a scale model of a folding chair, because the design process involves decision-making:

> I began by complaining that when visitors came to my house there were not enough comfortable arm chairs to seat them

all. Was it a similar problem in their houses? What was the solution to this problem? The children suggested buying a larger house, sitting on the floor, knocking a wall down here and there and inventing blow-up chairs that could be deflated and packed away. This led us to the idea of a rigid fold-away arm chair that could be stored in a cupboard when not in use.

At this point I helped the children define the problem they were to solve. 'Design and make an attractive, folding chair for use in a lounge. The chair should fold flat and be as comfortable as possible.' (Rob)

Ann's pupils knew that "eighteen hen's eggs were due to be delivered this particular Wednesday in March ... we were ready for the business of hatching chicks". Before that,

I had already had discussions with the class about egg-turning (essential to the well-being of the embryo because it prevents 'sticking'), following the children's 'planned discovery' that two library books differed in the recommendations given. Why? Did only one book provide the 'correct' information leading to successful hatching and, if so, which one? Or could both be accepted, since each book recorded a healthy number of chicks born as a result of their preparatory work? What, then, was to be our decision on egg-turning over the 21 day incubation period? After a lively session the view of the majority was accepted, that the eggs should be turned three times daily. Making our own decision, which did not match either text book, meant that we had the opportunity really to learn 'firsthand'. (Ann)

The work started because the school was asked to make a musical and dramatic contribution to a concert for primary schools in the area. (Chris)

When they are making a book and have to get the cover to fit the pages, they learn more about length and measuring and angles than they do in a whole term of exercises. And when we go out anywhere we always cost it — public transport, fees and so on, or we make a game of it. For example, when we went to the museum, they made a board game ('Get on the wrong bus: lose a turn') and they learnt a tremendous amount from that, like counting, measuring, area, probability. (Lynne)

The topic was rounded off by concentrating on the import-ance of the cycle of agricultural care year by year to con-serve the land, then by contrasting this with the conditions in famine areas in the Third World. The children agreed that it would be a good idea to perform once more in the village church in a concert in aid of a Third World Appeal. (Chris)

I read this story with my eyes only, telling him I was afraid to spoil it by misinterpreting his intentions. Would he read it to me? No. Would he read it into the tape recorder? Yes, if the room were completely empty ... (Gill)

Often, the children adopted the teacher's ideas, but then de-veloped them. The teachers actively encouraged this process, want-ing their pupils to raise their own questions and pursue their own answers to them, to undertake activities which had individual mean-ing for them or to have the opportunity for creativity or self-expression:

I encourage them to ask questions. When we were looking at where they all came from — Ireland, Bradford, Bangladesh or Brighton — or why their aunties had moved to Australia, Spain or Birmingham, we had lots of discussion about race. They asked all sorts of questions that *they* wanted to know the answer to, like 'Why are there so many white people on telly?' and 'Why is it always the Bengalis who have fire put through the letterbox?' (Lynne)

John showed his own view of how the character of Yell should be interpreted and then created his own recording of his experiment. I began to feel more hopeful. (Gill)

When the eggs arrived they were a source of enquiry in themselves. Nine were 'average-sized' creamy white, five were slightly smaller ones, and four were about the size of bantam eggs and of the softest blue. Weren't duck eggs pale blue, though much larger than these? Didn't they take longer to incubate? What could these be? (Ann)

Within the groups each child chose a character from their picture and wrote about him or her, describing the work. Most wrote in the first person. They then drew and coloured their character. (Later they went on to develop the work of the individual whom they had adopted so that) 'the final presentation was a combination of the children's own music, mime and rhymes'. (Chris)

The problem now was what to do with the empty television carcasses which filled the classroom. Necessity prompted invention ... We found that many of the components could be used to make sturdy and realistic models of steam engines, robots, satellites, monsters or lunar modules, especially after being sprayed with metallic paint. Others could be used for unusual collages or mobiles, or making plaster impressions or printing with acrylic paints. The glass screens were used to make simple wormeries and the wooden cabinets were utilised as puppet theatres or hamster cages. (Roger)

Opportunities for purposeful learning often arose from the children's direct experience, because the latter stimulated interest, provided real-life problems which needed solving and gave pupils reasons for becoming actively involved. Ann's children handled, albeit with instruction and supervision, eggs and chickens, used thermometers and scales, watched the hatchings and visited a farm. Class visits and outings were an integral part of Lynne's curriculum. Roger's pupils used tools to dismember electronic equipment, then utilized its components to make their own radios and models. Chris took her children to see and sketch a period house and encouraged them to participate in raising money for charity. Rob's class handled 'real folding chairs — loungers for the garden, fishing stools, deck chairs and so on', administered their own questionnaire, used tools and varied materials to construct models. Gill gave her 'non-reader' the opportunity to read aloud to his sister and challenged him to find books in the library which did not 'look boring'.

Embedded in these accounts are three related assumptions which provide reasons for this stress on purpose and meaning. All these teachers appeared to believe that motivation, concentration and retention are increased when people perceive their activities as purposeful, that individuals should therefore be encouraged to develop and take responsibility for their own learning and for activities contributing to it, and that the development of the capacity for autonomous learning is an educational end in its own right. As far as possible therefore teachers should ensure that learning is perceived as serving the immediate or long-term goals of individuals, that it will help them to go on learning and that it will equip them to be active and self-directed learners. For all these reasons it should also be within their capacity.

In consequence, the teachers' emphasis was upon what their pupils learnt as they pursued their individual ends — that is upon process — rather than upon the learning outcomes — that is, upon product. But this is to suggest a dichotomy which they did not accept. They cared about the quality of the outcome — live healthy chickens, radios which worked, the ability to read confidently, a polished dramatic performance, well-designed, technologically appropriate chairs, beautifully produced books written in grammatical, correctly spelt English. However, they saw these outcomes as important not so much in themselves, but because they were vehicles for the learning of worthwhile attitudes, knowledge and skills. They also valued them because they increased the learners' self-confidence and self-esteem, and thereby motivated them to undertake further tasks.

Yet, though none of these teachers polarised process and product, they differed in the extent to which they felt it helpful to decide in advance what the learning outcomes might be and in the amount of guidance which they thought the children would find valuable. Rob was clear that inexperienced design students needed plenty. By contrast, Roger felt that:

> The work can only be described in retrospect ... it was a qualitative experience for us all in which we simply found answers to *our* questions. There was no initial aim, only a sense of commitment or improvisation, with neither the children nor myself knowing where we were going until we had arrived, on a journey that could never quite be repeated or pre-ordained ... (Roger).

In between these two, the other teachers had 'a broad idea of what I'd like to do' (Lynne) and encouraged the children to add to or modify this so that the final outcome was jointly negotiated, agreed and pursued.

To say that these teachers were committed to purposeful and therefore to individual learning is not however to suggest that they saw it as a solitary process. They all encouraged their children to work together and to learn from one another:

> We began by looking, in groups, at contemporary pictures of the sixteenth century farming year ... Each group painted a large background picture on which the characters,

their animals, buildings and implements were mounted. This created a set of seasonal pictures for the Calendar of Farming. Autumn showed ploughing, harrowing and sowing; winter, chopping trees, killing animals, baking; spring, tending sheep and haymaking; and summer, harvesting, threshing and winnowing ... (working with the music specialist, other children) developed musical themes in groups to accompany each task and with the musicians we then worked on the movement and mime for each task. (Chris)

The work was organised in small groups, on the grounds that a single group using all the available tools was more productive than children having to improvise. (Roger)

We do a lot of work in groups ... I encourage them to work together — reading books together or to each other, making a game for maths, putting a story onto the word processor, deciding what questions they want to ask when (the visitor) comes. ... I want them to realise they can help and support each other, that other people's ideas are important, that they can take pride in something everyone's contributed to. (Lynne)

During one of these sessions John was joined in his usual isolated writing place by Peter, a creative, literary boy. The two chatted and seemed to be working in a relaxed way. I didn't approach. At the end of the session John had drawn his main character and written a page of narrative. (Gill)

We began by discussing the proportions of the chair. They would have to fit a Mr. or Mrs. Average. Here we cheated a bit and decided to find the average proportions of the children in the class. The children worked with a partner to measure forearm, thigh, neck and head and so on. The results went on the blackboard and calculators were used to average the measurements. We then scaled these down to one fifth size and proceeded to make a jointed, cardboard, average person. Later we used this model to draw around on our design drawing. (Rob)

Since not every child could have an equal share in the egg-turning, we agreed among us that the duties of thermometer and incubator water-tray monitoring should also be allocated. (Ann)

Children were also invited, tacitly or openly, to view adults as helpers, participants, sources of knowledge. Every account mentioned at least one person other than the teacher whom pupils used as a resource:

A local secondary school lent an oscilloscope as a means of showing that sounds could be converted into electronic signals. The local librarian produced a number of books ... we borrowed tools from parents, ransacked the attics of the neighbourhood ... Nothing was unused — and even the television tubes could be used as bottle gardens once the vacuum had been safely released by an expert Dad 'in the trade' ... Dads popped into the school with tools or advice (and this in a neighbourhood historically antipathetic to schools). (Roger)

The village drama group lent costumes which gave additional colour and atmosphere. (Chris)

The hatching out was a marvellous experience shared by all who were nearby, including our crossing patrol lady. (Ann)

I knew a teacher who was going to Africa and travelling round the continent on her bike, so I sent a note round the whole school saying anyone could come and ask any questions they wanted to ... It went very well. (Lynne)

More immediately, in classroom terms, teachers felt that they too were an integral part of their pupils' learning. Indeed, in writing about their teaching they referred to themselves and their classes as a unit, as 'we'. They also made frequent reference to their own involvement as the work progressed:

This left the responsibility for weekend supervision (of the eggs) still to be accounted for. Numerous offers were forthcoming but when I stressed the difficulty of transferring school keys from one person to another the children agreed that I should 'man' the three Saturdays and Sundays involved. But they wanted me to make two daily visits to the incubator, instead of three, 'to prevent me getting tired': I assured them that should any weekend prove difficult I would appoint one of the children, accompanied by his or her parents, to do the work. (Ann)

We spent the remainder of the afternoon sorting the components according to materials, shape or symmetry, and generally conjecturing on Baird's inventiveness. It was a world as strange to me as it was to the children. (Roger)

I encourage them to make their own books and read each other's ... After we've had a big discussion, I sometimes make what they've said into a book and illustrate it myself and they read that too. (Lynne)

The fact that the teachers identified so closely with their classes' learning is indicative of the social and emotional relationships which existed between them. These relationships had several characteristics, each of which helped to free the teachers from the felt-need to 'teach formally' all the time. First, they felt secure, that is 'in control' (Gill), 'free from the constant need to shout' (Lynne), 'not feeling I have to impose myself on the class all the time' (Rob). Whenever they felt that they were in a state of latent, potential or actual conflict with their pupils they were aware of the need to act a role, to be a 'policeman', a 'boss figure', 'the teacher'. By contrast, when they felt 'relaxed', 'easy', 'not frightened any more', that is, when they could 'be themselves' in the classroom, they were ready to pass more and more of the responsibility for learning to their pupils. In other words, a classroom climate in which teachers feel secure appears to be a necessary condition for the establishment of self-directed, purposeful learning on the part of pupils. For Roger, this meant, among other things, that he and his class could share a joke:

We dismembered the school's television on a wet Friday afternoon. It seemed an appropriate end to a television which had behaved so irresponsibly and provocatively over the last few months. It was a gleeful joint act of retribution, in place of the timetabled sortie onto the games field.

Being a 'knowledgeable' class of perky New Towners, the children were soon pointing out conclusively where the weather man lived — suitably miniaturised of course — but were less sure where Goldie slept at nights. Kevin was particularly dubious, arguing that there was no trace of dog biscuits in the receiver ... (Roger)

Of course what we cannot tell from accounts like these is where causality lies, whether the introduction of learning which the children perceived as purposeful and under their control reduced for their teachers the need to impose 'discipline' or whether, as the latter gained more experience, they became more self-confident and consequently felt less anxious to dominate their classes. Rob related this question to school organisation:

> One of the great problems is the group in a large class who have run out of steam or got stuck and whom the teacher can't reach because of pressures elsewhere. This group can easily become disruptive. In a smaller class the teacher can keep all the children going. It's easier too for a classteacher because those children can be directed onto another area of their work. This safety valve isn't available to specialist teachers who only see their classes for timetabled lessons, maybe once a week.

Secondly, the relationship was characterized by friendliness and mutual acceptance, atrributes which the teachers felt facilitated learning. They made children more open than they might otherwise be to suggestions from the teacher about learning and behaviour and helped the latter to build effective links between home and school. Most important of all, they opened the way for genuine communication between the adult and the child; as teachers they felt that it was through and because of their close and accepting relationship with individual pupils that they were able to help them learn:

> If you're going to support the children in their learning instead of imposing your ideas on them, you've got to have the sort of relationship which enables you to say, 'How's your mum today?', 'What happened about that cat?' or 'Can you sort out that argument together or do you need me or another friend to help you?' (Lynne)

> I could help John because I knew about what he was good at in school and about his family, what he did at home, how he felt about his sister. (For example) I knew that he watches many cartoons and films on TV and video and that the visual element is his prime enabling factor. I obtained some, what I hoped would be, interesting picture books, and began to read one each day to the whole class. The first one aroused his interest and, after other children had re-read it, he took it home 'to read to his sister'. So far he has taken home four of these. (Gill)

> We had soon gained sufficient reputation for Kevin's dad to bring in the family television for repair. (Roger)

Thirdly, some teachers made explicit their feeling that for this relationship to be authentic, it had to be reciprocal (for example, 'I expect it to be a two-way thing — for example, if I've been away ill, I want them to ask me how I am' (Lynne)). Others simply enjoyed the fact that they could be open with their classes, that they could share some of their own feelings with them, be it excitement, amusement, exasperation, wonder, pleasure or, more rarely, frustration and disappointment. As Lynne said,

> What teaching this way means for me is that I'm happy. I feel cared for. I don't feel as if I'm acting. I don't feel stressed or bored, I never look at the clock, I don't have to fight for control — and I have the satisfaction of knowing that I do the job better, that I'm a better teacher. (Lynne)

Within this overall atmosphere of openness, mutual security and trust the teachers' functions and the way they carried them out varied with their pupils' activities. Certainly, they were not afraid to be directive when they felt their children would benefit. Lynne was clear that

> I prefer to see myself as supporting children's learning ... Sometimes that means I show them or tell them or ask them to practise a skill, but that's because I can see they will get on better if they can do something or because they've discovered for themselves that they need help. I don't just sit back and watch them make mistakes. But as far as I'm able I try not to teach things just because I or somebody else thinks they're important. (Lynne)

Rob made a similar point, after helping his pupils define a design problem:

> If the children had been let loose at this point some of them might have known how to proceed, but others would have foundered and become discouraged. With this in mind I set about guiding them through a series of research exercises which would (a) give them time to think about possible solutions to the problem and (b) give them facts and figures to help in their design. Finally, I showed them some simple techniques for hinging pieces of wood, card or plastic together. (Rob)

At one point Chris's class were asked to amass 'information from books and slides lent by the County Library, with particular reference to tools and machinery and the care of animals' so that their mime could be more accurate and realistic. (Chris)

Recently John has begun to draw cartoons labelled with cryptic words and will flesh them out with a lively narrative if pressed. (Gill)

Often, however, their activities were more oblique. They stepped in to guide, help, correct, stimulate when interest was flagging, when the inevitable frustrations of problem-solving seemed likely to overcome an individual's desire to learn or when they judged that the learner's satisfaction would be increased if the quality of work were improved. Ann helped her young children sustain their interest over three weeks by drawing attention to minute changes in the eggs:

On the seventh day, as a child checked the thermometer reading, a change was noted — the temperature registered slightly under 104°F for the first time. Could this be our first piece of evidence that the embryo was forming within some eggs? We re-set the thermometer to 102°F (to allow it to rise much above 104°F could cause the eggs to 'cook') and waited for further developments. On the fourteenth day, the temperature again bordered on the 104°F. Surely there must be life here! On the twentieth day, we noted a 'pin-prickly' feel to a number of eggs, and also detected the faintest 'cheeping' sound within the incubator. We could hardly contain ourselves. (Ann)

Other teachers stepped in with assistance:

There were moments of frustration when the technology of folding chairs hadn't been completely mastered, but with help from me (and from each other) these were overcome. (Rob)

When I notice a child has finished something or can't go any further, I try and sit down with him/her then and there. With spelling, for example, first of all I ask them to underline the words they think they haven't got right and then I go through these with them and I show them the ones that were right after all and work with them on the others. (Lynne)

Gill also wanted to help, but her task was more difficult:

John then re-erected barriers. During class story time he sat physically removed from the group behind a low cupboard. He arranged plane geometric shapes into a rocket whilst I was reading. I act the story as much as possible and give the characters very different voices. The other children listen with bright eyes and alive faces and make pertinent interjections. John kept himself turned away. This happened for several days running. My attempts to make the reading a conversation with him seemed fruitless ... (Later) he asked me to read Sniff 'with me' and sub-articulated parts of it and 'told' some of it by remembering the plot with the aid of the pictures. We have done this often since, but I notice it is only when the classroom is noisy that he feels able to join in. Nevertheless it is involvement ... (later still) I read to them both a book on Fairground Machines which promoted discussion and a swapping of anecdotes, and then John volunteered to read 'The Egg'. I could now begin to make marks on the recording sheet. (Gill)

A marked characteristic of interactions such as these was that the teacher took on the role of critic rather than assessor. Error was valued as a means of self-diagnosis or a springboard for further development rather than being perceived as a sign of failure. Individual or group products were freely discussed with their creators:

If I think a child has done a poor job, I'll ask them if they're satisfied — often they aren't and I'll suggest ways it could be improved or extended and try to make sure they have the help they need. If I think they're trying it on, I'll tell them why I think it's crappy ... It's important that they do something as well as they can, then *they* get the satisfaction from it. It's *their* work but I tell them what I think about it. (Lynne)

Teachers gave their own views:

Gill:	To go back to the original question then, so you don't really know why I'm desperate for you to join the Reading Club?
Andrew:	No (John shakes head).
Gill:	Well, I'll try to explain to you. I think that to be able to get lost inside a book is one of the most magic things that there is, because you can shut the outside world out and you can go into anybody

else's world at all. ('um' from Andrew) Whatever is
happening in the story you get to be part of it so
you have all sorts of experiences that you can't have,
that you're not going to have yourself, but ...

John: Like Commander Bone.

Gill: Yes, lovely, just like Commander Bone ... but the
real excitement is writing your own and then reading it back?

Andrew: Cos I haven't finished mine yet, I've a lot more to
go.

Gill: That's good. You write quite slowly, so does John,
but John's been taking his home and he's done two
fabulous stories now, very lengthy and exciting
stories I can get absorbed in, so that's real writing,
isn't it ... (after discussion of these stories). How
can you say you're no good at reading when you
wrote a three page story and read it all back?

John: It were 'cos I writ it.

Sometimes the teacher came alongside the children not just as a
critic but as a fellow learner:

My own knowledge of electronics was negligible, even suspect. Like one of Thurber's characters who '... lived the
latter years of her life in the horrible suspicion that electri-
city was dripping invisibly all over the room', I viewed the
venture with sheer apprehension ... (and, after the work
was over) I noted the growth of particular children — of
Scott, of Kevin, of Samantha, of Gary — 'non-academics'
who found a maturity and newborn confidence as they led
our mutually enthusiastic advance into new territories.
(Roger)

The next stage was to ask the children to sketch a number of
possible ideas for the chair. This gave them the chance to
consider more than one solution to the problem before
committing themselves to a single solution — an important
step in the design process ... Generally they showed origi-
nality; in fact they surprised me with some of their ideas.
(Rob)

Interventions, whether of guidance, help or criticism, depended
for much of their effectiveness upon their timeliness. The teachers
stressed the importance of being willing to leave a child or group to

work unaided on a problem, to struggle, even to fail, but at the same time of knowing when to join in, to offer assistance or suggest a new line of endeavour:

> You often do the most through a quick word as you move around the classroom. It's being in the right place at the right time (which often means you aren't, of course) and that means knowing them so well as individual learners, as people, that you can gauge quite quickly if they need help and if they do, of what sort. (Gill)

> I see myself as a resource, but not the fountain of all knowledge. As a white middle-class woman, I often cannot answer their questions or concerns, but I can refer them to other children or grown-ups who have a similar experience to themselves. When they get stuck, they need someone to refer to. They learn most from me if I'm able to be there at the right moment. So you have to be alert, on the lookout all the time for the signs that will tell you someone doesn't understand, or a group can't get it together, or somebody wants encouragement or reassurance. (Lynne)

> Although our activities that afternoon were mostly exploratory, there was sufficient enthusiasm for me to feel we could develop the ideas further. (Roger)

Finally, but crucially, they acted as resource-providers. They anticipated the need for and provided (or stimulated the children to provide) the resources without which the latter would have found it difficult to work accurately or authentically. These included the tools of literacy and numeracy (such as paper, pens, pencils, books and visual material of all sorts, measuring instruments of various kinds), standard equipment for other areas of the curriculum (for example, magnets, batteries, woodwork tools, craft materials, simple musical instruments, paint), and items to meet more specific needs, for example,

> a purpose-built chicken run, with an infrared lamp adjusted in height over the central area to give a temperature of 100°F. (Ann)

> diodes — tiny components about a centimetre in length — which were the modern electronic equivalent of the POW's 'cat's whisker'. (Roger)

Work of this sort could not be constrained by epistemological definitions or divisions imposed by the adult world. To be sure, it sometimes took its impetus from a recognizable subject area. For example, Rob's design work was timetabled as 'craft' and for Chris:

> Our focal point was Thomas Tusser who had lived in our village in the sixteenth century. In 1571 his work, *Five Hundred Points of Good Husbandry* was published, 'being a calendar of rural and domestic economy'. This book, perhaps one the earliest of its kind, as a treatise on farming, was written in verse. (Chris)

In general, however, whatever its genesis, curriculum content developed from and was subordinated to the fulfilment of ends which derived from the problem, enquiry or activity, that is from the individual's pursuit of purposeful learning. The careful observation, recording and treatment of the eggs in Ann's class could be described as 'science', but while it was going on 'work also continued, within and outside the classroom, around the general theme of "change" and,

> as the nine chickens grew and arrangements for their transfer, at five weeks to a nearby farm, were finalised, some points were explored together: How would their farm environment be different? What natural dangers might they encounter? Had we overhandled them so that they were now too 'trusting'? Could they survive? We were able to follow up these enquiries a month later, when the class spent a morning on the farm. (Ann)

Roger's work might also be described as 'science' because

> we used a magnet to examine the different types of metal and a battery to find which components allowed electricity to pass through them (Roger),

even though it went on to encompass history (for example, Baird, the 'jury-rigged length of World War II telephone cable, acquired from an army surplus grave-yard'), art and technology. In any case the study of particular curriculum areas was peripheral to the main concerns of both teacher and children:

> Several days later the voice of Jimmy Young crackled unsteadily through the ether from a pair of army headphones. The reception was fitful, but excitement remained unbounded as one by one the seven radios came 'on air'. (Roger)

Similarly, though Chris' project involved history, art, music, movement, drama, geography and economics, as curriculum areas these were means rather than ends.

This kind of work also bridged in other ways divisions which often appear in the primary school curriculum. The basic skills of numeracy and literacy were learnt, applied or practised as a natural part of each undertaking. For example, the youngest group wrote their names, recorded temperatures, made written observations and accounts, read library books, worked on the measurement and sequencing of time, used a thermometer, recorded their findings in graphical forms. And the oldest compiled, administered and analyzed a questionnaire, consulted magazines and catalogues, measured, recorded their findings, worked out and used averages, proportion, scale and percentages. The groups in between engaged in similar activities.

Secondly, in order to fulfil their aims the children acquired and practised the kinds of cognitive skill which underpin work in all curriculum areas. Every teacher mentioned comparing and contrasting, Roger, Gill and Ann encouraged their children to classify by reference to varied criteria, Ann's and Chris's pupils had experience of sequencing. Chris's class interpreted pictures and Ann's, Roger's Chris's and Rob's used graphical representations to record and to communicate with others. Chris encouraged her children to collect evidence from several sources and collate it. They all gave their classes opportunities to ask questions, speculate, conjecture, imagine, propose ideas, make decisions and formulate hypotheses. In addition, the pupils in Roger's and Rob's classes tested their hypotheses through the construction of working models.

Most of all, perhaps, every teacher provided ample opportunity for and encouragement of the development of oral skills. As the work in each class took shape, its next stages were discussed and decided upon, either with the teacher or by groups of children working without him/her. Children listened to each other, to visiting adults, to their teachers. They had practice in speaking for different purposes — to inform, share ideas, ask questions, speculate, contribute to joint decision-making, entertain, persuade. Lynne, in particular, gave instruction and practice in the skills of discussion:

> We often sit down in a circle on the carpet for a discussion. I don't decide what we're going to talk about (though sometimes I start them thinking with a question); the content is

their ideas and experiences. But the discussion is governed by rules which we all adhere to. For example, no-one can say more than three things, or you have to try to answer the previous speaker's question before you say what you think. I chair the discussion, in that I help it along or point out when something's going wrong, but mostly I want them to talk about things they think are important and above all to listen to each other and keep an open mind about the things that other people are saying. (Lynne)

Lastly, learning practical skills was also perceived as important. Ann's infants 'gently sprayed the eggs with tepid water, to soften shells for the "breaking-out" process ... The chickens were fed, watered, cleaned out, lifted and held for weighing and measuring'. Lynne's children learnt to use public transport, to visit and make use of public places, to bind a hardback book and use a word processor, Roger's class learnt constructional and other manual skills, Chris' children sketched, drew and painted in different media for a variety of purposes, wrote and performed music, and synthesized it with movement and mime, Rob's class followed the design process through to the construction of working models and, 'because my group was a relatively small one, they were able to use woodwork tools and had a free choice of materials from paper and card to wood and wire'. Gill's 'non-reader' drew, acted, tape-recorded, and used the library.

❖ ❖ ❖ ❖ ❖ ❖ ❖

It is commonplace that teachers seldom see one another in action, and discuss their classroom methods and the assumptions underlying them even less frequently. Yet the accounts given by these six experienced teachers have much in common despite their different education, training and career history, and the varying contexts in which they were teaching. There might be several reasons for this, for example, a conscious or unconscious desire to supply me with responses of which they thought I would approve; shared socialization into a common professional culture; similar influences during training which, though in different institutions, took place for five out of the six between the mid-1960s and mid-1970s.

It is also possible, however, that they had a common view of education, forged from their own experience of working with children in situations which did not require them to instruct, direct or dominate. Their accounts suggest that as experienced practitioners they were guided by educational principles relating to learning, teaching and the context in which both take place which were the same irrespective of the school and the pupils in which and with whom they were working. These principles themselves may be rooted in a set of beliefs about the nature of knowledge and how it is acquired, but since I asked the teachers to describe their practice, not to examine the philosophical origins of it, without further information my analysis must be speculative. Notwithstanding, at the heart of their descriptions seem to lie two related beliefs — that knowledge is actively constructed by each learner rather than being passively received or stored and that it is therefore in two senses individual, being both personal and unique. It follows from these beliefs that the function of the teacher is to encourage each learner to engage actively with the material to be learned. This in turn requires that learners have the will to become and remain involved in constructing their own knowledge — that they are, in short, motivated to learn. So, much teaching becomes a matter of arranging the optimal conditions under which each learner can, in the often-quoted words of the Plowden Report, become 'the agent of his own learning'. The teachers' work is likely to include directing learners to material which will engage their attention and be within their capacity, helping them to set themselves appropriate goals, assisting them to talk purposefully about and monitor their progress towards these ends and organizing the context, direction, pace and scope of their endeavours. In such a situation the organisation of time, space, resources and attention must be flexible, learners should be free to seek help, guidance and stimulation from many sources. Moreover, since in schools one teacher has the task of simultaneously helping many pupils to construct their own learning, it is imperative that the latter learn to help one another as well as themselves; in the crowded, dense conditions of the classroom, learning must be co-operative as well as autonomous.

Whether or not this summary expresses the epistemological beliefs of these teachers, they certainly wanted their pupils to assume responsibility for and take control of their own learning. To these ends they tried to ensure that classroom activities were perceived by their pupils as having meaning, purpose and value (whether or not the impetus came initially from the learner or the teacher). In particular, they therefore sought to involve them in direct experiences, from which they could draw and to which they could impart their own meanings, and in practical activities, by means of which they could act upon, interpret, transform and make sense of their experiences. In these senses, as Rowland (1984) persuasively argues, they encouraged their children's classroom learning to resemble their play.

However the resemblance does not stop there. Like play, the learning in these classrooms was both individualistic and collaborative. Self-directed and self-controlled learning is, by definition, egocentric; it serves personal ends and is achieved by the expenditure of individual effort and resources. While accepting and to some extent encouraging these characteristics of individualized learning, these teachers also encouraged interaction. They arranged for children to work with partners and in groups and to have access to other adults. Wherever possible they also participated in the children's activities themselves, as co-learners, by presenting alternative viewpoints and new ideas and as critics of the emerging end products. Implicit in these arrangements is the idea that the development of autonomous learning depends upon discussion; the self can best develop through challenge from and with the support of others.

There is a further similarity between self-directed classroom learning and children's play; neither are constrained by adults' ways of organizing knowledge. These teachers encouraged their pupils to draw upon all the curriculum areas with which they came in contact. Their learning ranged widely, guided by their felt need for specific information and skills and not by their teachers' desire that they should attain specific learning outcomes. Yet, because they were learning in a collaborative context, they were open to suggestions and intervention from their teachers who permeated the curriculum with opportunities to learn, practise and apply both the basic skills of numeracy and literacy and more complex cognitive skills such as classification, comparison, conjecture and the making and testing of generalizations. In short, what the children learnt was the outcome of interaction and negotiation between their own interests and the guidance of their teachers.

Negotiations of this kind could only go on, however, in an atmosphere of mutual trust. Teachers wanted to know their pupils very well and to have a relaxed, informal relationship with them not only because it created a pleasant working atmosphere for all of them, but also because it was through that relationship that they could, as it were, enter into their pupils' play and influence their learning. In other words, teaching went on by means of, rather than simply as a consequence of, the open communication which existed between teachers and pupils. Their relationship enabled learning to be negotiated rather than imposed, but was at the same time the tool by which this was accomplished.

Now it is not easy for teachers to sanction, let alone encourage, playlike activities in their classrooms. They are expected to discipline the children in their care and are accountable for their learning. Moreover, an essential part of 'being' a teacher is to feel in control of the classroom (Nias, 1988). Yet, paradoxically, it was confidence in that control that enabled these teachers to behave as they did; it is only those who are secure in their power that can afford to give it away. So, 'good relationships' with pupils served a second purpose. By helping teachers to relax and 'be themselves' they facilitated the transfer of control over learning to pupils themselves. To put it another way, for teachers to feel 'in control' may be a necessary condition for the development of autonomous learning among children. It is small wonder, then, that inexperienced or insecure teachers find it hard 'not to teach formally'.

Moreover, there is ample evidence from recent reports of Her Majesty's Inspectorate that even experienced teachers at present need encouragement to use in the classroom the natural capacities for learning which children display in their play. As the 9–13 Middle School Survey (HMI, 1983) points out, pupils in these schools were given more opportunities in extra-curricular activities than they were in any other aspect of school life to learn and display social responsibility, cooperation, independence, initiative, decision-making, choice. Yet 'the quality of their responses to (such) opportunities indicated that schools could profitably extend their range' (4.6). We need seriously to consider why teachers evidently find it easier, or consider it more appropriate, to cultivate important qualities such as these in their pupils' 'play' but not in their 'work'.

Moreover, the view of learning and teaching which emerges from these accounts is not new. It has been current in educational thinking, in Europe and North America, for at least 200 years, expressed as it is in the work and writings of educationalists such as Rousseau, Pestalozzi, Froebel, Montessori, the McMillan sisters, Dewey, Isaacs and Neill. It has found frequent expression in private schools, from the more widely-known such as Abbotsholme and Bedales to a multitude of suburban kindergartens. It has appeared and reappeared in state education, its practice documented by teachers such as Holmes (1952) and Tustin (1950) and advocated both by educational writers (for example, Caldwell Cook, 1917; Catty, 1949) and by official reports (in particular, the Hadow Report (CCBE, 1931), and the Plowden Report (CACE, 1967). More recently, it has run as one thread through all the recent surveys of primary and middle schools by Her Majesty's Inspectorate and through the Report of the Education, Science and Arts Committee (1986), notwithstanding the fact that they are set in the context of accountability, assessment and cuts in resources. It supports the notion that classrooms can be places in which pupils are actively engaged in constructing their own learning and solving their own problems, guided and assisted by teachers with whom they enjoy a relaxed but mutually respectful relationship, exploring many aspects of human experience without losing hold of 'the basic skills'. In this sense it is not radical.

It is, however, controversial. There are other, equally time-honoured views of the nature of knowledge and thus of teaching and learning. Whereas the practice described in these accounts is consistent with Piagetian psychology (according to which active learners pose their own problems and construct knowledge for themselves through the struggle to resolve them), it conflicts with principles derived from rationalist and behaviourist conceptions of knowledge. These posit passive learners, dependent upon teachers to decide for them the ends of learning and to assess their progress towards them, motivated by extrinsic rewards and sanctions and heavily reliant in their learning upon repetition and practice. It is a view of education which has dominated much classroom activity in both state and private schools for hundreds of years and which is currently enjoying a fresh vogue among politicians and administrators. Recent official documents such as the White Paper *Better Schools* (DES, 1985) and the DES curriculum publication *The Curriculum from 5 to 16* (HMI, 1985c), point in the direction of a centralized national curriculum, divided into 'subjects', taught by specialists, planned by reference to objectives which, once set, are beyond the control of either teachers or learners, and assessed by externally administered criterion-referenced tests. Such developments would make it very difficult for teachers and learners to work together in the kinds of ways which are described in this chapter. They take control of learning out of the hands of the learner, prescribe goals, content, directions and standards and, in so doing, set limits to both aspirations and achievements. By vesting knowledge in the teacher, they ensure an assymetrical power relationship in the classroom and in the process determine the nature of the communication between teacher and pupils.

This is not the place to pursue the epistemological, philosophical and psychological implications of the debate between these conflicting educational viewpoints. There are, however, important pragmatic reasons for continuing to allow teachers to work in ways which are consistent with their belief systems. Recent enquiries (comprehensively presented in Fullan, 1982) into the failure of curriculum innovations seriously to change the classroom experience of many pupils make it clear that teachers change their behaviour only when they have had the opportunity to examine, try out, modify, selectively reject and absorb proposed changes, that is, when they feel that they 'own' them. Further, as I have argued in Nias (1984, 1985 and 1987), teaching is a personal activity, shaped by individual perceptions, perspectives and judgments which are deeply protected from challenge and change. There are few grounds for supposing that these teachers would be any more susceptible to external direction than many others have been. The imposition of a set of educational principles different from those espoused by the people who wrote these accounts is no guarantee that their fundamental attitudes and therefore their behaviour would change.

Moreover, they are experienced members of their profession. All of them have been promoted, five of them to the post of deputy head. Although we have no way of 'measuring' their success in helping children to learn there is a *prima facie* case for claiming that they would be among those who would find approval from the appraisal schemes advocated in *Teaching Quality* (DES, 1984) and *Better Schools* (DES, 1985) and who would be rewarded as 'effective teachers'. Why then should we discount their convictions and the practice by which it is informed?

Instead I wish to leave the last word with them. In his response to my analysis Roger wrote: '(My fear is that) the qualitative strands that you teased out from all the accounts ... may be contradictory to a system which requires finiteness and quantitative 'measurability' in order to function efficiently ... The work on crystal radios could *only* have matured within an atmosphere of freedom — without intervention or restriction from headteacher, timetable or the DES.' Rob responded, 'I feel your conclusions are right, but we still have a long way to go. Can the children wait that long?', while Gill replied, 'I don't want to alter anything you have written. It is too dear to my heart.'

Garden or Jungle? Teacher Development and Informal Primary Education

Robin Alexander

Language, Consensus and Power

Changing Words, Changing Deeds?

Certain words have acquired a peculiar potency in primary education, and few more so than 'informal'. Never properly defined, yet ever suggestive of ideas and practices which were indisputably right, 'informal' was the flagship of the semantic armada of 1960s Primaryspeak, whose vessels, somewhat tattered now, are beginning to disappear over the educational horizon: spontaneity, flexibility, naturalness, growth, needs, interests, freedom, the whole, the seamless robe, the child's view of the world, thematic work, integration, individualization, self-expression, discovery ... and many more.

On whither they are heading — for immortality, for oblivion (or for a refit) — we shall have to await the verdict of history.

It was probably pointless to try, as some did, to define any of these words as exact operational concepts. If, for example, 'informal' indicates (as the dictionary tells us) a situation lacking or eschewing publicly established and agreed norms, forms and conventions, celebrating instead private idiom and idiosyncrasy, then to seek to 'formalize' informality in this way is not so much practically problematical as logically impossible.

Yet the paradox of formalized formlessness was in a sense achieved, at least at the level of the public language of primary education. Primaryspeak became at one and the same time nebulous but normative, obscure but ordained, imprecise but imposed.

For the situation was (and is) about rather more than terminological fuzziness. Primaryspeak was never simply a descriptive or technical language comparable to that used, say, by doctors, though it included a technical element, particularly in relation to children's cognition and learning and to the more highly codified curriculum areas like reading and mathematics. It was a language generated against the historical backdrop of a professional community seeking to distance itself from its Victorian roots: a language of persuasion and solidarity, an ideological shorthand.

It was also a language which served a function in relation to professional hierarchy: it exerted a subtle but irresistible pressure towards consensus, conformity and cohesion; and it strengthened the power base of heads and advisers.

So, what has changed? We know that informality has been on the defensive since the mid-1970s, certainly in the pure form that we used to be told made British primary education, like British democracy, British broadcasting and the Great British Breakfast, the 'envy of the world'. The gulf between the sometimes overblown claims and the classroom realities, the 'myth of progressivism', was confirmed by a succession of empirical studies[1]. Some of the most strenuously defended tenets of informality were challenged on the grounds of their practical viability as well as their educational effectiveness: the assertion that the class teacher, simply by virtue of being with all the children all the time, knows each of them to the extent necessary for devising curriculum experiences which exactly 'match' their abilities, needs and potentialities[2]; individualized learning and group work[3]; and the principle (in some places more a dogma than a principle) that the only valid pattern of classroom organization is one where several different curriculum areas are being pursued simultaneously[4].

Moreover, as I noted above, the language of informality is of itself on the move. The kind of child-centred sloganizing that would have produced a standing ovation only ten years ago is now as likely to make listeners shift uneasily on their chairs. But is the old language being replaced by one which has a greater degree of neutrality, aptness or precision? Somehow, I think not. It is true that where protagonists once espoused 'freedom', 'flexibility', 'spontaneity' and 'discovery' they may now espouse the apparent rigour of 'skills', 'concepts', 'match' and 'standards'. Where they endorsed 'creativity', 'self-expression' and 'making and doing' they may now endorse 'problem-solving' and CDT. 'Individualization' has been replaced by 'collaborative group work'; 'professional autonomy' by 'collegiality'; the 'seamless cloak' of the thematically-based curriculum has ceased to be *de rigueur*, and 'subjects' are no longer taboo.

Such terminological adjustments undoubtedly mirror genuine shifts in consciousness and practice. But equally, they may sometimes be little more than a prudent updating of public professional vocabulary, having a fairly tenuous relationship with private classroom practice and allowing the latter to proceed undisturbed. For an activity as complex as teaching, where individual knowledge and skill are built up slowly and sometimes painfully over many years, simply cannot be transformed as rapidly as these verbal shifts imply, and indeed to claim such overnight transformation is to diminish rather than enhance teacher professionality.

Every example above of 1980s Primaryspeak is problematic in at least two senses: firstly, the terms are capable of sustaining any of a large number of meanings, yet they are (as in the 1960s) too seldom defined; and secondly, even if or when given a stipulative definition each has still to be put into practice. Thus: what *is* a 'skill'? Can one conceive as readily of imaginative skills as one can of manual skills? And if so, which is doubtful, how does one teach them? Or, what kinds of professional relationships and responsibilities are indicated by 'collegiality'? How do these accommodate to the head's contractual accountability to governors and the LEA? How do they accommodate to the value-divergence which is the essential heart of all educational discourse? What is the right balance between individuality and uniformity in teaching and how is it to be achieved? Is collegiality, in short, as easy, or as cosy, as it sounds? The speed and scale of terminological changes such as these, and the all-too-frequent failure, now as in the 1960s, to treat the terms as conceptually or operationally problematic, suggest to me two themes concerning the professional situation and development of primary teachers which are worth pursuing and which, indeed, will be pursued in this chapter.

'For Want of Well Pronouncing Shibboleth'

The first is the *function* of the public professional language of primary education. If terms manifestly in need of definition are not in fact defined, that suggests either that everyone knows exactly what they mean, which is clearly not the case, or that in the context within which such terms are used their meaning does not much matter.

I have referred elsewhere (Alexander, 1984, pp. 210–6) to the contrast between 'academic', 'everyday' and 'ideological' language in primary education, to the dominance of the latter, and to the barriers this dominance can place in the way of meaningful professional discourse. A particular component of ideological language is the recurrence of key words and phrases such as those I have exemplified. Scheffler (1971) characterizes these as 'slogans', but this conveys only part of their force; rather, they seem to function as shibboleths:

> In that sore battle when so many died
> Without reprieve adjudged to death
> For want of well pronouncing Shibboleth.
> (Milton, *Samson Agonistes*, lines 287–9)

While a slogan, then, fosters collective solidarity among the troops, a shibboleth has a more self-serving function in relation to the recognition and advancement of the individual. Of course, the stakes for primary teachers are not so high as they were for those 42,000 Ephraimites, though there are not a few teachers who can attest to careers frustrated because of their failure to conform to the LEA or school orthodoxies of the day, just as there are a fair number who are seen by less successful colleagues to have gained advancement less by merit than by 'saying what the head/adviser wanted to hear' — and of course the fact that appointments are made on the basis of verbal performance at interview rather than operational performance in the classroom legitimates and indeed celebrates the shibboleth. (It is true that we have witnessed in recent years an encouraging move away from so one-dimensional an approach to appointments, at least where senior posts are concerned, with appointing bodies viewing candidates in action in the classroom, but there too the focus of attention may be less the nature and quality of children's learning than the visual equivalents of verbal shibboleths — what in the trade is so ingenuously but revealingly termed 'display'. Thus, conscious of this, Sue, one of the teachers I refer to in the second half of this chapter: 'Teaching needs to be visible: I play the game.')

So although the power context in which shibboleths operate in primary education is less overtly adversarial, more subtle and indirect, than that portrayed by Milton, it may be none the less as pervasive. We are dealing not so much with an ideological blunderbuss pointed directly at teachers' heads (though even that, both locally and nationally, seems now to be happening) than with what for some may be the inexorably engulfing shroud of pseudo-consensus.

Power changes hands, ideologies are superseded: so too are shibboleths. Primaryspeak has updated itself in keeping with the political climate: the language of educational openness and liberalism has given way to a tougher-sounding language of quasi-instrumentality. But its functions are as before.

Public Language, Private Practice

The second theme which this consideration of professional language requires me to pursue is rather different. Like the first, it is offered as a hypothesis. It runs as follows. Despite the profession's ritualistic use of the words 'practice' and 'practical' in ways which suggest that teaching is little more than a simple manual activity, the job does in fact require a high degree of cognitive engagement. If there are such evident discontinuities between public language and classroom practice, and if such public language so obviously and grossly oversimplifies the job the teacher actually does, might this not suggest two other possibilities? The first is fairly readily verified: that until recently, and even today in many schools, the primary teacher's world was a relatively private one, in which there was little incentive and no requirement to explicate to others one's ideas, beliefs and practices except at the deliberately (and maybe necessarily) level of bland and uncontroversial anecdotes over coffee in the staffroom or the strategic exchange of shibboleths at job interviews. The second is that perhaps there is something about teaching in general, and primary teaching in particular, which makes precision and neutrality in professional discourse difficult to achieve. Might not some of the confusions, paradoxes and contradictions to which commentators can so devastatingly point be not so much 'failings' in teachers as inherent properties of the task to which those teachers are committed? Might not the job of primary teaching be in reality far more subtle, complex and sophisticated than either of the public linguistic forms so far available — academic/technical and ideological — can convey?

To answer these latter questions, and to get inside some of the processes and themes identified in this introductory section, we must talk with and examine the activities of teachers themselves, so it is with their work and thoughts that much of this chapter will be concerned. I shall seek to show how some of the problems of discourse and practice raised above manifest themselves as tensions and dilemmas which individual teachers have to confront, resolve or come to terms with during their professional development; how while some of these tensions and dilemmas are intrinsic to teaching, others are created or at least exacerbated by the grandiloquent vagueness of the language and expectations concerning classroom practice as proclaimed most characteristically by people who do not (or no longer) have to implement them; and how the individual teacher's encounters with such tensions, dilemmas and expectations also mirror — and of course are inevitably tied up causally with — the history and development of primary education as a whole.

We start with the latter — macro, historical — context, entering it, (appropriately, in view of the discussion so far) via a 1980s update of one of the most hallowed of all metaphors in the lexicon of informality.

Alternative Metaphors and Alternative Realities

The Garden: The Power of Metaphor

One of the abiding characteristics of the language of primary education is its use of metaphors in general and organic metaphors in particular. This is not really surprising, given that the one unalterable fact about primary education, regardless of changing ideologies, priorities and procedures, is its concern with children who are growing and developing.

But for Froebel, and many others for whom his ideas had a particular resonance, 'growth' and 'development' were depicted in botanical rather than zoological terms — hence of course the kindergarten, with children as plants and teacher as gardener, and the associated horticultural imagery with which we are all so familiar — natural, ripening, unfolding, budding points, nurturing and so on[5].

A garden is not, except in so far as it contains plants, a 'natural' environment. Rather, it is a contest, man's taming of nature, in which plants are placed, shaped, bred and cross-bred in accordance with human notions of form and order; most obviously so in the case of Le Nôtre's manicured geometric formalism, more gently so in the English pastoral tradition of Capability Brown. But even in the latter landscape it is a man-made re-ordering of nature, rather than nature untamed, which is on view.

Thus, in the garden metaphor *order* and *authority* are as important as the more familiar notion of growth. The educational garden is enclosed and protected; it is free from weeds and impure strains; it is visually pleasing; it is harmonious; in it everybody and everything knows and accepts its place. There is more than a hint here, as Dearden pointed out two decades ago (1968), of authoritarianism — and, one might add, of eugenics.

This is not the digression it may begin to seem. For these kinds of images and associated assumptions are peculiarly pervasive (deeply-rooted, one might say) in primary education: not just where teacher–child relationships and the curriculum are concerned, but also in our inherited view of the primary system as a whole, past and present. Notions like 'flexibility', 'spontaneity', 'enrichment' and so on have been treated as self-evident, unproblematic and efficacious, and practices like thematic work, the integrated day and groupwork have been regarded as incontestably 'right' for young children, not because of any conceptual subtlety or operational inviolability (far from it) but because to challenge such specifics was to threaten the whole — the entire interconnected package or edifice of ideas, practices, institutions and roles, the professional consensus by which these were sustained and, in turn, the professional power structure through which consensus was achieved, enforced and regulated.

There has been, therefore, a tendency to slide from the organic, unificatory concept of the young child's education (which may well have a great deal to commend it) to the view that the system as a whole has the same kind of preordained and 'natural' coherence (which is manifestly not the case).

There are many examples of the consequences of failing properly to separate for analytical purposes the educational ideology from the institutional context, and the world of childhood from the world of teacherhood. One such is what I term elsewhere (Alexander, 1984, chapter 5) the 'correspondence' approach to curriculum preparation in initial teacher education — the notion that the teacher needs to experience in terms of quantity, proportion and character a grown-up version of what is offered to the child: a view which has only relatively recently begun to be challenged at an official level[6]. Another example, a different aspect of the same problem, is the almost universal failure to question the existing curriculum pecking-order in primary schools, with its dominance of what I call (1984, chapter 3) 'Curriculum I' — the 'basics' of numeracy and literacy — over the 'Curriculum II' of environmental and social, personal and moral, physical, aesthetic and expressive development and understanding. Such questioning as does occur is more often at the level of rhetoric (of course everything is equally important, it is asserted) than at the level of practice, where the discrepancies in time and resource allocation, in teacher expertise and above all in quality of learning and seriousness of professional intention tell a different story[7]. Or there is the matter of the class teacher system, unquestionably the 'best' way of educating children of primary age, we are told, and woe betide any band of HMIs that dares to suggest otherwise[8].

Many of those involved in primary education will confirm how difficult it is to prise open this package of certainties. Yet of course there is nothing inevitable, incontestable, let alone 'natural' about them. The Curriculum I/II divide and the class teacher system are no more than enduring throwbacks to the ancestors of today's primary schools, the nineteenth century elementary schools: to the sternly utilitarian '3Rs' curriculum on the one hand, and, on the other, to the form of organization devised to secure delivery of that curriculum as cheaply and efficiently as possible.

Stepping Outside the Garden

I would suggest that the time has come not only — as this book seeks — to reappraise informality as an approach to the education of young children, but also to re-examine the sanitized, ahistorical, consensual and unproblematic version of primary education as a whole which informal ideology, by a process of hegemony, seems to have generated.

To help us on our way (and with the garden not forgotten) I would suggest that if we must proceed on the basis of metaphor we should at least have some alternatives to enliven the debate and challenge the consensus. My alternative to the ordered garden, for the sake of consistency, would also be botanical, but it would be rather more rampant. It would be the jungle.

The jungle of primary education is vast, dense and rambling. It is at once open and secret. Its sights and sounds invite and welcome, the display of some of its species attract and seduce; yet further in it becomes inpenetrable, able to be negotiated only with knowledge of shibboleths and hidden pathways; its surface harmony barely camouflaging on the one hand a surprising diversity, and on the other, myriad struggles for space and survival.

If the metaphor seems extreme, that is only because we have conditioned ourselves to accept metaphors, images, versions of primary reality and history which overstate order, harmony and consensus. The truth lies somewhere in between, but — however portrayed — it must, I suggest, more explicitly acknowledge and accommodate diversity, disagreement and compromise than hitherto. For in primary education, values and beliefs about children, curriculum and pedagogy diverge and compete. The curriculum is at best an uneasy compromise between competing but precariously co-existing values, and at worst (as now) a no-holds-barred political battleground. Children's potentialities, far from being recognised and nurtured by an all-seeing teacher-gardener, may sometimes remain undetected, unaroused, unrealized, even suppressed. Children, as do teachers, evolve or fail to evolve their own strategies for coping, surviving or succeeding[9]. Power and rewards are unevenly distributed and, for many, the pursuit and maintenance of power, influence and status are overriding preoccupations.

The Jungle of Educational History

The jungle metaphor can prompt an alternative perspective not just on schools and the situations and careers of children and teachers but also on the history and current disposition of the system as a whole. The idea of primary education's encapsulating different and sometimes competing traditions and ideologies is not new. Blyth in 1965 showed how the 'elementary', 'developmental' and 'preparatory' traditions had come together in post-war primary education. Richards (1982), contrasts the ideologies of 'liberal romanticism', 'educational conservatism', 'liberal pragmatism' and 'social democracy'. Golby (1986) replaces the 'preparatory' tradition in Blyth's list by 'technological'.

I suggest that we can now fairly readily identify seven distinct ideologies which have been prominent at different points in the history of primary education and which are all, though to varying and shifting degrees, discernible in current primary discourse and practice. They are presented here in tabular form for ease of reference.

Some Dominant Ideologies in Primary Education

Ideology	*Central values in respect of curriculum*
1 ELEMENTARY	Curriculum to meet society's economic and labour needs, and to preserve the existing social order. Education as a preparation for working life.
2 PROGRESSIVE	Curriculum to enable the child to realize his/her full potential as an autonomous individual. Childhood a unique phase of development, not just a preparation for adulthood. Curriculum open and negotiable.
3 DEVELOPMENTAL	Curriculum to be structured and sequenced in accordance with the child's psychological and physiological development and learning processes.
4 BEHAVIOURAL/ MECHANISTIC	Curriculum defined and structured in terms of hierarchies of observable and testable learning outcomes.
5 CLASSICAL HUMANIST	Curriculum about initiating the child into the 'best' of the cultural heritage, defined chiefly in terms of disciplines or forms of understanding: the arts, sciences and humanities.
6 SOCIAL IMPERATIVES: ADAPTIVE/ UTILITARIAN	Curriculum to meet society's economic, technological and labour needs, to enable the child to adapt to changes in these, and to preserve the existing social order.
7 SOCIAL IMPERATIVES: REFORMIST/ EGALITARIAN	Curriculum to enable the child both to fulfil individual potential and to contribute to societal progress. The latter defined in terms of plurality, democracy and social justice, as well as the economy.

A chronological sequence of sorts can be inferred here: for example, it is clear that the progressive tradition was in part a reaction against the instrumentality and rigidity of elementary education, that it in turn was buttressed by the emergent discipline of developmental psychology, and that by the 1980s the wheel seemed to have come full circle with the Thatcher government's espousal of a utilitarian and cost-cutting ideology which resembled none more than that of elementary education a century earlier. But such sequencing should be minimal, for the important point in the context of the present discussion is this: ideologies do not come in single file, one replacing another, but compete, interact and continue in juxtaposition. Some are modified, some are driven, temporarily or permanently, underground, minority viewpoints become majority ones, and vice versa. Different ideologies continue to influence the system in different ways and to differing degrees.

Thus, the residual but powerful legacy of the elementary system is ever present, as I have already argued, in 'Curriculum I' — the continuing allegiance to a particular (though now expanding) notion of 'basics' — and the class teacher system. The progressive tradition has had a profound impact upon the physical and interpersonal milieu of primary schools which political centralization and pre-scription are unlikely to diminish. The developmental tradition, especially through Piaget's work, has transformed our views of children's cognition and of the kinds of learning activities and ex-periences which are appropriate at different stages of development. Behaviourism, having had minimal impact on primary education when first imported here from the USA, is experiencing a new respectability with the current emphasis upon prespecified objec-tives, agreed and measurable 'benchmarks' or 'targets' of attainment for given ages of pupils, and national testing procedures[10]. Even classical humanism, a public/grammar school import, is detectable in HMI's liberal 'areas of learning and experience' approach to the 5–16 curriculum (HMI, 1985c). And while all political parties at both national and local levels agree on the need for education to be socially relevant and responsive, they differ sharply on how such 'relevance' is to be defined and on which aspects of society and culture demand a curricular response[11].

So while each of the seven traditions/ideologies above has emerged at different points during the history of primary education, every one of them is detectable to some degree and in some aspect of the system as it now stands. The juxtaposition may in some cases be a trouble-free one (progressivism and developmentalism, for example, have forged a powerful alliance) in which case the garden metaphor will suffice and the process is one of hybridization: mixed ancestry but a viable organism[12]. But in other cases where the ideologies conflict — most notably perhaps in the 1980s debate about the curriculum, the jungle metaphor is more apt. In such a climate the essential incompatibility of some of the ideologies is exposed; so too are the Darwinistic consequences of their juxtaposition — with the arts, to take just one current example, having to adapt by redefining themselves in accordance with prevailing social relevance criteria (hence the emphasis on 'skills' and 'design' rather than 'self-expression') or face extinction.

Informal education, as a conception, is a progressive/developmental hybrid; but as practice, even in those schools claiming to manifest informality at its purest, it is a considerably more complex mixture.

The current struggle in the primary jungle seems to involve on the one hand a rearguard action by grassroots progressivism in the face of government utilitarianism, with behaviourism opportunistically waiting in attendance on the latter and an updated classical humanism available from HMI as a compromise[13]. On the other it is for many teachers a struggle whose protagonists are less clearly identifiable because the more pressing problems concern time, space, resources, recognition and survival. The language of primary discourse — in any staffroom, on any course, in the educational press — echoes the contest: spontaneity/planning; openness/aims and objectives; growth/standards; balance/relevance; themes/skills and concepts; autonomy/accountability; compartmentalization/subjects; self-expression/CDT; topics/science; life-skills/the world of work; cooperation/competition ... And so on. (The pairings are not, I hasten to add, mutually exclusive — as they are sometimes presented — but given their differing genealogies their resolution requires effort.)

Professional Development in the Primary Jungle

The Randomness of Experience

And so to the teachers, whose individual development, I suggested, while not mirroring exactly the processes and cross currents explored above, at least offers parallels and counterpoints. It is they who have to make practical sense of the competing ideas and claims and have to come to terms with the jungle — to hack a path through it, to learn to accept and perhaps exploit its confusion and luxuriance, or be overwhelmed by it.

From here on, I shall be drawing on data collected as part of a research project on professional knowledge-in-action which involved an intensive programme of observation, videotaping, individual interviewing and collective discussion with experienced primary teachers in Leeds, Bradford and Calderdale LEAs[14].

Professional development often tends to be conceived in terms which highlight formal career events and moves — initial training, induction, changes of school, promotion, inservice activities and courses — and which sees these passage rites as what, centrally, 'develops' a teacher. Thus, development becomes firstly an intermittent succession of events rather than a continuous process, and secondly something which is handed down by others (advisers, heads, teacher educators) rather than initiated or executed by the teacher himself/herself[15].

In contrast to this somewhat managerialist view, teachers themselves tend to highlight 'experience' as the main agent in their development, though because experiences are unique and the word itself is so nebulous it tends not to be explicated further and therefore loses ground to what can be formalized. Moreover, everyone is only too familiar with the cautionary adage about 'experience' ('Is it thirty years' experience or one year repeated thirty times?') which reminds us that learning from experience requires receptivity, predisposition and effort on the part of the learner. Working closely with experienced teachers one becomes aware of how random and serendipitous, in contrast to the tidy and top-down training-to-retirement sequence, professional development actually is. For some teachers, initial training has a major impact; for many, a negligible one. Inservice activities, similarly, can inspire or frustrate. But more important than either seem to be the school contexts within which teachers happen to find themselves: the children, heads and fellow-teachers with whom they work and the professional climate and affiliations which such communities engender. Circumstances and outcomes, then, have a large chance element.

Teachers as Agents in Each Others' Development

Such influences can be positive or negative. Thus while Graham attests to the impact of two very different heads on his classroom practice and professional relationships, Peter talks despairingly of having encountered only 'anti-models' during his career so far — teachers whose values he did not share, whose perceived parochialism he despised and from whose practice he wished to distance his own as far as possible.

For all these teachers, colleagueship — day-to-day communion with fellow-teachers whom one likes and respects and from whom one can learn — was something to be prized. Yet all too often, as Nias's work also shows (Nias, 1984 and 1985b) the individual primary teacher feels isolated and at variance with the prevailing professional culture of a particular school. In such cases, an alternative reference group might be available outside the school, or it might not be, and the teacher's development would be frustrated by the denial of such stimulus and support.

How one learns from others varies, of course. Some blossom in a combative, even a rebarbative relationship; others may seek the security of consensus or even of paternalism. For professional development is as much about the teacher's personal attributes and capacities as it is about the professional experiences and people encountered. Thus, Sue, from her own schooldays on, has always been intensely competitive, and as a teacher needs colleagues among whom she can shine yet who will also stimulate and acknowledge her. Jenny, Pam and Graham have a restless, questing mentality which makes them intensely impatient with those who are too easily satisfied. In contrast, Sheila has a more relaxed outlook on colleagues, and values their company for its own sake, exemplifying the kind of tolerance she seeks to foster in her pupils.

Professional Development as Personal Journey

Equally inseparable are non-professional, particularly family influences. Several teachers' own sometimes traumatic experiences of failure at school seem strongly to have coloured their approach to the children they teach and particularly to those they see as less able, disadvantaged or withdrawn. Several admit to identifying particularly with those children who are 'like me as a child' — whether boisterous and mischievous, or introverted and earnest.

The family is a powerful influence — whether being the child of one's parents and enacting in one's teaching the kinds of relationship and qualities one most valued in them; or being oneself a parent and seeing in the children one teaches resonances of the anxieties, foibles and pleasures of one's own offspring. Equally, it must be said, there are those who never manage to 'only connect' their own and others' experiences and situations in this way.

So professional development is less fundamentally an institutional sequence of formally-designated activities than a personal journey, in which individual personality, experience and maturation, and teacher growth, are not easily separated and where the key influences extend, contextually and temporally, well beyond the knowledge, let alone the control, of professional development agents or agencies.

Professional Development and Classroom Decision-making

Another way of viewing professional development is as a process of coming to terms with the kinds and contexts of *decision-making* that the job of teaching demands. Calderhead (1984) distinguishes 'immediate', 'routine' and 'reflective' classroom decisions, and Jackson (1968) 'preactive', 'interactive' and 'postactive' phases of teaching. Putting these together we can see that the interactive phase — that which takes place in the classroom, with the children — has an intensity, complexity and pressure that thinking, planning and talking away from the classroom never have. In a busy primary classroom the teacher has relatively little time for reflection: decisions must be taken quickly. By trial and error he/she learns which decisions work and which do not, so that what start early in one's career as immediate decisions may soon become routine. The teacher also routinises some of the decisions during the preactive and postactive phases, thus allowing more time for reflection on other aspects of the job (or simply for living). Interactive decision-making becomes smoother and less fraught, and time is opened up for immediate decisions, however rapid, to be grounded in some degree of reflection.

That at least is how it looks in theory. In practice, much depends on the teacher's individual skills, attributes, circumstances and commitments. Thus, Bennett's (1984) criticism of the tendency towards 'crisis management' in primary classrooms, on the grounds that it restricts opportunities for the kinds of careful one-to-one diagnostic interactions that match of learning task to child requires, is probably, in many cases, fair. But for some teachers, queues at their desk are not necessarily a symptom of any kind of organizational crisis, and they may feel no particular lack of diagnostic time or space. For these, the more that is routinized, the easier the job becomes, the less it has to be thought about outside the classroom, and indeed the less incentive there is for such reflection, particularly of a questioning or critical variety, since it only 'makes waves'.

For others, however, the extent of reflection does not diminish, and carries its own impetus, rewards and penalties. For a start, as Graham points out, every situation and encounter in teaching, however familiar, is also unique, and previous experience can never provide a blueprint. Citing what he felt to be a mishandled approach to a child with behavioural problems he said:

> You only progress as a teacher if you take each experience, evaluate it and try to improve upon it . . . (Yet) no matter how many experiences, no matter what your bank of experiences is . . . you're still going to come across (a situation where) you'll never have quite the right answer, and that's where I feel my problems are in professional development. We do want to do things properly, but there's no real yardstick for how you actually deal with any one situation.

For teachers with this kind of reflective commitment, the routinising of some aspects of teaching may actually make the job more rather than less taxing, though in a different way. For the inexperienced teacher, the challenges are immediate and clear-cut: content and control — what shall I teach them and how shall I secure and maintain their cooperation? As through experience one acquires a content and control vocabulary for answering these questions in a variety of circumstances, so one creates cognitive space to re-examine firstly the very aspects of the job one has routinized and the routines one has adopted, and secondly aspects or layers of the task of teaching which one hitherto may have treated as 'givens' and subjected to little thought.

Sue illustrates this graphically. Now with ten years' experience behind her, she has developed a considerable interest in curriculum as a professional issue, and in particular in the need to secure for 'Curriculum II' areas like art and environmental studies the attention to conceptual structure and underlying cognitive processes which she sees as more usually restricted to mathematics and language. She is prepared (in the face of prevailing primary ideologies) to assert that while she is no less child-centred than her colleagues she now finds thinking about curriculum matters more challenging and rewarding. But, recalling her first years in teaching:

My major concern at that time was control. I mean it was a case of 'sod the curriculum' ... how you're going to cope with the day and make sure these kids don't walk all over you before four o' clock and if you got out at the end of the day and felt reasonable then you'd succeeded.

Learning From Experience: Does the Job get Easier or Harder?

Sue *had* succeeded, yet now, like Pam, Sheila, Judith and others, she saw the job as getting harder rather than easier. One telling man-ifestation of this was the way several of them, for all their accumu-lated banks of experience, ideas and resources, spent if anything longer in mid-career planning away from the classroom than they had as trainees or probationers. But whereas in the early days the main effort went into producing workcards and other materials to keep the children occupied, now the emphasis was more upon reflecting on individual children, keeping records, devising more and more sophisticated strategies for maximizing the time that with a class of thirty could be devoted to each child; engaging with curri-culum less in terms of 'What shall they do?', more in terms of 'What precisely do I want each of them to learn? What kinds of concepts and skills? How can I ensure that they do so?'; probing the mine-field of 'match', and so on.

For some, the associated emotions arising from a combined sense of the problematic nature of the task, once one honestly faced it, and the inevitable shortfall between aspirations and outcomes, could be uncomfortable: words like 'uncertainty', 'pressure', 'responsibility', 'muddle', 'quandary' were common; so too were more self-lacerating terms like 'obsession' and 'guilt'.

As I suggested earlier, the central factor in professional de-velopment is the kind of person the teacher is. Teaching becomes harder, more complex and problematic only if one chooses or is disposed to see it that way (as Sue remarked: 'They don't have to be problems. I could just get on and ignore them'), so for many teachers the job does in fact become easier. But it is worth com-menting here on another contributory strand too often neglected in discussion of professional development: the teacher's age and life-situation. Our teachers ranged in age from 30 to 50, but most were between 36 and 44, the period during which what Erikson (1967) terms one's 'ego-identity' begins to be tested, and during which one becomes increasingly conscious of one's shortcomings, of lost opportunities, of failures in relationships, of career frustration, of the mortality of one's parents and hence of oneself, of the end of the relative idyll of parenting young children . . . and, for some, of the proximity of despair.

The case, however, must not be overstated. Teaching, like many other jobs, is intellectually and situationally demanding. It poses challenges and problems which have to be and in fact are resolved. While with experience and maturity a teacher's apprehension of these challenges and problems may become keener and more subtle, and the focus of his/her reflection and preparation may shift to deeper levels, and while earlier certainties may begin to be questioned, for most teachers this can fairly readily be accommodated, and nothing detracts from the pleasure, the regenerative power and what Lortie (1975) calls the 'psychic rewards' of being among young children. In any case, an alternative line of professional development is available, that leading to habituation, complacency and intellectual ossification.

Competing Imperatives and Teacher Development

Let us take stock for a moment. The theory being evolved so far is of professional development as in part a deepening consciousness of and response to the problematic nature of teaching. All our teachers, though to varying degrees, were aware of being caught between different versions of how they ought to act, what we came to call *'competing imperatives'*. Some of these competing imperatives were situational — to do with the constraints of a school building and its resources; or the differing and not necessarily compatible or personally acceptable expectations of a head, or an adviser, or parents; or the values and styles of the colleagues with whom one is obliged to work; or of course the particular children one teaches and the physical circumstances in which one teaches them. Many of the competing imperatives were value-related — to do with reconciling alternative views of children's needs and capacities or contrasting views of curriculum priorities. Some were uncomfortably pointed up by the professional power context — finding oneself at variance, for example, with school or LEA orthodoxy, but feeling obliged to toe the line or at least to pronounce the shibboleth.

This idea has something in common with the Berlaks' (1981) idea of 'dilemmas' in primary schooling — a set of sixteen 'control', 'curriculum' and 'societal' polarities (for example, public vs personal knowledge, knowledge as content vs knowledge as process, extrinsic vs intrinsic motivation) which they see as underlying the schooling process in general, at the macro, societal level, and therefore confronting and needing to be resolved by each teacher at the micro level of the classroom. There are difficulties here: it could be argued that for a dilemma to exist for a person he/she must be conscious of it, whereas the Berlaks presented little evidence that this was so in individual cases, seeing the dilemmas as inescapably 'in the situation' as they as outsiders defined it. Moreover, their dilemmas were presented as mutually exclusive polarities, which in real life they rarely are. However, the idea is a potent one, and offers an important bridge between societal values and the situation of the individual teacher.

A different notion of professional 'dilemmas' is provided by Argyris and Schön (1974): for them the dilemma is a mismatch within a professional's 'espoused theory' (the ideas 'to which one gives allegiance and which one communicates to others') or between such espoused theory and one's 'theory-in-use' (the ideas which actually, regardless of what one claims to others, govern and inform one's actions). A dilemma in this sense is an intellectual tension or inconsistency, which it may cause discomfort to oneself to acknowledge and which, because of this, one may respond to by any of a number of strategies: keeping the two kinds of theory firmly apart (progressive ideology and shibboleths for others — the staffroom and job interviews — and theory-in-use for oneself); changing the one but not the other; selectively ignoring or suppressing anything that points to such an inconsistency; redirecting blame for such an inconsistency away from oneself to others — parents, children, colleagues for example.

This version of dilemmas is also useful. The idea of an espoused theory/theory-in-use mismatch, given the idealistic nature of some of the former in primary education, is particularly important, and the coping strategies are readily observable.

The present idea of 'competing imperatives' is looser and more eclectic than in either of these models, and tries to capture a sense of tensions, many of which the teacher is well aware of, emanating from and within many sources and levels — primary ideology, central government, HMIs, LEA advisers, parents, head, colleagues, one's particular physical and interpersonal situation as a teacher, and oneself. In this more generalized usage what is being argued is (a) that the teacher is at the intersection of many such competing imperatives; and (b) that teachers may become more conscious of, and indeed conscious of more, such competing imperatives as they become more experienced and their increased executive competence opens up to them deeper levels of awareness about the nature, and the problems, of the job they are doing.

The link with primary ideology, whether 1960s informality or its 1980s update, should by now be fairly clear. Such ideology is essentially an array of values, beliefs and prescriptions concerning children, knowledge and society and how these should be translated into appropriate curriculum content and teaching strategies. Values are not absolutes: they are by their nature contestable and contested; they yield, or are generated in deliberate opposition to, alternative values. In the case of primary education, as I showed above, the amalgam of progressive and developmental ideas that has constituted 'informality' is but one of a number of concurrent and perhaps conflicting value systems which generate pressures and demands that the teacher has to reconcile in his/her practice.

'Competing imperatives' are a more cerebral representation of the primary jungle, and among these imperatives some of the hardest to cope with are those which are especially pervasive in informal ideology: imperatives which are accessible, attractive and indeed irresistible as generalized values, but which are rather less easy when it comes to translating them into viable classroom practices; yet, because of their status as power-backed orthodoxies, they are also difficult for the ordinary teacher to question or resist.

This process can now be illustrated by reference to four professional themes: teachers' response to the generalized sense of an obligation to demonstrate 'flexibility' and 'openness'; their approaches to planning; the question of whether and/or when the teacher should 'intervene' in children's learning; and the organizational devices of grouping and group work. Space permits only these four illustrations, but the project from which these come generated many more which will be discussed elsewhere[14].

Competing Imperatives, Informality and the Experienced Teacher: Examples

Openness and Flexibility: The Informal Paradox

As so much of the language of informal and post-informal primary education centres on an opposition of 'openness' (desirable) to 'structure' (undesirable), whether in curriculum content, pedagogy or the school building itself, it is not surprising that the imperatives thereby created for teachers can be prominent and problematic. Our teachers fell into three groups: those who espoused flexibility but whose patterns of classroom practice seemed relatively fixed, yet for whom the possible paradox was not an admitted problem; those for whom the paradox was apparent, yet who felt under a sense of obligation to strive for the ever-receding ideal of flexibility and thereby faced an acute sense of the mismatch between ideal and reality; and those who recognized the paradox but had ceased to worry overmuch about it, had become more accepting and realistic and had thereby achieved flexibility in a rather different sense.

So, for example, Joyce's work with a class of 5-7-year-olds was a highly efficient implementation of a procedure termed the 'flexible day' which she saw as having official endorsement. Flexibility here (as with the integrated day, which it resembled) had two aspects: different curriculum areas pursued by different groups of children simultaneously, and a degree of individual choice. The procedure was complex and professionally demanding, and was sustained by very firm teacher control, and an emphasis upon 'discipline' and 'routines' to which children were expected to conform and in which they were trained. The curriculum was divided three ways: language, mathematics and the rest (art, topic, science and craft) which was designated 'choosing'. Children spent equal amounts of time, in rotation, on each.

The organization, therefore, classically reflected the Curriculum I/II problem as I have analyzed it elsewhere (Alexander, 1984, chapter 3). Flexibility and choice were in fact restricted to Curriculum II ('choosing') while Curriculum I was non-negotiable. Since the three areas fitted the typical primary school day — three relatively uninterrupted sessions punctuated by play or dinner-time, and a fourth for PE/games/story/finishing off/administrative odds and ends all additional curriculum demands — science, drama, music and so on — had to be accommodated in the three-way structure. In practice, because of the protected status of Curriculum I, this meant acute pressure on the one area where flexibility and choice actually existed, 'choosing' (Curriculum II).

Joyce's situation, operationally impressive though it was, enshrined a paradox which could not really be acknowledged, since both the term 'flexible day' and this form of organization — which seemed to gainsay usual definitions of 'flexible' — had been officially endorsed.

Janet, a teacher of 6-7-year-olds, was well aware of the potential for this kind of paradox and such consciousness made her somewhat uncomfortable, even guilt-ridden. For she had acquired a notion of 'flexibility' not as a specific form of organization but as a moral absolute which her teaching must at all costs demonstrate in order to gain approval (from herself as well as others) as 'good informal practice'. Janet had learned to treat anything not 'flexible' as 'rigid' — a polarity, which like so many in primary education, carries a strongly disapprobatory loading. This meant that since she had set herself a virtually unattainable ideal of flexibility the spectre of 'rigidity' hung (quite unjustifiably for us who observed her) over much of what she did. So, for example, even a modest degree of subject-separation in the curriculum opened up the risk of 'little boxes' and 'compartmentalization', while in operationalizing 'flexibility' through a system of groups undertaking different activities simultaneously the danger she perceived was that her need closely to monitor children's progress represented some kind of 'imposition' upon them.

But alongside 'flexibility' as shibboleth — and, except through inflexibility, an unattainable ideal — was another, more personal version. Janet, as an experienced teacher on the way to headship, was increasingly conscious of the fact that her abiding anxiety, over many years, to meet others' expectations of how she should teach, in fact contradicted the idea of 'flexibility' in its truest sense. Janet, therefore, was moving towards a version of flexibility as being less about conforming to an approved style than about freedom to think and act independently of such preconceptions, to evolve her own version of flexibility.

Such emerging autonomy was always constrained by external requirements and demands. Janet, like Andy, Jenny and several others, found the ubiquity of published mathematics schemes a distinctly double-edged benefit. On the one hand they provided a framework and prop in a curriculum area having a high and very public profile in primary education and for which they, like so many primary teachers until recently, lacked the extent of personal proficiency, and therefore, confidence, they wished. On the other hand, such schemes 'imposed' a 'rigid structure' of the very kind that they sought to reject, and in the most prominent area of the curriculum, at that. Since working through the schemes was mandatory, the dilemma seemed unresolvable. Janet's partial resolution was to accept this contradiction and constraint, to identify instead those curriculum areas where she would be free to develop her own

style and interests, and there to enact 'flexibility' in a more individual sense. Topic work provided the required context: it was the
area where she could freely enact her own 'personal view of the
world . . . views on how to bring up children . . . on what's important in life' free from external expectations and constraints. She, like
several others, felt liberated in topic work to an extent which
seemed impossible in mathematics and language. Indeed, these
teachers accepted that to some extent themes for topic work were
often chosen to reflect the teacher's rather than the child's interests.
Perhaps, therefore, the case made by HMI in the primary and first
school surveys (HMI, 1978 and 1982) against randomness and
repetition in topics is not quite so clear cut as it seems, for against
the apparently inexcusable idiosyncrasy of such arrangements one
should maybe set this kind of personal commitment and enthusiasm,
from which, surely, children must benefit.

As we worked with Janet, over two terms, we (and she) perceived a gradual loosening of the earlier grip of the shibboleth of
'flexibility'. Janet moved, and felt herself moving, from an outer-
directed to an inner-directed approach in this and other respects
which made her less educationally fashion-conscious and confor-
mist, more relaxed, less insecure and guilt-ridden. Having admitted
to us what she could obviously not admit to the primary hierarchy,
that flexibility in teaching, at least in the absolutist, utopian form
presented in the informal rhetoric, was unattainable, she became
more realistic and accepting of herself — and thus more truly
flexible.

Sheila was also conscious of tension here but had less room for
manoeuvre. Teaching in a brand new fully open-plan school, her
curriculum and organization had to reflect in every way not just
'flexibility' (which does at least imply some boundaries) but 'openness' (which seems to imply none at all). Her recurrent phrase was
'freely-flowing': children had to be able to move freely from one
part of the building to another and from one kind of learning,
unencumbered by subject labels, to the next; curriculum areas had
to merge into each other imperceptibly; the whole had to be thema-
tically unified; staff relationships had to be open, frank and collaborative. This ideology was one, it should be emphasized, to
which she herself was totally committed: it accorded with her personal values, and the consistency made her seem a happy and
fulfilled professional.

Yet the now familiar paradox and tensions were evident, for
what Sheila sought was what we came to term a 'non-framing

framework' or a 'non-structuring structure': some kind of formula for planning and organizing children's learning in her section of the school which enabled individual children's programmes to be planned, implemented and monitored in accordance with prior commitments to appropriate experiences in the designated areas of mathematics, language, 'creativity' and 'investigation', but which admitted of no such conceptual or organizational boundaries.

There was a constant and recurrent tension in Sheila's interviews between 'freely-flowing' as an elusive ideal and 'bittiness' as ever-present danger — the Scylla and Charybdis of competing imperatives in informal primary education, perhaps. For the very procedures which had been designed in order to promote, exemplify and enact flexibility — large open spaces, shared curriculum/resource areas, collaborative teaching — in fact made the open curriculum more rather than less difficult to achieve than for one teacher in a box classroom. The complex logistics of one space, four curriculum areas, three teachers and sixty children dictated considerable forward planning, and, in particular, prior agreement on the use of time and space so that children and curriculum could 'freely flow' without collision. 'Spontaneity', the usual adjunct of 'openness', was therefore ruled out except in a limited sense, and 'flexibility' was somewhat circumscribed.

Sheila was well aware of the challenge of reconciling ideology with physical and professional circumstances, and of the added pressure on her of having to prove, as deputy head, that such physical and organizational circumstances, having been designed to deliver flexibility and openness, would do just that, but because she identified so unequivocally with the value-system she accepted both the challenge and the consequent tensions and problems.

Peter, a teacher of 10–11-year-olds, shared Janet's sense of guilt (a word used by several of these teachers) about having or displaying structure in curriculum and pedagogy. Like Janet, too, he had learned to worry less about demonstrating allegiance to text-book informality and those who dictated it, and more about evolving his own style. But he also hinted at the limits to such independence when he suggested that one reason why this issue was less problematic for him now was that 'structure is no longer a dirty word ... we are emerging from the dark days of the polarity between progressive and traditional'. 'Structure', therefore, may well become not just respectable but transmuted into orthodoxy and accorded shibboleth status: as overused and eventually as meaningless as 'informal'. We shall see.

Planning, Anti-planning and Teacher Psyche

The flexibility/openness/structure tension applies at the preactive (planning) as well as at the interactive stage of teaching. Informal ideology dictates to teachers that they avoid what Calderhead (1984) terms 'comprehensive' planning, as incompatible with flexibility and spontaneity. The particular objections seem to be firstly to writing one's plans down on paper (except in the form of a topic web, since that has the informal virtue of being limited only by the size of paper one writes on and the notional topic web stretching towards infinity is ideologically very sound). Planning in the sense of ongoing reflection away from the classroom about what one has done and what one intends to do — 'one plans (thinks about teaching) all the time' — is accepted as inevitable and proper. The second objection is to the pre-ordinate nature of the written plan, which is seen to 'tie down', 'constrain', 'predetermine' to excess what teacher and children can do. In contrast, writing up what one has done, say at the end of a week, is deemed ideologically acceptable — even though planning after the event, if one thinks about it, is something of a logical curiosity.

Despite all this, however, most of our teachers not only planned in advance but planned in detail and in writing too. Moreover, several of them attested to planning now, in mid-career, in far greater detail than they had as inexperienced teachers (though, as I have mentioned, their focus of attention in such planning had changed). For this sometimes massive task — the number of hours per week for some of them frequently went into double figures — no official guidance was available, for being ideologically suspect, written planning was rarely discussed.

So individuals had to evolve their own planning styles. Some of them imported and applied models they had encountered on courses — topic webs and checklists of skills were common — but such everyday models, like the behavioural objectives model endorsed by academics in the 1960s (and now experiencing a renaissance) are only applicable in certain circumstances, and Calderhead's (1984) assertion that planning is dominated by the particular classroom context and focusses upon learning activities rather than learning outcomes, which our experience supports, underlines the limited usefulness of the few handed-down planning paradigms that teachers encounter. What Calderhead's review of teachers' planning underplays (and the theoretical models themselves ignore) is the impact of factors in addition to those of children, classroom and resources usually included in 'situational analysis' approaches. In particular, planning in primary education varies quite markedly (a) from one curriculum area to another — different paradigms are implied and used for mathematics, art and topic work, for example; and (b) according to teacher personality and development.

Some teachers, therefore, felt a psychological need to plan in great detail in advance (two spoke of their fear of chaos, others of their need for security) while others were happy planning 'incrementally'. For some, even, planning became almost obsessive. But, ideology apart, there seems no good reason why individual teachers should not plan in whatever way, and to whatever level of detail, makes them professionally confident and efficient when they enter the classroom.

It should also be mentioned, because this is where the anti-planning rhetoric is particularly unrealistic, that the comprehensive planners never felt enslaved by their plans. On the contrary they seemed to be liberated by them. They frequently deviated from them, sometimes to a marked degree, and some of the most relaxed, 'spontaneous' and 'flexible' teaching we saw had been preceded by the most detailed planning. The planning then, does not dictate precisely the form of the action, but it ensures that one thinks through possibilities and contingencies and provides a resource on which one can draw if necessary. There is an analogy with the performing artist's practice and training — the more thorough the preparation, the more confident and apparently effortless is the performance, and the greater the capacity to take those risks which give a performance flair and make it move and excite rather than merely interest its audience. It is an imperfect analogy, but on the other hand the notion of teacher as artist is — in the light of emerging analysis of the way that experienced teachers actually operate — a lot more convincing than that of teacher as scientist.

The relationship of planning style to curriculum areas is also significant, not only in the obvious sense that teachers see mathematics, art and topic as implying different planning paradigms, but also because there may be a direct correspondence between a teacher's knowledge of a curriculum area and the extent of his/her planning. It can cut both ways: the less one knows, the more one needs to plan to ensure security/the more one knows the less one needs to worry; or, the more one knows, the more learning possibilities one can envisage and the more one feels the need to structure learning in advance to ensure that these are actually encountered/the less one knows the less one can envisage and therefore plan.

Robin Alexander

Walking the Ideological Tightrope: The Teacher as Intervening Non-interventionist

Next to some competing imperatives arising in the interactive phase of teaching. It is a measure of the power of informality as a historical phenomenon and as a shaper of teacher consciousness that of all the words in the educational vocabulary even 'teaching' itself should have acquired pejorative overtones in the primary sector ('We mustn't teach: we must let them learn').

Underlying this is a simple confusion of 'teaching' with 'telling' which can readily be sorted out. Once that is done, a genuine pedagogical issue remains: the degree and nature of the teacher's mediation in the child's learning. I use 'mediation' as the most neutral term available because of course the linguistic minefield here is a pretty extensive one and many of the other words in common currency carry a strong adverse loading — 'direction', 'intervention', 'pushing', 'interfering', 'forcing', 'intruding'. The competing imperatives, therefore, are clear and situationally acute. While ideology dictates a teacher role of facilitator and encourager, common sense (not to mention recent classroom research) indicates the benefit for children of purposeful intervention by the teacher, especially of a kind which generates cognitive challenge.

To some degree, there has always been an infant/junior divergence here, with the belief that 'children learn at their own rate and when they are ready ... we shouldn't interfere' more strongly espoused where younger children are concerned (King 1978: see also his chapter in this volume). For two of our teachers, this aggravated the problem therefore.

Sue had worked mainly with juniors but was now deputy head and in charge of infants, with a class of 6–7-year-olds. She was highly ambitious, for herself and the children, and believed firmly both in detailed forward planning on the basis of a clear conceptual map of each curriculum area and in setting up and closely directing experiences to maximise children's learning in accordance with such maps. She was irritated by what she saw as colleagues' rationalizing espousal of wait-and-see 'readiness'; was eager to 'push as hard as I can to see what I can get back' and to demonstrate that, given engaged and knowledgeable teaching, some notions of what infants can do (or, perhaps, cannot do) are misconceived; yet at the same time she was anxious about seeming to 'push' or 'overstretch' the children. Behind this dilemma lay her strong commitment to planning, structure and process in the curriculum. This led her to place high priority on advancing and deepening her own curriculum understanding, to the extent that she had come to the view that the main reason why some colleagues resisted 'intervention' and demanded what she saw as too little from the children was that they had little idea what to demand.

Pam expressed similar anxieties. As a reception teacher she had imbibed both informality and non-intervention. Her practice, in fact, (like that of most of the other teachers in this group) displayed the external characteristics by which 'good informal practice' is usually defined — diversity in activities at any one time, grouping, busyness, display and so on — and indeed she cited the Plowden genealogy of much of her thinking, together with a random array of other influences, which underscores my earlier point about serendipity in professional development. Pam both operated within, yet was profoundly critical of, informality.

Her central aims — of fostering children's independence, their willingness and capacity to ask questions, their positive attitude to learning — were familiar enough. The problem for Pam was that her lively and honest intellect made her constantly aware of the danger that such goals might slide into rhetoric. Yet with a class of twenty-two 'reception' children, some of whom had arrived in September and the rest in February, she felt — for all her considerable experience — that numbers, lack of time and professional isolation would combine to subvert her goals. Watching and listening to colleagues, she was critical of the various coping strategies she felt that they adopted in the face of these constraints, and suspected herself of using such strategies also: undervaluing the capacities and interests that children bring to the classroom; levelling them down to a providable-for mean, and labelling and grouping them accordingly; encouraging passivity and conformity to ensure stability and cohesion; responding disproportionately to the children who are most visible or who demand attention; identifying 'what children cannot do rather than what they can do' in as far as it is easier to remedy a deficit than exploit a strength.

To compensate, Pam invested immense amounts of time and energy in detailed planing — yearly, termly, half-termly, weekly and nightly — then, ever alive to the pervasiveness of informal ideology, was duly defensive about having done so. Apologies for teacher intervention are prominent in her interview transcripts: she worries about 'pushing', 'imposing', 'putting too much in', 'giving too much input', 'intervening', 'over-organizing', being 'over-ambitious', entertaining 'over-expectation'. And she was also alive to the possibility — again, perceived as a failing in fellow-teachers — that she might be planning for notional and generalized 'levels' of ability rather than with individual children's capacities in mind: 'All the planning's there before they've considered the children'.

Every organizational challenge honestly confronted raised such tensions, and a feeling that it is actually far easier to survive as a teacher by ignoring them. Thus, to intervene is necessary: but to intervene is to make work for oneself. To match curriculum experiences to a child's abilities and needs requires that one should pitch work above rather than below what one initially diagnoses those abilities and needs to be, and that one should be 'unwilling too readily to accept the children's responses' as they stand: yet to do so is perhaps to make it more likely that children may 'fail' or at least feel themselves doing so. And, Pam believed, children themselves may consciously underachieve in order (a) to attract the approval they need; and (b) to get comfortably by (a point discussed in Maurice Galton's chapter in this volume).

It is important to remember that this critical analysis was offered not by an academic researcher seeking to demystify or debunk primary teaching and its associated ideologies, but by a committed and talented teacher whose ideas and practice, far from being maverick, were firmly embedded in the progressive/developmental tradition, yet whose experience and personal qualities had increased her pessimism in respect of the actual achievability of that tradition's ideals.

Grouping: Simple Recipes, Complex Repercussions

The central pedagogical challenges — of diagnosing children's needs, fostering their learning and monitoring their progress; and of doing so in the context of large numbers and the ambitious curricular and organizational expectations associated with prevailing ideology — provoked different responses and strategies in our twelve teachers, though all were conscious of them as overriding but not easily reconciled imperatives.

The one strategy they did have in common was grouping. The number of groups we saw operating at any one time ranged from three to eleven (in the latter case a 'group' could be two children working together). More often than not, the groups would be working in different curriculum areas. Sometimes groups were relatively fixed and had names or numbers; elsewhere their membership varied according to the nature of the learning task and the needs and characteristics of individuals and/or the dynamics and cohesion of the group as a whole. The groups were, variously, of comparable ability, of mixed ability (i.e. less comparable ability — the notion of a 'single ability' group is surely unsustainable), based on friendship or on what the teacher saw as likely, socially, to work. Sometimes, following Tann's (1981) distinction arising from the ORACLE project, children were grouped and sometimes they were doing group work: that is to say, physically grouped and working individually on the one hand, physically grouped and working collaboratively on the other. Most of the teachers had varied combinations of grouping and group work, though deliberate strategies for actually promoting collaborative activity were less common.

Sometimes groups followed a relatively standard routine of moving from one activity to another in rotation and at more or less fixed intervals, while elsewhere there was less routinization and teachers would need to spend some time explaining the procedures for the particular session, day or week to the children. Some teachers delivered these instructions by bringing the whole class together; others went round each group in turn; elsewhere the groups' tasks for the day or week were listed on a sheet or the blackboard, or on cards, and the children simply settled themselves down in accordance with such instructions as soon as they arrived in the morning.

And so on. The point demonstrated by this catalogue, arising from the work of a mere twelve teachers, is that the blanket term 'grouping' is capable of being operationalized in a large number of ways, not just across different classrooms, but within a single classroom by one teacher. And yet, considering the ubiquity and diversity of the practice, the term as it is offered to teachers — as shibboleth and quintessential feature of the informal package — is an astonishingly (or typically) unqualified and monodimensional one. There seems simply to be an overriding assumption that grouping is one of the minimum conditions of 'good primary practice' and that no more needs to be said.

As will now be clear from other examples already discussed, I am arguing that this combination of generalized ideological pressure and vagueness about operational detail can generate high levels of anxiety and guilt among teachers and can cause some to place quite unrealistic and inappropriate demands on themselves.

Among our teachers, the perceived imperatives where grouping was concerned were four-fold:

1 Children should be grouped.
2 At any one time each group should be doing something different, and preferably working in different curriculum areas.
3 The teacher should as far as possible give constant and equal attention to each group.

To these, for some of the teachers, was added a more recent imperative:

4 Children in groups should be working cooperatively.

The last of these, of course, stems mainly from the ORACLE research. Whatever the intentions of Galton's and Simon's team, the message increasingly being received by teachers, perhaps via advisers and teacher educators rather than from direct reading of the project's publications, is that unless children are interacting and collaborating within their groups, there is little point in grouping them. This message seems to have been delivered to, or at least received by, teachers working with every age of child from reception to top juniors, despite the fact that the children in the ORACLE study were no younger than 8+.

It is of course a questionable message in this form. Why shouldn't teachers, when grouping children, have purposes in mind other than to promote cooperative learning?

Taken together, and expressed concisely as in the list above, it will be seen that grouping, so conceived, can never be less than a major challenge to the teacher's skill, particularly where the inexperienced teacher is concerned.

Equally serious is the way that this particular aspect of primary ideology and practice reveals the price teachers have to pay for having their own ideas on such matters ignored. For the ORACLE research, like some other observational research of the past decade or so — and indeed the HMI surveys — takes little account of teachers' intentions in offering its characterizations and critiques of their practices. Yet intentionality in pedagogy is surely of critical importance: firstly in the obvious sense that a teacher needs to have good reasons for working in a particular way; and secondly because practice can only be fully understood if one engages with the thinking that underlies it (the rationale for the project from which this material is drawn). Practice is not just observable, codable and measurable behaviours but an array of ideas, values and intentions; and, in action, diagnoses, decisions and judgments. Practice is thought and thought is practice.

Grouping: There's Still Only One Teacher

Space does not permit me to portray here the various ways in which our teachers responded to, or liberated themselves from, the established or emergent imperatives associated with grouping, but it is instructive in the present context to draw attention to one issue: that of how they dealt with the need, in the context of a complex pattern of organization, to give adequate supervision and attention to each child.

Three patterns emerged. At one end of the continuum was the highly routinized and controlled procedure associated with the 'flexible day' arrangements already described. Here the teacher monitored children's progress mostly from a fixed point in the centre of the room which gave her sightlines to every corner, and circumvented the problem of queues, which diversity in grouping tends to generate, by rules and procedures governing the number of children allowed out at once, how they should wait for attention, what they should do having finished a piece of work, and so on. At the other end of the continuum, a large number of groups undertaking very diverse activities (though all loosely related to a common 'theme') generated a considerable monitoring challenge which could be responded to either by what Andy called 'buzzing around' at a sometimes frantic rate from group to group and child to child, or by an apparently random monitoring of those children who overtly demanded attention. In the latter case, children might wait in queues for some time — not necessarily in the way that Bennett reports, at the teacher's desk — but peripatetically, following the teacher as he/she moved round the room, with attention divided between this moving tail and those children still seated.

At a mid-point in this supervisory continuum, between what we came to call its 'Queen Bee' and 'Bluebottle' poles, were teachers who adopted what we termed a 'high investment/low investment' strategy. That is to say, they set up groups in such a way that, because of the nature of the work being undertaken, one or at the most two groups at any one time required their close attention. So, for example, Judith spent the best part of an hour seated with a mathematics group, interacting with them both collectively, in a 'group instructor' mode, and individually, with only occasional forays to other groups. Such movement would be judged necessary on the basis of intermittent scanning.

The argument presented by Judith, Sue and others who adopted this kind of strategy was that such concentrated attention on a relatively small number of children over a sustained period was more productive in terms of both diagnosis/match and children's learning than the brevity and superficiality of the interactions which result from seeking to give all children equal attention. Provided that such a strategy is carefully planned and monitored, the teacher can ensure that over, say, a week, every group and every individual within a group gains a significant amount of undivided and concentrated attention of the kind that can produce the 'higher-order cognitive interactions' that the ORACLE and ILEA teams[16] regarded as the prerequisites for purposeful learning. The procedure is comparable to the idea, now, since Bullock, fairly well established, that the ever-nagging primary imperative of 'hearing children read' is best responded to on the basis of 'sustained and occasional' rather than 'little and often'.

There is nothing new or revolutionary about the high/low investment strategy: many teachers of the kind who manage to remain unimpressed by swings in educational fashion regard it as 'just common-sense'. But it is not dilemma-free. There is the initial anxiety that it is manifestly contrary to the 'equal attention' imperative and others out, or up, there might disapprove. Then some felt that the kind of learning activity that could be undertaken with relatively low teacher investment of attention might necessarily be somewhat undemanding for the child, and that this could scarcely be defended. In fact, as we observed and discussed with the teachers who had most extensively developed this strategy, this is not inevitable. On the contrary, an activity which makes little demand on the children often ends up demanding a lot from the teacher because children finish quickly or become bored and restless.

One way through seemed to be to make pupil activities in the low teacher-investment groups to some degree self-monitoring, in other words to devise tasks for these groups which required and encouraged collective problem-solving and decision-making, so that children would turn to each other rather than to the teacher.

That is easier said than done, however. As Sue commented: 'if the work is high demand cognitively for the children, then it's high investment for me as teacher.' All the same, we believe we saw examples of children who were to a large degree self-directed yet, because of the care taken in devising the learning task, were also working at a high level cognitively.

The other dilemma is more fundamental and takes us back to the question of the curriculum as a whole and the relatively unshakable nature of the Curriculum I/II structure. As other teachers, not in this group, have commented when discussing the high investment/low investment strategy, 'Well, you'd only do this in maths and language work, wouldn't you?' Our teachers admitted that it was all too easy to respond to the perceived pressure to concentrate on the basics by making these the 'high investment' groups and allowing children undertaking Curriculum II activities like art, craft or topic work to get on more or less unsupervised, perhaps rationalizing the lack of teacher investment in terms of the post-ORACLE shibboleth of cooperative group work (which, indeed, topics in an obvious way seem to lend themselves to). In this event, lack of teacher expertise would give the differential a further twist: as Graham said, the work in, say, science, might be undemanding simply because the teacher did not know what questions it was possible to ask.[17]

Sue was conscious of this danger, and of what she saw as her not wholly convincing response to it. She had a considerable personal commitment to art, and her teaching in this area was nothing if not demanding of children's intellectual as well as expressive capacities, so that her conceptual and pedagogical framework was one which, ideally, combined high demand for the children with high teacher investment of an interactive kind. But this commitment tended to be overridden by her consciousness of Curriculum I as an irresistible imperative so that, firstly, children were invariably grouped for mathematics/language but generally not for art, and secondly, if they were grouped for art as well as for mathematics/ language she would tend to concentrate her attention on the latter groups, while feeling guilty, because of the clash with her personal values, for doing so.

With these teachers we evolved a number of hypotheses concerning group work which will be developed at greater length elsewhere. One final point needs to be made before I pull the strands of this chapter together and offer some conclusions. It is clear that it is not adequate to make inferences and judgements about teaching on the basis of behavioural observation alone. Teachers' theorising repays close attention, for not only does its study enhance our — and their[18] — understanding of this complex and demanding job, but it may also be, as theory, as sustainable as any which outsiders offer, and certainly far more so than the unfocussed rhetoric of informality (or whatever succeeds it). In the present example, concerning grouping, several of these teachers had evolved operationally viable and theoretically coherent strategies for meeting the challenge of providing individual diagnosis and attention in the context of large classes. Yet they comformed neither to the older 'equal attention all the time' imperative nor to the more recent imperative that all group work should be 'cooperative'. At the same time the teachers' anxieties in the face of ideological and other kinds of external expectation made the successful operationalisation of their experientially-derived theories more difficult than was necessary.

Conclusion

This chapter has raised a large number of issues and it is not sensible to try to summarize every single one of them. Rather, let me highlight five of the main strands.

The first is professional development. I have departed from conventional practice by presenting professional development as a personal journey rather than a formal sequence of pre-service and in-service events and activities. In emphasizing the person within the professional I have noted a number of issues, each of which has implications for how we conceive of and structure formal professional development activities: the power, but the randomness, of individual experience; the influence — good, bad and indifferent — of teachers on each other; the inseparability of professional development from personal growth and from individual temperament, intellect, imagination, values and beliefs; and the way, therefore, that it is not just the teacher that changes, but also the job, in as far as increased understanding and expertise in relation to classroom decisions and practices allows that job to be, for and by each teacher, redefined. I showed how this redefinition can take any of a number of forms, but how while for some the job becomes easier and more routine, for others it becomes more complex, challenging and perhaps difficult — though in different ways and at deeper levels from those confronting the younger teacher.

The job of primary teaching, then, is not a pre-ordained, standardized reality but an individual, shifting and therefore (considering how much it is talked about) a surprisingly elusive construct.

Clearly, this has implications for formal agents and agencies of professional development and appraisal — advisers, heads and teacher educators in particular. Proper account needs to be taken of the teacher as person: in fostering personal growth and autonomy; in encouraging the individual to develop a professional style which exploits rather than opposes his/her personal characteristics and strengths; in matching initial/in-service experience to where a teacher is, developmentally; and in encouraging, respecting and building upon each teacher's own articulation of the job of teaching as he/she progresses through his/her career. We need, therefore, to examine carefully the degree of congruence which exists or might exist between professional development as an officially defined and provided procedure, and professional development as an experienced human process. This is not to re-state familiar arguments (or slogans) about the 'relevance' or otherwise of pre-service or in-service activities to the 'real world', the 'chalk-face' of practice 'as it is'. Such versions of practice as are offered or implied in this kind of context tend to be arbitrary or even stereotypical. More serious, in the light of this discussion, is the way in presenting the job of teaching as 'out there' they fail to acknowledge either its reflexive, subjective character or the way as reality it changes as the teacher changes.

This would suggest that teaching 'as it is' may have more meaning for, say a student teacher when defined and explicated by a probationer than by a head. I do not argue that students cannot learn from experienced teachers — on the contrary, the thrust of this chapter is that they can and should (and IT/INSET schemes show how — Ashton *et al.*, 1982); rather that they will learn most when the job as conceptualised and enacted for them is not too far removed from their existing perceptions and capacities (which is only to apply a basic learning principle which is familiar enough in the primary classroom). Similarly, the potential benefits of procedures whereby experienced teachers can learn from each other seem to be considerable. Yet these benefits remain largely unexploited: it is true that teachers talk about teaching away from the classroom, but how often are they given opportunities to observe and enter into each others' ideas and practices within it?

The second strand was the societal context of British primary education within which the individual teacher operates and which, too, is also a powerful influence upon the way he/she defines, enacts and evolves his/her professional role. Here again I emphasised diversity, change and conflict — not to be perverse, but because these are facts of the educational present and past which are too often ignored. I offered a view of primary education today in which ideologies and traditions which have emerged at different times during the past century or so are still very much with us, in an agglomeration of ideas, values and practices which are far from coherent, consistent and harmonious, but which schools and teachers have somehow to reconcile and present as such. Sometimes the juxtaposition (of progressive and developmental ideas, for instance) is a reasonably comfortable one, but elsewhere (for example in respect of central questions, encapsulated as the Curriculum I/II tension, concerning what children should learn) the dilemmas are constant and perhaps unresolvable.

Again, it seems to me, we help ourselves by viewing diversity and divergence in primary values, ideas and practices not as an uncomfortable problem but as a fact of life. These values are not, as so often in the primary world they are portrayed, extraneous and unreasonable 'demands' and 'pressures', irritants or irrelevances which frustrate those who simply want to 'get on with the job', but an essential and necessary part of the package: they are the job. This fact, too, has to be confronted by those responsible for organizing professional development and training procedures, and it is not an easy matter to deal with. The trainee teacher should certainly be aware of the value divergences and dilemmas embedded in the job, and that the particular curricular and organizational arrangements he/she happens to come across are by no means pre-ordained; but he/she also needs security, confidence and a basic framework for classroom action which works and can be justified, otherwise the questioning will undermine the very capacities it is intended to enhance.

I brought together the first two themes — personal/professional development and value plurality — through the idea of 'competing imperatives' as the third main strand of this chapter: the hypothesis that teachers are confronted on a day-to-day basis not only by 'practical' choices and options of a more or less resolvable kind, but by more fundamental dilemmas and tensions which have their roots partly in the diverging and competing values which constitute primary education as a whole, partly in each teacher's particular school and classroom contexts — very powerful influences and constraints upon what one does, obviously — and partly within the teacher himself/herself, as a unique and changing individual.

The fourth strand, and a pervasive one, was the public language of primary education in general and of informal primary education in particular. This language is so singularly unhelpful to dispassionate professional discourse about the day-to-day detail of classroom practice that, I suggested, we probably have to acknowledge that this is not its main function. In any case, I argued, it is possible that none of our existing ways of talking collectively about primary education — including the academic — yet has the capacity to grasp the full subtlety and complexity of classroom processes; and if this is our objective, which it surely should be, it can be achieved only by taking far more account of everyday teacher theorizing than we have hitherto, and that in turn dictates that we penetrate well beyond the 'espoused theory' which the public primary language tends to restrict itself to.

This language, I suggested, notwithstanding the way that informal Primaryspeak is currently being superseded by an ostensibly more instrumental and precise vocabulary, is more about solidarity and power than meaning. To point up these functions I introduced and exploited the 'shibboleth' idea, those key words and phrases which pepper primary professional discourse, which teachers feel obliged to use to demonstrate their professional allegiance and which, in their practice, they have somehow to enact. The language of primary education, then, is the medium through which not a few of the competing imperatives are conveyed, and I showed how the vagueness of the language can cause the teacher serious problems at the point of operationalisation, yet, because the imperatives arrive as officially-endorsed orthodoxies backed by hierarchic power, they cannot easily be questioned.

A more sophisticated, precise and neutral language, then, is the minimum precondition for promoting the kind of professional dialogue upon which school and teacher development depend. The chicken-and-egg problem here, of course, is that it is the dialogue which will generate the language — it will have little meaning or validity if evolved away from the classroom. Perhaps there are grounds for optimism here in the apparent shift, encouraged by the enhancement of the curriculum consultancy role, towards more 'collegial' relationships in primary schools (though since that word is currently one of the most prominent of all the new wave of 1980s shibboleths we must be extremely cautious about assuming any correlation between frequency of use and change of practice).

All of these strands were illustrated by considering the responses of a number of experienced teachers to some of the central elements and challenges of informality — openness and flexibility, planning, 'intervening' in children's learning, and the central organizational device of grouping. Many other illustrations are possible, but space does not permit them: one cluster, for example, concerns 'balance' in the curriculum as a whole (like grouping, a shibboleth currently in the process of being updated); another concerns 'community', whether this means children working together, team teaching, or collegial approaches to school policy-making — the latter two, again, coming to the forefront of official and professional consciousness at this moment.

The final strand was my linguistic excursion into the 'jungle' as an alternative metaphor for capturing the tensions, dilemmas, conflicts and paradoxes within primary education at both societal and classroom level, but which also, in a positive way, evokes primary education's richness and diversity. The 'jungle' is offered as a corrective to that pseudo-consensus which has been so salient a feature of primary education since the 1960s and which has proved so frustrating both to meaningful and productive debate about educational purposes and processes and to the personal/professional development of individual teachers in the sense it has been defined in this chapter. But the 'jungle' bears on professional development in another, more fundamental way: for professional development, as inseparable from personal maturation, is about coming to terms with the inner as well as the outer world, with resolving the tensions of the psyche as well as the dilemmas of the classroom. The jungle is in each of us. So too is the need and urge to make sense of and impose order upon the outer world in order to achieve inner equilibrium, to turn the jungle into a garden.

In this respect, two final points can be made about the particular collection of ideas and practices connoted by the word 'informal'. One is the empirical observation, that — regardless of semantic connotations or official ideals — 'informal' as successfully operationalized by experienced teachers is highly structured, conceptually and organizationally; the word 'informal', therefore, is singularly inappropriate if it is taken to imply 'without form or order'. The second point is that as shibboleth 'informal', and those of its associated terms which suggest an unbounded openness and flexibility, may have placed an unreasonable and in some cases intolerable burden on those teachers for whom among all the competing professional imperatives the overriding one was the personal need to avoid or resolve uncertainty, ambivalence and dissonance, to know and be convinced about what they were doing and why. The reality of primary education may sometimes be nearer the jungle than the garden, and we do not help ourselves by pretending otherwise, but this does not invalidate the garden as symbol of a basic and necessary human quest.

Notes

1 See Simon in Simon and Willcocks (1981), pp. 7–25; HMI 1978, 1982, 1983 and 1985b; Galton, Simon and Croll (1980); Galton and Simon (1980); Bennett (1984); ILEA (1986).
2 HMI (1978); Bennett (1984).
3 Galton, Simon and Croll (1980); Galton and Simon (1980).
4 ILEA (1986).
5 See Blyth (1984a), pp. 9–11 for a discussion of Froebel's use of the 'garden' metaphor; and Jenkins (1975) for a more general exploration of this and related metaphors; also Taylor (1986).
6 For example, in the criteria (DES, 1984) subsequently imposed by the Council for the Accreditation of Teacher Education (CATE) that all primary BEd students should spend half of their course on 'subject studies at a level appropriate to higher education' which could then form the basis for subject consultancy in the primary school.
7 See Alexander (1984) chapter 3.
8 See, for example, the NUT response (1979) to the 1978 HMI primary survey. But things are changing here: LEAs and schools, responding to strong DES and HMI pressure, are now introducing curriculum leadership/consultancy quite rapidly.
9 See Jackson (1968) and, of course, John Holt's pieces, but also Maurice Galton's chapter in this volume.
10 Consider, for instance, the work of the Assessment of Performance Unit since its establishment in 1974, but, more particularly, the national curriculum attainment targets and age-related tests (at 7, 11, 14 and 16) announced by the Thatcher government in 1987 (DES, 1987).
11 It is instructive to compare the tension between central government and some LEAs during the 1980s in these terms. For central government, 'relevance' has been defined mainly by reference to the 'world of work'; for some LEAs, especially large urban authorities in areas of high unemployment, 'relevance' has to do more with improving job prospects, halting inner-city decline and redressing discrimination against and disadvantages among minority groups. HMI's (1985c) list of 'essential issues' (for example, information technology, political understanding, economic understanding, the world of work, careers education, equal opportunities, ethnicity, health education, environmental education) holds the middle ground: it seems something of a hotchpotch, but is in fact a serious attempt to identify the range of social imperatives to which the curriculum should respond. For a further discussion of social imperatives see Blyth (1984a) especially pp. 31–3 and 45–7.
12 Maurice Galton suggested this usage of hybridization to me.
13 At the time of going to press, the government's national curriculum proposals appear to represent the apotheosis of utilitarianism and final, legislated, confirmation of the curriculum I/II divide: to the established curriculum I of mathematics and English is added science (as I predicted in Alexander, 1984), and these are sharply demarcated from

the remaining 'foundation' subjects in terms of a quantified pecking order and assessment programme.

14 *Professional Knowledge-in-Action; The Conceptual Basis of Primary Teachers' Practice*; a project funded by, and based at, the University of Leeds. It is hoped to publish the main report in book form during 1988. The willing cooperation and support of the teachers involved is gratefully acknowledged. For obvious reasons they are referred to here by pseudonyms. My co-researcher was Kay Kinder.

15 But see some recent literature on teachers' lives and careers which begins to explore professional development in a more active or interactive sense; Ball and Goodson (1985); Sikes, Measor and Woods (1985).

16 See Galton and Simon (1980); ILEA (1986).

17 The extent to which the teacher's curriculum understanding is one of the critical factors in successful small-group teaching is pointed up in another project I am directing. In evaluating Leeds City Council's Primary Needs Programme (PNP) we have found many instances of PNP's enhanced primary school staffing being used to facilitate collaborative teaching, often involving one teacher working with a small group of children for long periods of time. Such staffing enhancement, of course, is what primary schools have long demanded as a means of reducing the unrelenting pressures of the class teacher system. However, it is clear that small group teaching can pose its own problems, not least because 'sustained questioning and discussion require the teacher to have a clear framework of the kinds of understanding she wishes to promote' (Kinder, 1987, p. 17).

18 In the professional knowledge project (see 14 above) we also monitored the impact on the twelve teachers of their being involved in such an intensive programme of observation, recording and discussion. We also brought them together for viewing and discussing each others' videotapes. They strongly endorsed (and in their transcripts demonstrated) the potential of such procedures in a professional or school development programme.

Conclusion

Alan Blyth

The purpose of this book is not, it will be remembered, to provide a comprehensive survey of informal primary education in England today, still less to pass a verdict on its merits as such, but rather to illuminate thinking about what informal primary education claims to be, and about what considerations should now be borne in mind when the question of informality in primary education is seriously discussed. In the preceding chapters, many issues have been left open, or even prised further open. Yet there is one point in which all their authors are at one, namely the legitimacy and importance of serious, dispassionate analysis as a basic element in the formulation of policy. It may well be that the extent of serious study revealed through these chapters and their bibliographic references is daunting to teachers engaged in the considerable daily demands of primary education, and bewildering to parents and others for whom education is only one, albeit an important one, of many concerns. Daunting and bewildering it may be, in which case it is incumbent on those of us who specialise in such matters to make them intelligible and to demonstrate their relevance and helpfulness. Specious and negligible it certainly is not, and that, we hope, we have shown. We want to see primary education set on sure foundations.

The 'variations' that made up the body of the book were wrought separately and without reference to the five aspects of informality discussed in the Introduction and in chapter 1. However, they contribute to an understanding of how those five aspects have figured in developments since Plowden. A survey of those developments may help to illuminate the current status of informality in English primary education.

Informality in *pedagogy* was identified in chapter 1 as the earliest and most prominent of those aspects, and it still commands much of the attention focused on informality in general. Evidently there are able, experienced teachers, such as Nias' subjects, who have indicated that they could not happily teach without finding an important place, alongside more formal procedures, for work that involved the excitement of collective exploration of themes that arose from discussions with the children themselves, that could not be planned in advance by objectives or otherwise, and that were conducive to self-directed learning on the children's part. These features, rather than the label 'informal', were to them the important consideration. That is encouraging. There is considerable evidence, reinforced by Galton and indeed by the ORACLE studies on which he draws, as well as by Bennett's major reports (Bennett 1976 and 1984) that any simple dichotomy between formal and informal, progressive and traditional, becomes increasingly inadequate as a classification either of teachers' intentions or of their actual be- haviour. This further emphasizes the increasing maturity in profes- sional understanding required to outgrow simplistic ideologies of the sort whose persistent influence can be traced in particular in King's and Alexander's chapters, or the process of serendipity by which, as Alexander indicates, teachers' views are often modified. This is where common sense can and should combine with profes- sional wisdom in the formation of an independent, responsible member of a teaching staff.

Meanwhile, as Gammage and Kelly indicate, technological adv- ances are making impacts on every aspect of primary pedagogy, so that earlier classifications are in any case likely to be superseded in important respects. It is equally essential to take note of Galton's important message, that informal pedagogies may suit some teachers more than others, and some pupils more than others, and some situations more than others; and, as King suggests, this is not simply a question of cultural background along the social-class lines adum- brated by Bernstein (1975). So the emphasis may be moving away from informality as such in pedagogy towards the evolution of personal teaching styles, capable of adaptation to professional growth, beliefs, and commitment, as well as to changing circum- stances. It could well be this trend, as much as some quasi-political swing of the pendulum, that accounts for the apparent partial retreat from informality in pedagogy in recent years that several of the authors have remarked.

If that trend is associated with professional maturity, this could help to explain why the teachers in Nias' study appeared to associate sureness of touch in informal teaching with the confidence bred of experience. It is interesting to set this possibility alongside the view often expressed by sceptics, that informal pedagogy is suited only to a few able and experienced teachers[1] and to bear in mind also that in Alexander's sample it appeared that increasing experience brought about a greater awareness of the incompatibility between received ideology and evolving practice and thus of the need for the systematic rethinking which he, and others, advocate.

Alexander (1984) maintains that, for this purpose, a more adequate psychological basis for pedagogy is required, one from which a coherent and satisfying approach could be wrought. The same contention is put forward, in different ways, by Gammage, Blenkin and Galton, and runs parallel with current trends in educational psychology developed by Stones (1979), Noel Entwistle (1987) and others who have used theoretical models directly in investigations of classroom practice such as Bennett (1984). Certainly, psychology can no longer be expected to underwrite informality with the ready insouciance that was once assumed by enthusiasts; but neither can it be wheeled on in support of didacticism. The nature of learning and of motivation is too complex for that.

One useful line of advance might be to look carefully at those instances, such as Nias', where informality in pedagogy does appear to have been markedly effective, and to locate the factors that appear to account for that effectiveness. Her account shows something of the personal qualities that may be relevant. The contextual concomitants of effectiveness remain less easy to identify. King, in his contribution, lays more stress on the possible links between informality and socio-cultural circumstances, though he also warns against any over-ready assumptions about such links. He also demonstrates, as in his own previous work (King, 1978) and Alexander's (1984), that there is a more thorough-going, if sometimes self-contradictory, commitment to informality in pedagogy among infant teachers than among junior teachers, one which can be traced back to the origins of universal primary education, but one whose consequences for teachers, parents and children is not always recognized. The contradictions in this commitment may also reflect Kelly's contention that, even when informal pedagogy appears successful, it may mask logical contradictions in teachers' thinking that adherents of a radical developmental approach would soon detect.

The strongest arguments in favour of informal approaches to *curriculum* are presented by Blenkin in her innovatory chapter on the earliest years, and by Kelly in his examination of later pre-secondary education. Both rest their cases on a thorough-going developmental approach to curriculum. Blenkin emphasizes the necessity for congruence between developmental psychology and curriculum planning and brings out, with admirable clarity, the way in which Bruner's modes of representation and their relation to instruction, enriched by Eisner's multisensory and affective emphasis, can link development with a curriculum for competence[2]. This almost Herbartian conception adds significantly to the view of curriculum as intervention in the interaction between development and experience, to which I subscribe (Blyth, 1984a). Kelly links a process approach to curriculum with a reconstructionist epistemology that owes much to Dewey, though perhaps the forms-of-knowledge approach to curriculum need not be envisaged in such an elitist guise, or necessarily linked with high-status knowledge as defined by an exclusive academic establishment. From this firm base, he throws shrewd light on the spate of documents that have preceded the planning of a national curriculum and its accessories, and it is necessary that this view should continue to be considered, as the statutory framework is introduced. To both Blenkin and Kelly, the formation of the autonomous learner, and the construction of knowledge by the learner, are the prior considerations, and Nias' teachers echo a similar view. It follows that, for them, as for others since Rousseau and Froebel, particular subject-matters and forms of understanding acquire significance not objectively in their own right, but subjectively if and when the learner is impelled to look towards them. For this basic purpose, informality in curriculum is likely to be a major instrument, especially in the earlier years; but it is not an end in itself.

Of the other contributors, none takes a clearer stance on curriculum than Blenkin and Kelly. King's infant teachers regard informality, as it has developed over the years, as a datum. At the junior level, the division clearly persists between what Alexander has identified as Curriculum I, consisting substantially of language and mathematics which are relatively immune from informality in curricular assumptions, and Curriculum II, consisting of all the rest, where greater informality is offset by lesser status. Meanwhile Galton shows the range of actual curricular structures that operate across junior and middle schools, thus throwing further light on earlier data such as those provided by Ashton *et al.* (1975) and Bassey (1978). Gammage chronicles the drift first towards informality in curriculum, and then again away from informality, that has in recent years paralleled the drift in pedagogy, and suggests that both drifts reflect a growing expertise and professional understanding rather than mere vacillation or the reflection of fashion, though Alexander fears that fashion may have something to do with it as long as teachers feel obliged to allow deference rather than self-confidence to prevail where curriculum and pedagogy are concerned.

It is to be hoped that expertise based on confidence will develop strongly enough to meet the demands that are being made, and will be made, for the inclusion of more and more specific issues in the primary curriculum, the social imperatives whose increasing importance Alexander notes. These include matters such as multi-cultural and anti-racist education, anti-sexist education, various forms of health education, and economic awareness, none of which were so prominently emphasized in the Plowden era, yet all of which are now expected to figure within or alongside a national curriculum based on different premises. The danger here is that more emphasis than ever will be laid on the core, Curriculum I with science added; less, but still some, demands on those parts of Curriculum II that will uneasily enjoy protection as foundation subjects provided that they display most of the features of a formal curriculum; and finally a reluctant and chilling admission of any other embodiments of informality to the outer zone of the curriculum, just within the perimeter fence. In considering the support that has been mustered for such a curricular structure, it has to be admitted that, especially in Curriculum II, informality has sometimes been made an excuse for wanton ignorance in planning and sloppiness in 'delivery', while more frequently defects have arisen through the sheer difficulty met by teachers in trying to keep abreast of knowledge in so many fields, a requisite that is, incidentally, increased rather than reduced by the demands of an informal curriculum. A defensible professional response to a national curriculum as proposed must include not merely the building up of self-confidence in curriculum planning among groups of teachers (it cannot be a purely individual matter any more) but also the raising of awareness of the nature and importance of aspects of curricular knowledge and the improvement of the means of access to that knowledge. Here the concept of 'consultancy' in an informal curriculum, has a legitimate place embodying mutual assistance between teachers and not the teaching of separate subjects to children. In such ways, public concern about whether children know enough, can do enough, and can behave well enough can be reconciled with a genuine professional understanding of how they learn to learn and behave at all, and why they should.

Informality in *organization* is considered in the earlier chapters in a number of ways. Gammage brings out the relatively substantial and continuing move away from streaming and from differential selection for secondary education, which could be said to constitute a systemic increase in informality. Interestingly, in his analysis of the Plowden Report, he does not refer to the claim that a change in the ages of transfer, allowing the introduction of a flexible three-tier system with first and middle schools, would promote informality in organization within schools, or to the patchy response made by LEAs to this claim, or to the persistent survival of first and middle schools in a significant minority of LEAs (Blyth 1984b; Hargreaves, 1986).

As regards informal organization within classes, Nias' teachers were obviously inclined towards it through the very nature of their work; Galton makes it a central feature in his differentiation between teaching styles and puposes; and King identifies informality in class organization as one of the criteria that distinguish the infant ideology. Alexander goes further, examining in some depth the nature and purpose of grouping within the classroom, a question which Gammage also discusses, stressing the close link that must exist between informality in organisation and informality in curriculum (as with Nias). Certainly there has in recent years been a tendency to laud grouping for grouping's sake, or on the basis of dubious evidence, and it is clearly necessary that there should now be a closer consideration, especially in the light of Galton's work, of just how children do behave in groups in school, and of how these can benefit cognitive and social development in various situations (see for example Armstrong, 1981; Rowland, 1984; Pollard, 1985).

One point that receives little direct attention in these chapters is the question of informality in organization at the level intermediate between class and system, that of the school. It seems likely that, where teachers differ in their views on pedagogy and curriculum, it will be difficult for them to cooperate in a fully informal school, especially one whose informality is reinforced by open-plan architecture (Bennett *et al.*, 1980). This situation could indeed be worsened if the appointment of specialist postholders (Campbell, 1985) were to be used, as Kelly fears, to reinforce formality in the curriculum rather than to foster more informal roles. Here, much depends on the skill, enthusiasm and understanding of the headteacher. It is to be hoped that the current heavy emphasis on management in primary education will take account of such matters, rather than being seen as simply 'against' informality in organization.

Informality in *evaluation* does not receive much specific consideration. Galton, perhaps, indicates something about differences in styles of evaluation when writing of differences in styles of pedagogy and of learning. Gammage, Blenkin and Kelly all indicate ways in which primary education as a whole could be evaluated from different informal standpoints, while Nias and Alexander convey how teachers' professional growth and development could enable teachers to evolve means of informal self-evaluation. Yet at a time when national testing is being adumbrated as an adjunct of a national curriculum, it will be necessary to go beyond the span of this volume and to design procedures of appraisal and assessment of children's progress that are built on the best of primary experience, including informal monitoring, rather than being based on the demands of secondary education or on imperfect memories of what primary education used to be like. Here, the work of the Assessment of Performance Unit and in particular of Harlen in primary science (Harlen, 1983 and 1985) gives rise to many useful suggestions. Already, there are signs (DES, 1987) that some flexibility will be permitted when national criteria are spelled out and that some continuity in assessment, through profiling at the secondary stage, to the new procedures associated with GCSE may be encouraged — provided that time and resources are sufficient to permit a thorough programme of development that is not itself simply a response to administrative directives.

As for informality in *personal style*, this is more difficult to identify from the contents of this book. Nias' teachers, at least, clearly demonstrated and valued some informality in style as a conscious part of their practice, though not in any irresponsible sense. Galton indicates that personal style, too, varies with variations in classroom interaction styles, and that within the complex range available, junior children select, and have a right to select, what demeanours they consider appropriate in a teacher: clearly, they accepted his! The same is true of infants, though they may express it differently. Meanwhile, a lofty pedantry in style would hardly be consonant with Blenkin's or Kelly's approach to curriculum. Kelly, too, remarks on the contrast between the formal stance of many secondary teachers and the open approach of primary teachers as a whole, whereas King, once again, draws from observation a comparable contrast between junior and infant teachers, with the latter displaying informal styles derived from their distinctive professional ideology. Thus King and Kelly each draw attention to a major interface in personal style, corresponding to a point of transition in the administrative structure of primary education and its sequel, and incidentally suggest the tensions that may be caused in this respect where first and middle schools modify that structure. Their contentions both ring true. Maybe there are few other countries where they do both ring true, in quite the same historically-determined way. Meanwhile that other dichotomy in personal style, between the libertarian and collectivist emphases mentioned in chapter 1, finds little place in later chapters apart from King's criticism of oversimplified forms of Marxist explanation.

What finally emerges from these essays and studies, and indeed from other recent and current developments and opinions, is that events are outstripping conventional categories and that the straight choice betwen formal and informal approaches to primary education is no longer a meaningful one. Alexander indeed emphasizes the need for teachers to transcend the cherished stereotypes that have often constrained professional thinking. The issue now is not whether to be informal, in whatever sense, but when to be informal, and how, and with whom, and why, in order to effect the best match between teachers' styles and convictions on the one hand, and children's styles and growth on the other. The teachers in Nias' and Alexander's accounts were coming to terms with that issue. No doubt informality in pedagogy, curriculum, organization, evaluation and personal style will continue to have a place, and an enhanced place at that, within primary education; but then so will direct instruction, access to established and emerging forms of knowledge and understanding, initiation into new technologies and media of expression, large-scale participation in organized physical and expressive events, some forms of specific assessment especially of a criterion-referenced or self-referenced nature, and some styles of pupil–teacher interaction based on ritual relationships and on mutual dignity and respect. In addition, it seems likely that the scope of primary education itself will be widened, demanding communication with parents and clergy and politicians, employers and trade unionists, and with the adult community in general. This is in one sense a new role for primary teachers; but in another sense it is also a very old one, for it harks back to that tradition of informal education whose ancestry is much longer than that of formal schooling itself. It is not quite a sixth aspect of informality; but it does involve both a kind of informal adult education and also a mobilization of communities as a resource for the education of children.

This wider repertoire of primary teaching, involving the whole community and calling for a strenuous response from all children irrespective of endowment or experience, can transcend mere eclecticism or serendipity through the consistent and rigorous application of the professional knowledge, skills and discipline for which this book consistently calls. Just as children nurtured in the best of informal primary education are equipped to explore experience, so teachers who build on the best of that tradition should be equipped to explore education itself, and to revise and enlarge their perspectives as the years pass.

For some, that exploration and enlargement are their own justifications and their own ends. For others, the motivation to explore is itself derived from a range of religious and political values that transcend exploration. As primary education comes of age, it must also come to terms with conflicts and divergences within its own realm of expertise. As Alexander emphasizes, dilemma-language rather than garden-language is appropriate to a mature professional outlook. The resolution of dilemmas is not always easy or even possible. What is possible is the sharing of professional experience and expertise in a rapidly-changing world, the amicable definition of areas of agreement and of disagreement, and a willingness to be confidently self-critical and to change. This, rather than polarisation around the categories of formality and informality, marks the way ahead for the study and practice of primary education today. The collective aim, as we approach the twenty-first century, should be to look beyond past controversies and present parsimonies and directives and to assert the need to support, resource, enrich and dignify the education of young children through the endeavours of those who, whatever their deep differences in belief and practice, share to the full a commitment to the education of those future citizens of the world.

It is appropriate that a book concerned with primary education, especially informal primary education, should end by emphasizing the view of the children themselves (Blyth, 1984a, chapter 8). As Gammage emphasizes, they are not to be mere consumers of education made in their elders' image, however benevolent that may be. Galton's study and Nias' in particular indicate that the children's own aims and objectives, their hopes and dreads, their classroom strategies and their affective responses are centrally important. It is sobering, too, to recall that their continuing immersion in that age-old world of informal community education, to which primary teachers may now increasingly turn, leaves the whole of schooling as minority time in their lives. In this particular sense, all schooling is necessarily child-centred, and nobody can make it otherwise. For informal education, this should be a welcome truth rather than an unwelcome interference. Even if the Plowden Report exaggerated somewhat in suggesting that schools belonged to the children, it is certainly true that their education does; and so it should, if they are to become 'agents of their own learning' and understanding, feeling and loving. So it must be the interaction between the teachers' and the children's perspectives that really lies 'at the heart' of the processes of learning and teaching and living; and it is this interaction that deserves the scrutiny, the energies, the courage and the commitment of teachers, parents, laymen, and all of us who are concerned with the success of primary education today and tomorrow.

Notes

1 Such comments were made, for example, in the *Black Papers* series by authors distinguishing between the theoretical basis of informal education and its apparent practical outcomes.
2 For another recent and relevant analysis of the developmental basis of infant education, see Tamburrini, J. 'Trends in developmental research and their implications for infant school education: in place of ideologies' in Davis *et al.* (1986), pp. 23–38.

Bibliography

Note: Titles under the authorship of Her Majesty's Inspectorate of Schools (HMI) are listed separately from those of the Department of Education and Science (DES). There is, or has been, a difference.

ALEXANDER, R.J. (1984) *Primary Teaching*, London, Holt, Rinehart and Winston.

ANTHONY, W.S. (1973) 'Learning rules by discovery', *Journal of Educational Psychology*, 64, pp. 525–8.

ARCHAMBAULT, R.D. (Ed.) (1965) *Philosophical Analysis and Education*, London, Routledge and Kegan Paul.

ARGYRIS, C. and SCHÖN, D. (1974) *Theory in Practice: Increasing Professional Effectiveness*, San Francisco, CA, Jossey-Bass.

ARMSTRONG, M. (1981) *Closely Observed Children*, London, Writers and Readers Co-operative and Chameleon Press.

ASH, M. (1969) *Who Are the Progressives Now?*, London, Routledge and Kegan Paul.

ASHTON, P.M.E. *et al.* (1975) *The Aims of Primary Education: A Study of Teachers' Opinions*, London, Macmillan Education.

ASHTON, P.M.E. *et al.* (1982) *Teacher Education in the Classroom: Initial and In-Service*, London, Croom Helm.

ATKIN, J. and HOULTON, D. (1986) *Qualified — But What Next?*, A Survey of Primary Teachers' Views on Award-Bearing In-Service Courses, Nottingham, University of Nottingham School of Education.

AUSUBEL, D. (1978) 'In defense of advanced organisers: A reply to the critics' *Review of Educational Research*, 48, pp. 251–7.

BALL, S.J. and GOODSON I.F, (Eds) (1985) *Teachers' Lives and Careers*, Lewes, Falmer Press.

BANTOCK, G.H. (1968) *Culture, Industrialisation and Education*, London, Routledge and Kegan Paul.

BANTOCK, G.H. (1984) *Studies in the History of Educational Theory, Vol. 2, The Minds and the Masses 1760–1980*, London, George Allen and Unwin.

BARKER LUNN, J. (1982) 'Junior schools and their organisational practices', *Educational Research*, 24, 4, pp. 250–61.

BARKER LUNN, J. (1984) 'Junior school teachers: Their methods and practices', *Educational Research*, 26, 3, pp. 178–88.

BARNES, D. (1982) *Practical Curriculum Study*, London, Routledge and Kegan Paul.

BASSEY, M. (1978) *Nine Hundred Primary School Teachers*, Slough, NFER.

BECKER, H.S. *et al.* (1968) *Making the Grade: The Academic Side of College Life*, New York, John Wiley.

BENNETT, N, *et al.* (1976) *Teaching Styles and Pupil Progress*, London, Open Books.

BENNETT, N. *et al.* (1980) *Open Plan Schools*, Slough, NFER.

BENNETT, N. *et al.* (1984) *The Quality of Pupil Learning Experiences*, London, Lawrence Erlbaum Associates.

BENNETT, N. and DESFORGES, C. (Eds) (1985) *Recent Advances in Classroom Research*, BJEP Monograph (2), Edinburgh, Scottish Academic Press.

BENT, A. (1966) *Steps in the Life of a Teacher*, unpublished account for Sarah Bancroft Clark, Street, Somerset.

BEREITER, C. and ENGELMANN, S. (1966) *Teaching Disadvantaged Children in the Pre-School*, New Jersey, Prentice Hall.

BERLAK, A. and BERLAK, H. (1981) *Dilemmas of Schooling: Teaching and Social Change*, London, Methuen.

BERNSTEIN, B.B. (1961) 'Social class and linguistic development: A theory of social learning' in HALSEY, A.H. *et al.* (Eds) *Education, Economy and Society*, New York, Collier-Macmillan.

BERNSTEIN, B.B. (1975) 'Class and pedagogies, visible and invisible' in BERNSTEIN, B. (Ed.) *Class, Codes and Control*, Vol. 3, London, Routledge and Kegan Paul.

BERNSTEIN, B.B. and DAVIES, W.B. (1969) 'Some sociological comments on Plowden', in PETERS, R.S. (Ed.) *Perspectives on Plowden*, London, Routledge and Kegan Paul.

BLENKIN, G.M. (1983) 'The basic skills' in BLENKIN, G.M. and KELLY, A.V. (Eds) *The Primary Curriculum in Action*, London, Harper and Row, pp. 29–56.

BLENKIN, G.M. and KELLY, A.V. (1987) *The Primary Curriculum*, 2nd edn, London, Harper and Row.

BLOOM, B.S. (Ed.) (1956) *A Taxonomy of Educational Objectives. 1: Cognitive Domain*, London, Longmans.

BLYTH, W.A.L. (1965) *English Primary Education: A Sociological Description*. 2 vols. London, Routledge and Kegan Paul, reprinted with a postscript comment on Plowden in Vol. 1, 1967.

BLYTH, W.A.L. (1984a) *Development, Experience and Curriculum in Primary Education*, London, Croom Helm.

BLYTH, W.A.L. (1984b) 'The English middle school' in GORWOOD, B. (Ed.) *Intermediate Schooling, Aspects of Education* 32, Hull, University of Hull, pp. 23–39.

BOND, G. (1986) 'The changing Anglo-American scene', *International Primary Education*, in (journal of) *National Association for Primary Education*, 17, pp. 8–10.

BORKE, H. (1983) 'Piaget's mountains revisited: Changes in the egocentric landscape' in DONALDSON, M. *et al.* (Eds) *Early Childhood Development and Education*, Oxford, Basil Blackwell, pp. 245–59.

BOWER, T. (1971) 'Early learning behaviour', *Times Literary Supplement*, 7 May.

BOWER, T. (1974) *Development in Infancy*, San Francisco, CA, Freeman.

BOWER, T. (1977) *The Perceptual World of the Child*, London, Fontana Open Books.

BOYDELL, D. (1975) 'Pupil behaviour in junior classrooms', *British Journal of Educational Psychology*, 45, 2, pp. 128–9.

BRADBURN, E. (1988) *Margaret McMillan: Portrait of a Pioneer*, London, Croom Helm.

BRANDIS, W. and BERNSTEIN, B.B. (1974) *Selection and Control*, London, Routledge and Kegan Paul.

BRITISH PSYCHOLOGICAL SOCIETY (1986) 'Achievement in the primary school: Evidence to the Education, Science and Arts Committee of the House of Commons', *Bulletin* of the BPS, 39, pp. 121–5.

BROPHY, J.E. (1979) 'Advances in teacher research', *Journal of Classroom Interaction*, 15, 1, pp. 1–7.

BROPHY, J.E. and GOOD, T. (1986) 'Teacher behavior and student achievement', in WITTROCK, M. (Ed.) *Handbook of Research on Teaching*, 3rd edn, New York, Macmillan.

BROWN, A.L. and DeLOACHE, J.S. (1983) 'Metacognitive skills', in DONALDSON, M. *et al.* (Eds) *Early Childhood Development and Education*, Oxford, Basil Blackwell, pp. 280–9.

BROWN, G. and DESFORGES, C. (1979) *Piaget's Theory: A Psychological Critique*, London, Routledge and Kegan Paul.

BRUNER, J.S. (1968) *Towards a Theory of Instruction*, New York, W.W. Norton.

BRUNER, J.S. (1981) 'The pragmatics of acquisition' in DEUTSCH, W. (Ed.), *The Child's Construction of Language*, London, Academic Press.

BRUNER, J.S. (1983) *In Search of Mind*, New York, Harper and Row.

CACE (CENTRAL ADVISORY COUNCIL FOR EDUCATION (ENGLAND)) (1959) *15 to 18* (The Crowther Report), London, HMSO.

CACE (CENTRAL ADVISORY COUNCIL FOR EDUCATION (ENGLAND)) (1967) *Children and their Primary Schools* (the Plowden Report) 2 vols., London, HMSO.

CALDERHEAD, J. (1984) *Teachers' Classroom Decision-Making*. London, Holt, Rinehart and Winston.

CALDWELL COOK, H. (1917) *The Play Way: An Essay in Educational Method*, London, Heinemann.

CAMPBELL, R.J. (1985) *Developing the Primary School Curriculum*, London, Holt, Rinehart and Winston.

CATTY, N. (1949) *Learning and Teaching in the Junior School*, 1st edn. London, Methuen.

CAZDEN, C. (1974) 'Play with language and metalinguistic awareness: One dimension of language experience', *The Urban Review*, 7, pp. 23–39.

CCBE (CONSULTATIVE COMMITTEE OF THE BOARD OF EDUCATION) (1931) *The Primary School* (Hadow Report), London, HMSO.

CCBE (CONSULTATIVE COMMITTEE OF THE BOARD OF EDUCATION) (1933) *Infant and Nursery Schools*, London, HMSO.

Child Education (1986) (June) 'Problems in schools'.

COHEN, A. and COHEN, L. (Eds) (1986) *Primary Education: A Source Book for Teachers*, London, Harper and Row.

COLEMAN, J.S. *et al. (1966) Equality of Educational Opportunity*, Washington, D.C., U.S. Government Printing Office.

COPPLE, C. *et al.* (1979) *Educating the Young Thinker: Classroom Strategies for Cognitive Growth*, New York, Van Nostrand.

CROALL, J. (1983) *Neill of Summerhill: The Permanent Rebel*, London, Routledge and Kegan Paul.

DAVIE, R. *et al. (1972) From Birth to Seven*, London, Longmans.

DAVIS, R. *et al.* (1986) *The Infant School: Past, Present and Future*, Bedford Way Papers 27, London, University of London Institute of Education.

DEARDEN, R.F. (1967) 'Instruction and learning by discovery' in PETERS, R.S. (Ed.) *The Concept of Education*, London, Routledge and Kegan Paul.

DEARDEN, R.F. (1968) *The Philosophy of Primary Education*, London, Routledge and Kegan Paul.

DES (1979) *Local Authority Arrangements for the School Curriculum*, London, HMSO.

DES (1981) *The School Curriculum*, London, HMSO.

DES (1984) *Teaching Quality*, London, HMSO.

DES (1985) *Better Schools*, Cmnd. 9469, London, HMSO.

DES (1987) *The National Curriculum 5–16: A Consultation Document*, London, HMSO.

DEWEY, J. (1938) *Experience and Education*, New York, Macmillan.

DONALDSON, M. (1978) *Children's Minds*, London, Fontana Open Books.

DONALDSON, M., GRIEVE, R. and PRATT, C. (Eds) (1983) *Early Childhood Development and Education*, Oxford, Basil Blackwell.

EDUCATION, SCIENCE AND ARTS COMMITTEE OF THE HOUSE OF COMMONS (1986) *Achievement in Primary Schools*, London, HMSO.

EISNER, E.W. (1974) *English Primary Schools: Some Observations and Assessments*, Washington, D.C., NAEYC.

EISNER, E.W. (1982) *Cognition and Curriculum: A Basis for Deciding What to Teach*, New York and London, Longmans.

EISNER, E.W. (1985) *The Art of Educational Evaluation: A Personal View*, Lewes, Falmer Press.

ELLIOTT, J. (1976) *Developing Hypotheses about Classrooms from Teachers' Practical Constructs: An Account of the Work of the Ford Teaching Project*, North Dakota Study Group on Evaluation, University of North Dakota, North Dakota.

ENTWISTLE, H. (1970) *Child-Centred Education*, London, Methuen.

ENTWISTLE, N.J. (1987) *Understanding Classroom Learning*, London, Hodder and Stoughton.

ERIKSON, E.H. (1963) *Childhood and Society*, Harmondsworth, Penguin Books.

ESLAND, G.M. (1971) 'Teaching and learning as the organisation of knowledge' in YOUNG, M.F.D. (Ed.) *Knowledge and Control*, London, Macmillan.

FULLAN, M. (1982) *The Meaning of Educational Change*, New York, Teachers College Press.

GAGE, N.L. (1981) *Hard Gains in the Soft Sciences: The Case of Pedagogy*, CEDR Monograph, Phi Delta Kappa, Indiana.

GALTON, M. and SIMON, B. (Eds) (1980) *Progress and Performance in the Primary Classroom*, London, Routledge and Kegan Paul.

GALTON, M. and SIMON, B. and CROLL P (Eds) (1980) *Inside the Primary Classroom*, London, Routledge and Kegan Paul.

GALTON, M. and WILLCOCKS, J. (Eds) (1983) *Moving from the Primary Classroom*, London, Routledge and Kegan Paul.

GAMMAGE, P. (1986) *Primary Education: Structure and Context*, London, Harper and Row.

GELMAN, R. and GALLISTEL, C.R. (1978) *The Child's Understanding of Number*, Cambridge, MA., Harvard University Press.

GOLBY, M. (1986) 'Microcomputers and curriculum change' in DAVIS, R. *et al.*, *The Infant School: Past, Present and Future*, Bedford Way Papers 27, London, University of London Institute of Education.

GORDON, P. and LAWTON, D. (1978) *Curriculum Change in the Nineteenth and Twentieth Centuries*, London, Hodder and Stoughton.

GRAY, J. and SATTERLY, D. (1981) 'Formal or informal? A re-assessment of the British evidence', *British Journal of Educational Psychology* 51, 2, pp. 190–3.

HARDIE, A.M. (1969) 'Let's return to sanity' in COX, C.B. and DYSON, A.E. (Eds) *Fight for Education: A Black Paper*, London, Critical Quarterly Society.

HARGREAVES, A (1986) *Two Cultures of Schooling: The Case of Middle Schools*, Lewes, Falmer Press.

HARGREAVES, D.H. (1978) 'Whatever happened to symbolic interactionism?' in BARTON, L. and MEIGHAN, R. (Eds) *Sociological Interpretations of Schooling and Classrooms*, Driffield, Nafferton Books.

HARLEN, W. (1983) *Guides to Assessment in Education: Science*, London, Macmillan Education.

HARLEN, W. (1985) *Teaching and Learning Primary Science*, London, Harper and Row.

HIRST, P.H. (1965) 'Liberal education and the nature of knowledge' in ARCHAMBAULT, R.D. (Ed.) *Philosophical Analysis and Education*, London Routledge and Kegan Paul.

HIRST, P.H. and PETERS, R.S. (1970) *The Logic of Education*, London, Routledge and Kegan Paul.

HMI (1978) *Primary Education in England: A Survey by HM Inspectors of Schools*, London, HMSO.

HMI (1982) *Education 5 to 9: An Illustrative Survey of 80 First Schools in England*, London, HMSO.

HMI (1983) *9–13 Middle Schools: An Illustrative Survey*, London, HMSO.

HMI (1984) *English from 5 to 16, Curriculum Matters 1: An HMI Series*, London, HMSO.

HMI (1985a) *Report by Her Majesty's Inspectors on the Effects of Local Authority Expenditure Policies on Education Provision in England*, No. 1874. DES, Stanmore, Middlesex.

HMI (1985b) *Education 8 to 12 in Combined and Middle Schools: An HMI Survey*, London, HMSO.

HMI (1985c) *The Curriculum from 5 to 16, Curriculum Matters 2: An HMI Series*, London, HMSO.

HMI (1985d) *Mathematics from 5 to 16, Curriculum Matters 3: An HMI Series*, London, HMSO.

HMI (1986) *The Response to Curriculum Matters 1: An HMI Report*, London, HMSO.

HOLMES, R.G. (1952) *The Idiot Teacher*, London, Faber and Faber.

HOLT, J. (1984) *How Children Fail*, rev. edn. Harmondsworth, Penguin Books.

HOOPER, R. (Ed.) (1971) *The Curriculum: Context, Design and Development*, Edinburgh, Oliver and Boyd in association with the Open University Press.

HUGHES, M. (1986) *Children and Numbers: Difficulties in Learning Mathematics*, Oxford, Basil Blackwell.

HUGHES, M. and GRIEVE, R. (1983) 'On asking children bizarre questions' in DONALDSON, M. *et al.* (Eds) *Early Childhood Development and Education*, Oxford, Basil Blackwell, pp. 104–114.

ILEA (1985) *Improving Primary Schools* (The Thomas Report), London, ILEA.

ILEA RESEARCH and STATISTICS BRANCH (1986) *The Junior School Project: A Summary of the Main Report*, London, ILEA.

JACKSON, P.W. (1968) *Life in Classrooms*, New York, Holt, Rinehart and Winston.

JENKINS, D. (1975) 'Classical and Romantic in the curriculum landscape' in GOLBY, M., GREENWALD, J. and WEST, R. (Eds) *Curriculum Design*, London, Croom Helm.

JONES, J. (1966) 'Social class and the under-fives', *New Society*, 221.

JOYCE, B. and WEIL, M. (1982) 'Against dogmatism: Alternative models of teaching' in LEE, V. and ZELDIN, D. (Eds) *Planning in the Curriculum*, London, Hodder and Stoughton.

KARABEL, J. and HALSEY, A.H. (Eds) (1977) Editor's introduction to *Power and Ideology in Education*, London, Oxford University Press.

KATZ, L.G. (1977) *Talks with Teachers*, Washington, D.C., N.A.E.Y.C.

KELLY, A.V. (Ed.) (1984) *Microcomputers and the Curriculum*, London, Harper and Row.

KELLY, A.V. (1986) *Knowledge and Curriculum Planning*, London, Harper and Row.

KINDER, K.M. (1987) *Teachers Teaching Together: Emerging Issues* (PRINDEP Report 4), Primary Needs Independent Evaluation Project, Leeds, University of Leeds.

KING, R.A. (1978) *All Things Bright and Beautiful? A Sociological Study of Infants' Classrooms*, London, John Wiley.

KING R.A. (1979) 'The search for the "invisible" pedagogy', *Sociology*, 13, 3, pp. 445–58.

KING, R.A. (1983) 'On the diversity of primary education', *Education 3–13*, 11, 2, pp. 41–4.

KUTNICK, P. (1983) *Relating to Learning*, London, George Allen and Unwin.

LASLETT, R. and SMITH, C. (1984) *Effective Classroom Management*, London, Croom Helm.

LAWTON, D. (1973) *Social Change, Educational Theory and Curriculum Planning*, London, University of London Press.

LAWTON, D. (1975) *Class, Culture and the Curriculum*, London, Routledge and Kegan Paul.

LAWTON, D. (1982) *The End of the 'Secret Garden'? A Study in the Politics of the Curriculum*, London, University of London Institute of Education.

LAWTON, D. (1984) 'Metaphors and the curriculum' in TAYLOR, W. (Ed.) *Metaphors of Education*, London, Heinemann, pp. 79–90.

LEWIN, R. (Ed.) (1975) *Child Alive: New Insights into the Development of Young Children*, London, Temple Smith.

LITTLE, A.N. et al. (1971) 'Do small classes help?', *New Society*, 18.

LORTIE, D.C. (1975) *Schoolteacher: A Sociological Study*, Chicago, University of Chicago Press.

LOVELL, K. (1968) *An Introduction to Human Development*, London, Macmillan.

McCANN, W.P. and YOUNG, F.A. (1982) *Samuel Wilderspin and the Infant School Movement*, London, Croom Helm.

MacDOUGALL, W. (1908) *An Introduction to Social Psychology*, London, Methuen.

McGARRIGLE, J. and DONALDSON, M. (1975) 'Conservation accidents', *Cognition*, 3, pp. 341–50.

MEADOWS, S. (1986) *Understanding Child Development*, London, Hutchinson.

MEASOR, L. and WOODS, P. (1984) *Changing Schools: Pupil Perspectives on Transfer to a Comprehensive*, Milton Keynes, Open University Press.

NATIONAL UNION OF TEACHERS (1979) *Primary Questions: The NUT Response to the Primary Survey*, London, NUT.

NETTLESHIP, R.L. (1935) *Lectures on the Republic of Plato*, London, Macmillan.

NEWSON, J. and NEWSON, E. (1977) *Seven Year Olds in the Home Environment*, London, George Allen and Unwin.

NEWSON, J. et al. (1978) *Perspectives on School at Seven Years Old*, London, George Allen and Unwin.

NIAS, J. (1984) 'The definition and maintenance of self in primary teaching' *British Journal of Sociology of Education*, 5, 3, pp. 267–80.

NIAS, J. (1985a) 'A more distant drummer: Teacher development as the development of self' in BARTON, L. and WALKER, S. (Eds.) *Education and Social Change*, London, Croom Helm.

NIAS, J. (1985b) 'Reference groups in primary teaching: Talking, listening and identity' in BALL, S. and GOODSON, I.F. (Eds) *Teachers' Lives and Careers*, Lewes, Falmer Press.

NIAS, J. (1986) *What is it Like to be a Teacher? The Subjective Reality of*

Primary Teaching, (mimeo), Cambridge, Cambridge Institute of Education.

NIAS, J. (1987) Seeing Anew: Teachers' Theories of Action, Geelong, Australia, Deakin University Press.

NIAS, J. (1988) On Becoming and Being a Teacher, London, Methuen.

NORTHAM, J. (1983) 'The myth of the pre-school', Education 3–13, 11, 2, pp. 37–40.

PETERS, R.S. (1965) 'Education as initiation' in ARCHAMBAULT, R.D. (Ed.) Philosophical Analysis and Education, London, Routledge and Kegan Paul, pp. 87–111.

PETERS, R.S. (1966) Ethics and Education, London, George Allen and Unwin.

PETERS, R.S. (Ed.) (1969) Perspectives on Plowden, London, Routledge and Kegan Paul.

PIAGET, J. (1951) Play, Dreams and Reality, London, Routledge and Kegan Paul.

PIAGET, J. (1955) The Child's Construction of Reality, London, Routledge and Kegan Paul.

PIAGET, J. (1969) The Science of Education and the Psychology of the Child, London, Longmans (1970 translation published 1971).

PINDER, R. (1987) Why Don't Teachers Teach Like They Used To? London, Hilary Shipman.

POLLARD, A. (1985) The Social World of the Primary School, London, Holt, Rinehart and Winston.

POLLARD, H.M. (1956) Pioneers of Popular Education 1760–1850, London, John Murray.

RICHARDS, C.M. (1975) 'Primary school teachers' perceptions of discovery learning' in TAYLOR, P.H. (Ed.) Aims, Influence and Change in the Primary Curriculum, Slough, NFER.

RICHARDS, C.M. (Ed.) (1982) New Directions in Primary Education, Lewes, Falmer Press.

RICHARDS, C.M. et al. (1985a) The Study of Primary Education: A Source Book Vol. 2, Lewes, Falmer Press.

RICHARDS, C.M. et al. (1985b) The Study of Primary Education: A Source Book Vol. 3, Lewes, Falmer Press.

ROSENSHINE, B. (1983) 'Teaching functions in instructional programs', Elementary School Journal 83, 4, pp. 335–1.

ROWLAND, S. (1984) The Enquiring Classroom, Lewes, Falmer Press.

RUSK, R.R. (1979) Doctrines of the Great Educators, 5th edn, revised by James Scotland, London, Macmillan.

SCHEFFLER, I. (1971) The Language of Education, Springfield, IL, Thomas.

SCHOOLS COUNCIL (1983) Primary Practice. Working Paper 75, London, Methuen Educational.

SCHUTZ, A. (1954) 'Concept and theory formation in the social sciences', Journal of Philosophy, 51, 9, pp. 257–73.

SELLECK, R.W.J. (1972) English Primary Education and the Progressives, London, Routledge and Kegan Paul.

SHARP, R. and GREEN, J. (1976) Education and Social Control: A Study in

Progressive Primary Education, London, Routledge and Kegan Paul.

SHIPMAN, M.D. (1971) 'Curriculum for inequality?' in HOOPER, R. (Ed.) *The Curriculum: Context, Design and Development*, Edinburgh, Oliver and Boyd in association with the Open University Press.

SIEBER, S. (1972) 'Images of the practitioner and strategies of educational change', *Sociology of Education*, 45, pp. 362–85.

SIKES, P.J., MEASOR , L. and WOODS, P. (Eds) (1985) *Teacher Careers*, Lewes, Falmer Press.

SIMON, B. (1986) 'The primary school revolution: Myth or reality?' in COHEN, A. and COHEN, L. (Eds) *Primary Education: A Source Book for Teachers*, London, Harper and Row.

SIMON, B. and WILLCOCKS, J. (Eds) (1981) *Research and Practice in the Primary Classroom*, London, Routledge and Kegan Paul.

SKILBECK, M. (1984) *School-Based Curriculum Development*, London, Harper and Row.

STENHOUSE, L.A. (1967) *Culture and Education*, London, Nelson.

STEWART, J. (1986) *The Making of the Primary School*, Milton Keynes, Open University Press.

STEWART, W.A.C. (1972) *Progressives and Radicals in English Education*, London, Macmillan.

STONES, E. (1979) *Psychopedagogy*, London, Methuen, (now re-issued (1984) as *Psychology of Education: A Pedagogical Approach*).

SYLVA, K. *et al.* (1980) *Childwatching at Playgroup and Nursery School*, Oxford Pre-School Research Project, London, Grant McIntyre.

TANN, S. (1981) 'Grouping and group work' in SIMON, B. and WILLCOCKS, J. (Eds) *Research and Practice in the Primary Classroom*, London, Routledge and Kegan Paul.

TAYLOR, W. (1986) *Metaphors of Education*, London, Heinemann.

TOBIN, J. (1983) 'Management of time in classrooms' in FRASER, B. (Ed.) *Classroom Management*, Education Research and Workshop Minograph No. 1, Perth, Western Australian Institute of Technology (WAIT).

TURNER, J. (1980) *Made for Life: Coping, Competence and Cognition*, London, Methuen.

TUSTIN, F. (1950) *A Group of Juniors*, London, Heinemann.

VYGOTSKY L.S. (1962) *Thought and Language*, Cambridge, MA, MIT Press.

WELLS, C.G. (1981) *Learning Through Interaction*, Cambridge, Cambridge. University Press.

WESTBURY, I. (1973) 'Conventional classrooms, open classrooms and the technology of teaching', *Journal of Curriculum Studies* 5, 2, pp. 99–121.

WHELDALL, K. (Ed.) (1982) 'Behavioural pedagogy: Towards a behavioural science of teaching, *Educational Psychology*, 2, 3 and 4.

WHITBREAD, N. (1972) *The Evolution of the Infant School: A Study of Infant and Nursery Education in Britain*, London, Routledge and Kegan Paul.

WHITE, J.P. (1968) 'Education in obedience', *New Society*, 2 May.

Bibliography

WHITEHEAD, M. (1985) 'On learning to write: Recent research and developmental writing', *Curriculum*, 6, 2, pp. 12–19.

WILLIAMS, G. (1986) 'Lies and damned lies', *Times Educational Supplement*, 13 June, p. 4.

WILLIAMS, R. (1961) *The Long Revolution*, London, Chatto and Windus (and Pelican Books 1965).

Notes on Contributors

Robin Alexander is Senior Lecturer in Primary Education at Leeds University. Educated at Cambridge, Durham, London and Manchester universities, he taught in various primary schools and a college of education before his present post, where he currently works on courses for intending and experienced primary teachers, and directs PRINDEP, a four-year evaluation of the impact on primary schools of Leeds LEA's Primary Needs Programme. His books include *Primary Teaching* (Cassell), *Change in Teacher Education* (with M. Craft and J. Lynch, Cassell), *The Self-Evaluating Institution* (with C. Adelman, Methuen), and three edited collections on aspects of teacher education.

Geva Blenkin is a lecturer in the Advanced Studies Department of the Faculty of Education at Goldsmiths' College. Her work and interests lie in the field of curriculum studies in general and the early years curriculum in particular. She was formerly headteacher of an infant school in the East End of London. She makes a major contribution to the higher degree programme in curriculum studies as well as to the initial education of nursery/first school teachers. Her publications include *The Primary Curriculum, The Primary Curriculum in Action* and *Early Childhood Education: A Developmental Curriculum*.

Alan Blyth was Sydney Jones Professor of Education in the University of Liverpool and is now Honorary Senior Fellow there. His interests and publications have been in the field of primary education, and especially in the primary curriculum. At present he is completing a study of appraisal and assessment of Humanities in primary schools.

Maurice Galton, Professor of Education at the School of Education, University of Leicester, has co-directed ORACLE project since its inception in 1975. He is co-author of *Inside the Primary Classroom* (1980), co-editor of *Progress and Performance in the Primary Classroom* (1980) co-editor of *Moving from the Primary Classroom* (1983) and a contributor to *Research and Practice in the Primary Classroom* (1981). Since 1985 he has been Director of the School of Education.

Philip Gammage was trained as a primary school teacher at Goldsmiths' College and taught in London for ten years before joining the staff at Bristol University. He has taught in N. America and Australia and is currently Professor and Chairman of the School of Education, University of Nottingham.

Vic Kelly is currently Dean of the Faculty of Education at Goldsmiths' College, London. His teaching experience, while mostly gained in the university and secondary school sectors, includes work with infant children and in adult and continuing education. He has written and edited a number of books on education and especially on curriculum. The prime concern both of his teaching and of his writing is to promote and maintain a properly rigorous debate on all aspects of the school curriculum. Thus his immediate preoccupation is with protecting that debate from the worst ravages of the Gerbill.

Ronald King is Reader in Education at the University of Exeter, where he teaches the Sociology of Education. His research has covered a range of educational institutions, including primary, in his book *All Things Bright and Beautiful? A Sociological Study of Infants' Classrooms* (1978). He is currently writing the account of a complementary study of junior schools.

Jennifer Nias is Tutor in Curriculum Studies at the Cambridge Institute of Education. In that capacity she plans, develops and teaches courses for experienced teachers which are based upon their enquiries into their own practice in classrooms and schools.

Index